NAMBA ROY

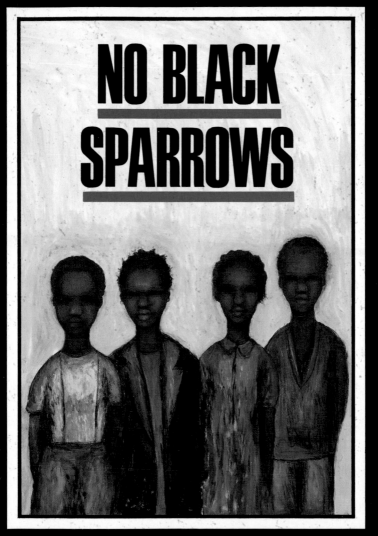

NO BLACK
SPARROWS

A vivid portrait of Jamaica in the 1930s

NAMBA ROY was born in Jamaica in 1910. He spent his childhood in Kingston and in Accompong in the Cockpit Country – a refuge where escaped Jamaican slaves, known as Maroons, lived as free men. Roy's grandfather and father were both traditional village carvers – a role passed down from father to son – and it was from them that Roy learnt about African folklore and the art of Maroon story-telling and carving.

Shortly after the outbreak of the Second World War, Roy joined the British Merchant Navy. Illness forced him to leave in 1944 and he remained in Britain where, in 1950, he met and later married English actress Yvonne Shelley, with whom he had three children. He died on 16 June 1961.

Roy, a prodigious painter, carver and sculptor, wrote two books and several short stories, including *Negro Creation*, an Afro-Maroon tale about the creation of the world, which was broadcast by the BBC in 1957. *Black Albino*, an historical adventure story about a Maroon community living in the mountains of Jamaica, was published by New Literature (Publishing) Ltd in 1961, shortly before the author's death. *Black Albino* was then published by Longman in 1986.

No Black Sparrows was written over the years 1956 and 1957. The book was important to Roy as it described his own childhood experiences in Jamaica.

NAMBA ROY

NO BLACK SPARROWS

Edited by Jacqueline Roy

HEINEMANN

Heinemann International
a division of Heinemann Educational Books Ltd
Halley Court, Jordan Hill, Oxford OX2 8EJ

Heinemann Educational Books Inc
70 Court Street, Portsmouth, New Hampshire, 03801, USA

Heinemann Educational Books (Nigeria) Ltd
PMB 5205, Ibadan
Heinemann Kenya Ltd
Kijabe Street, PO Box 45314, Nairobi
Heinemann Educational Boleswa
PO Box 10103, Village Post Office, Gaborone, Botswana
Heinemann Educational Books (Caribbean) Ltd
175 Mountain View Avenue, Kingston 6, Jamaica

LONDON   EDINBURGH   MELBOURNE
SYDNEY   AUCKLAND   SINGAPORE   MADRID

British Library Cataloguing in Publication Data
Roy, Namba, *1910–1961*
No black sparrows
I. Title   II. Series
813 [F]
ISBN 0–435–98812–3

PR
9265.9
R69
N6
1989

Phototypeset by Wilmaset, Birkenhead, Wirral
Printed in Great Britain by
Printed and bound in Great Britain by
Cox & Wyman Ltd, Reading

For Jacqueline, Lucinda and Tamba Roy.

*With special thanks to Lucinda Roy for her early
editing of the book, and to Anne Walmsley for
her belief and help, which have greatly contributed
towards its publication.*

PROLOGUE

He stood in the midst of the great whiteness, silent in wonder. Soundlessly it had come and had taken charge of the earth in a single night. He stretched down to pick up a handful of the whiteness around him, his hand seeming blacker by contrast. So this was snow!

He scooped up some more and started to press and roll it, but there was something in it that would not merge into roundness.

He thought it was a piece of wood and tried to separate it from the snow. As he brushed the powdery substance from the thing, he realized it was a bird . . . one of the kind that only the day before had been pointed out to him as a sparrow.

It lay stiff and cold with its claws drawn up in the palm of his hand. He stood for a while looking down on it, hoping that its death had been an accident. But there were no marks, no motor car had crushed the life from its body. The realization seemed to obliterate the beauty of the narrow back-street that had been so bleak and grey the day before the snow had fallen.

He drifted into a small park, still holding the bird which was becoming clammy in the warmth of his palm. The feathers were starting to lose their wooden appearance and the last of the whiteness had almost disappeared. He no longer heard the crunching of the snow beneath his feet, nor could he see the leafless trees and hedges which so closely resembled the Christmas cards he had once looked upon in wonder. The discovery of the dead bird had destroyed the magic of his first snow. Here in his hand was the symbol of God's promise. Yet, though the bird was sinless and innocent, it had been allowed to fall to the ground for want of food or warmth.

What did it say in the Bible?

'Are not five sparrows sold for two farthings and not one of them is forgotten before God?'

And again:

'Behold the fowls of the air: for they sow not, neither do they reap, nor gather into barns; yet your Heavenly Father feedeth them. Are ye not much better than they?'

As the words came back to him, it seemed that all around the air was filled with whispers and chants, and out of the whiteness came the dark faces of his people. He shivered, but not from cold. This chill took hold of him whenever he began to remember the past. He stood, cornered, as the familiar voices came from nowhere to taunt him, louder and louder until they burst into songs, hymns and chants. He looked over the low hedge to the street that ran alongside the park. The all-white crowd which passed him looked at his face with the curiosity of people looking at their opposite colour – perhaps for the first time. They could not see the faces that he saw. Now the voices became a roar, blocking out the noise of the passing buses and loaded lorries. Even the low-flying plane overhead only made its presence known to him by the shadow it cast across the snow.

The voices almost overwhelmed him. His heartbeat kept time with the chants. Bass voices, alto voices, tenors, baritones and the voices of children joined in so that he was rocked there in the ice-covered park with the force of the sound.

'God proteck de Sparrows! God proteck de Sparrows! God proteck de Sparrows!'

He looked down at the dead bird. When at last he was able to look up again, the faces – now certain that his resistance to these remembrances was crushed – began to fade, while the chant grew fainter and fainter until at last he was left alone with the dead bird and the memories of the past.

BOOK ONE

CHAPTER ONE

Sonna stood under the trees, watching and waiting. He was almost eleven years old and his head was a mass of tiny curls. His body was inclined to be plump but at present this was only a promise, for now – because of its watchful angle – his head seemed larger than normal. He had a roundish face and large eyes. On the top of his wide, flat nose, perspiration gathered and glistened against the darkness of his skin like a cluster of jewels on a cushion of dark velvet. His full lips, when parted, exposed purple-dark gums and strong, white teeth with a tiny opening between the centre pair. His clothes consisted of a bright, yellow T-shirt clinging closely to his body and a pair of short brown trousers, so short and tight that it seemed they must have belonged to a younger child. His dark legs shone except where his bare feet came in contact with the dust of the streets. Under his arm he held a shoebox, complete with lid.

Sonna talked to himself as he gazed intently across the park at the figures who were coming towards him.

'They say if you knees tremble and you press hard on it, that will make it stop.'

A pause, then: 'Don't look like it make any difference. Wonder if it mean I feel frighten? It's only three of them – and two is girls – and girls can't fight.' He knitted his brow, trying to size up his chances. 'That girl what wearing a man jacket over her frock, she look like a bad girl and she older than me – maybe a year older than me. The other girl must be 'bout ten. She can't fight at all for she is too slim.' He paused again and realized that he had not lost his shaking. 'But I not 'fraid,' he said.

'That boy, him look tough. Him must be eleven or twelve like the girl in the jacket, but I not 'fraid, it's only three of them and two is girls.'

The sun was in the middle of the sky and the tarred surfaces which served as paths between the grass and struggling flowers betrayed the heat by giving off a shimmering, ghost-like vapour. Not far away, the gong of a rickety, open-sided tram clanged impatiently, perhaps to warn a sun-drunk drayman to give it right of way.

3

Now Sonna saw the three move forward and was relieved. They were in no hurry, but there was aggression in the slow, deliberate steps they took towards him. The gap between them lessened steadily. They were ready to attack him now. Sonna noted with satisfaction that only the long wait had caused his nervousness, for now his legs no longer trembled. He grasped his precious shoebox even tighter under his right arm as he glanced around quickly to see if there was a place where he might hide it, but he realized he'd left it too late. They were almost upon him now, and only one arm was free for a fight. He hated to admit it but the girl with the man's jacket over the little red frock with the short, many-plaited head of hair looked like a fighter. She seemed to push out her chest as she came with the others. They spread themselves out so he could not run. Sonna stood his ground, perfectly still – his weight spread evenly on both legs – and changed the shoebox to his left arm.

The group seemed surprised that he was ready for a confrontation. The girl in the man's jacket called a conference. Sonna looked on calmly as they gathered together with their faces turned towards him. This girl was clearly their leader. Her many mounds of plaits were tied at each end with ribbons, black and red in colour. Sonna recognized these ribbons. He had found a bundle of them among some wastepapers behind one of the offices only that morning. A fellow salvage-seeker had explained it had no value for it was ribbon from a typewriter – the thing that girls use to tap out words as if by magic. It seemed to Sonna that the ribboned girl would be tough when she was angry. Her skin was shiny black, her nose almost bridgeless and her full upper lip turned upwards so that she seemed to have a slight snarl on her face at all times. Her ears were pierced and she wore a pair of round earrings in them.

Sonna looked at the other girl. Her appearance confirmed his first guess that she was slightly younger than he. She was slim and brown with hair that needed only half a dozen plaits. She too wore earrings and her print frock did not reach her bony knees. Although she tried to look as hostile as her two companions, the effect was unconvincing. Her wide mouth and heavy lips were contorted into seriousness. And yet her face was thin and sad. Instinctively, Sonna felt that he could trust this girl.

The boy now drew Sonna's attention. He must have been in endless fights for over his eyes, his lips, and even on the side of his pear-shaped head were old scars. He was – like the second girl – chocolate in colour, with a squat but not-too-flat nose, though his nostrils were extremely wide. He was taller than the rest and his body more fully developed than Sonna's. He wore an old, blue pullover without a shirt or vest, and his trousers were a man's cut-downs which puckered round his immature

4

waist and were held up by a piece of string. They were all barefooted and they all, like Sonna, had shoeboxes under their arms.

The vultures known as 'John Crows' cast their shadows as they circled and alighted on the branch of an old coconut tree nearby, attracted by the smell of the fish market not far away. The group came forward again and looked at one another as if trying to find an opening for their attack. Sonna did not help them. He started to hum a tune under his breath while the other three looked more like defenders than aggressors.

A signal passed between the boy and the girl in the man's jacket. Then the boy said, 'What you doing here?'

Sonna stopped humming. 'What you doing here youself?' he asked.

'I ask you first.'

'And I ask you back.'

A short silence followed. 'Where you come from?'

'Jamaica,' replied Sonna promptly.

'Damfool! All of we come from Jamaica. This is Jamaica!'

'Then if you know, why you ask where I come from?'

'You playing smart, *country boy*?'

'I not playing smart, I is smart – smarter than you and you friends as well!'

'Jesus! You hear him Mobel and Sista, him say him smarter than we. Make we laugh after him.' The others joined in the peals of forced laughter while Sonna bit his lip.

'That's all you can do,' he taunted angrily, 'can't do a thing but laugh like donkeys braying.'

They were stung by the scorn in his voice.

'You calling we donkey?' said the girl with the ribbons. She stepped forward until she was close to Sonna, her hands on her hips, her head tilted and her legs wide apart.

'If you feel I calling you donkey, that's what I say,' he answered boldly.

Without another word, the girl turned and handed her shoebox and her jacket to her girl companion. Then Sonna handed his shoebox to her also, as if he had been contemplating the gesture for some time.

The three were taken by surprise. 'We going to keep the box and share what inside!' shouted the boy. 'Give me the box, Sista.'

'No!' she answered defiantly, backing away from the boy's outstretched hand. But he followed, still bent on taking the box.

'Mobel! Tell Pazart to leave me alone with the boy box,' she cried.

'Leave Sista alone,' said Mobel.

5

The boy looked round angrily. 'You don't tell me what I must do,' he said, but he stopped trying to get hold of the box and returned to where he had been standing.

Sonna stood watching with arms folded and looked amused as Pazart continued to challenge Mobel's authority. She stepped menacingly to within inches of him, her arms akimbo, her face nearly touching his. 'You don't like what I say and do Mister Pazart?' she said.

'I don't want me and you to fight Mobel, don't talk into my face.'

'You want to do something 'bout it Pazart?'

He stepped back just a little from the threatening face. Sonna saw the retreat and made a mental note that the girl was feared. He wondered how a boy could allow a girl of his own age and size to shame him without fighting. He felt contempt for Pazart who allowed the girl to bully him and also for Mobel, whom he thought was showing off.

'You 'fraid to fight Mister Pazart?' asked Mobel, who had clearly won the unfought battle.

'I don't want to fight you Mobel,' he evaded.

Sonna thought it was time for him to butt in. 'You all don't know it's my box you want to fight 'bout?'

Pazart seemed to realize now that he had lost face before a stranger. Perhaps with the idea of regaining his self-respect by fighting Sonna, he looked out in the open space drenched with the blazing sun and pointed to the bald-headed vultures circling above.

'See them John Crows?' he leered into Sonna's face, pointing upwards.

'I see them,' replied Sonna softly, his body tense as he anticipated the insult that no West Indian child could hear without fighting.

'One of them fly away with you mother . . .'

The word 'mother' was barely out of Pazart's mouth when Sonna struck. He punched Pazart's nose, his head, his ears. Pazart reeled. It sounded to him like the whole world had exploded. He tasted the salty blood in his mouth and howled, 'Him killing me! Sista and Mobel, help me!' But his two friends remained where they were and said nothing while Sonna continued to strike until his opponent had lost even the courage to defend himself. The blows at last drove out any pride he had left.

'Don't beat me anymore,' he cried, 'I beg you pardon, I didn't mean what I say. You going kill me?'

At last Sonna stood panting over the boy who had insulted his mother. Pazart lay in the dust, with a bleeding nose and mouth. Mobel, standing as before, looked with disgust on her whimpering companion, but Sista placed the shoeboxes and Mobel's old jacket on the ground and walked forward to help Pazart to his feet.

'Go and wash you face under there,' she said, not unkindly, pointing to a water-pipe. The boys and girls who had stopped to watch the fight stood aside, jeering, while the loser staggered through them with both hands nursing his face.

Sonna was just about to step forward to ask Sista for his box when Mobel stepped in front of him, barring the way.

'Bet you couldn't do that to me,' she said, smiling slightly with her head tilted, her hands on her hips and her feet wide apart.

'I don't fight with girls,' said Sonna, making an effort to pass, but she continued to block his path.

' 'Fraid?' she asked softly.

' 'Fraid of a girl?' he returned scornfully.

'But I say you 'fraid Mister Man, 'fraid good and plenty.'

'You better get out of my way, else I forget you is a girl and do what I do to him!' Saying this, Sonna turned scornfully to bypass Mobel but she sprang forward and crashed her head to the side of his face, knocking him down.

Sonna wondered how it was he had not seen the trees and houses moving around him before. Dazed, he realized the girl had butted him. So that was why Pazart was afraid of this Mobel. He could hear the comments of the spectators.

'Him can't get up!'

'The girl beat him, man!'

'That girl buck like a cow!'

'The boy don't know where him is now.'

'All the same, I wouldn't like to know a girl beat me.'

'Girl never beat me yet.'

'You boys think you is the only one can fight? We can fight too, you see for youself!'

'You don't need to boast yet girl, it's only because the boy didn't expeck the girl to buck him.'

Mobel said nothing. She stood watching, ready to pounce as soon as Sonna got to his feet. He tried to remember the instructions his father had given him when he'd first learnt to fight, and had barely taken his hands from the ground when Mobel charged again. But this time he was prepared and stood up with arms stretched in front of him. Realizing that she would have to change her tactics, she braced herself against him. With bare toes clawing the earth they moved backwards and forwards fiercely, their breath coming out in gasps. Schoolchildren

7

going home for lunch joined the crowd of onlookers, the boys shouting for Sonna and the girls for Mobel. Suddenly it seemed that Sonna could not hold her. She prepared to give him the full power of her head but as she delivered the blow, he swung to one side, sending her sliding in the dust.

'Lawd,' said a voice, 'the girl don't have on any pants!'

As the crowd of children laughed, Mobel burned with anger. She drew her torn frock round her to cover her shame and pulled out a small penknife. Before she could prize open the blade, Sonna had knocked it from her grasp. He struck again and she fell backwards, winded. Then someone shouted, 'Police!'

The crowd scattered. Sonna instinctively started to run. Glancing back, he could see a figure standing over Mobel, who had not recovered in time to take flight. The man wore a leather armband with a crown on it. Sonna knew he was a District Constable. He stared. The man was tall but his girth made him seem squat. He wore a civilian khaki suit and an ordinary workman's cap; but for the badge on his arm and the heavy baton in his hand he would not have been recognizable as a Constable. Sonna knew him by his size; this was the famous Bangbelly, so named because of his paunch. He had been warned about this man. Although he was big, he was fast – the fastest of all the Constables. It was said that he took pleasure in making arrests – that he never pardoned anyone: children, the old, the market women, all came under his scrutiny. Everyone feared him.

Mobel looked into the face of the man above her and tried not to show that she was afraid. She had hurt her ankle in one of her falls and knew she could not escape. She thought of the children's prison where they sent orphans, delinquents and thieves. She had bad dreams about the place. Bangbelly would put her there, she knew. He'd often threatened to do it when she'd thumbed her nose at him from some safe corner. His cold eyes seemed to promise it. He folded his arms across his broad chest and shoved her roughly with his foot but he said nothing. He seemed to be enjoying this small triumph, prolonging the moment. Suddenly he spoke, the power of his voice making her jump.

'No need you try to run. I taking you to jail. Get up and if you know what good for you, you come easy.' He spoke quickly, each word seeming to run into the other, yet there was no emotion in his voice; it was toneless and brittle. He began to finger the baton that he was reported to throw between the legs of escapees to bring them to the ground.

Mobel began to move as if in acceptance of defeat and then she saw

Sonna crawling stealthily behind the Constable. He signalled to her to play for time and to distract attention, so she looked towards the crowd. Cautiously she turned towards the Constable again. She looked up at him imploringly, letting all her fear show now in the hope of drawing a response. She caught Sonna's eye and knew what she was meant to do. She raised herself into a kneeling position and then sprang without warning, her head butting the Constable's paunch. The force of the impact knocked him backwards over the crouching Sonna. His head crashed on an exposed root of a tree and he lay still.

'Run!' shouted Sonna to Mobel, who fled, despite the pain in her ankle.

The crowd roared its own encouragement. 'Run picni, run for you life! Run through the big gate, picni. Run before them shut you in!'

From out of the crowd, Sista ran too, still holding the boxes and the jacket. A whistle sounded and the children knew it was the signal for the chase. They passed through the gates just before they could be closed and fled through the crowded streets, urged on by the sympathetic market traders. But there was a policeman up ahead. 'Scatter!' shouted Sonna and he changed direction.

Looking back, Mobel could see that only Sonna was being chased now, just as he'd intended. She tried to run, though her ankle was hurting badly. Sonna was making for a cul-de-sac, she had to warn him. She cut across the street and headed them off, deliberately running straight into the policeman. He crashed to the ground, his pith helmet circling towards the gutter.

The children recovered quickly and ran once more, still spurred on by the crowd. Sonna gripped Mobel's hand; she was limping badly now.

'Go to the Dungle,' she said breathlessly. 'You run on.' They could hear the whistles close behind them. 'You go on,' repeated Mobel, 'I will manage.' Now they were in the quieter, narrow streets and there were fewer people. Mobel slowed down almost to a walk.

Sonna held her hand more tightly. 'Bear up,' he panted. 'If a policeman not in the nex' street you won't have to run so much.' He began to sprint again, pulling Mobel with him.

'Go,' she said fiercely, 'I say I is awright!'

Yet Sonna continued to run with her. She looked at him and saw he wouldn't leave her now, so although she drew her hand away she ran beside him meekly, trying to remember if she'd ever relied on anyone else for protection. Yes. Her father, before he had drowned. He had made her feel that nothing could happen when he was by her side. Yet this boy was her own age.

Still they hurried on, silently now, struggling for breath. At last the Dungle came in sight and they knew that they were safe. Up ahead they could see Pazart and Sista, already there, waiting for them both.

The half dozen or so inhabitants of the great dunghill known as 'Dungle' barely noticed as the children picked their way through the mounds of rubbish. Between one of these heaps sat an old man peering at the pages of a damp, week-old newspaper.

Someone stopped and asked him, 'What it say in the news, Marse Paperman?'

He looked over his string-tied pair of steel-rimmed spectacles and answered impressively, 'That man Hitler raising hell.'

'Think them will fight, Paperman?'

'Look like it.'

'You think England can beat him?'

'Maybe, but I was reading 'bout this place name Russia, and according to what I read, them have the men.'

'I was hearing something 'bout them myself, Paperman. Maybe them join up with Germany, the dawg would be dead for England!'

'That is true word.'

'What 'bout America?'

'She will fight for England but maybe she will wait 'til last like what she do before.'

'And what 'bout them son-of-a-bitch what murder Ethiopia?'

'Jesus! Man, I can't even bear to hear anybody call them, after what them done to we people!'

'You not the only one, Paperman. Every part of this Island go, as soon as you say Mussolini, everybody spit!'

'Hope them blow out him guts soon as war start. If I was not an ole man now, in spite of how England treat we who go and fight for her in the last war, I would go again; but this time would be because I want to revenge Ethiopia!'

'You talk sense, Paperman, same thing I say . . . Paperman?'

'Yes brother?'

'You think a war would help we?'

'Don't know. But it can't make things worst for we!'

'You talk truth, Paperman . . . it can't be worst for we . . .'

Mobel sat on the ground with her legs drawn up, scraping the earth with a piece of stick and relating their escape. Pazart sat a little way off, his lips swollen and his nose looking abnormally large. Every now and then, he discreetly raised his hand to feel the sore spots. Sista sat looking at Sonna with open admiration, while he looked away embarrassed, with a growing feeling of apprehension. He was starting to realize that they were not out of danger. The police would continue to look out for all of them.

'If them catch we, what would happen?' he asked.

The others looked surprised at the question, seeming to forget he was a stranger.

'Them would take we to jail, try we and send we to famitary,' said Mobel.

'Them can send we to famitary even when we don't thief?' he said.

Mobel answered with the authority of a law student, not a child of eleven. 'We don't have any license for the bootlace and pin we selling in we box. 'Sides, we don't have anybody, so if them catch we, even if we didn't do anything but sell, them would send us to famitary all the same.'

Sonna looked indignant. 'But we not thief! Famitary is a bad place for them what thief and do bad things. My father say it's a bad place. Even if you is good when you go there, you is bad when you come out.'

They all thought about the reformatory of Santa Lucia for a moment. Then Sonna said, 'How much for a license?'

'Five pounds for one year,' said Mobel.

'Gawd,' whispered Sonna in amazement. 'Think I would sell bootlace and pin and needle like what we have in we box if I have five pounds?'

The others shook their heads and they each thought of what they would do with five pounds . . . eat and eat and never be hungry for ever and ever . . .

They all looked again at their boxes and Sista got up and gave Sonna his box with a smile.

Sonna thanked her but looked down at the ground.

Pazart also wanted to make up for his earlier behaviour. 'I didn't mean what I say in the park,' he blurted suddenly, not sure where to look.

'That's awright,' said Sonna.

There was silence. Then Mobel said, 'You don't tell we you name.'

Sonna looked up in surprise. He told them as if he'd somehow expected them to know it already. It made him remember they were still strangers.

'You come to town with you people?' asked Sista with friendly interest.

'I not here with my people,' answered Sonna softly.

'But you have people in the country?' said Sista.

He nodded.

Sista felt that he was shy and her wish to put him at his ease made her pursue her questioning. 'But you have you father in the country?' she said.

'No,' replied Sonna abruptly.

Mobel saw that the hand which Sonna had on his shoebox was trembling. She wanted to warn Sista to stop asking questions but could not catch her eye.

'You mean you father and mother oversea'?' asked Sista persistently.

Sonna's agitation became apparent as his eyes began to fill. He looked fiercely at the three. 'All of you think I don't know my father and mother, that what you think. Awright, I will tell you. My father dead. Him dead in Santa Lucia prison but him didn't thief.' He fled from them suddenly, leaving his precious shoebox. He ran blindly over the rubbish heaps on the vast stretch of land and the others gave chase, certain that if they lost him now they would never find him again. Sonna ran on, aware only of his need for escape and comfort. Perhaps safety lay beyond the road he was approaching, or past the criss-cross of train lines, or a long, long way ahead by the beach, across the sea . . .

'Sonna, stop!'

'Wait, Sonna!'

'Don't cross the trainline, Sonna!'

But he did not hear, he just kept running, through the barrier over one set of lines and then between them as if he intended to challenge the train that was approaching.

Reckless in her desperation, Mobel dived under the barrier with her two friends close behind as the train thundered by a few yards from them. They could no longer see Sonna. But as the train passed out of sight and Sonna's mangled body did not appear between the lines they ran on again, through the next barrier and out on to the road. They hesitated for a moment, not knowing where to go next. Then a small boy waved and shouted to them, 'Him gone.'

'Where?' they called.

'That way,' answered the child, pointing to a narrow lane leading to the sea. They ran again, until they reached the fishermen's beach. There was no one to be seen at first, but then Mobel glimpsed a flash of yellow between the beached boats at the edge of the water. They ran towards it and found Sonna lying face down on the wet sand. A wave crashed up on the shore and then pulled back, drawing Sonna with it as he lay unresisting and compliant. Mobel waded in and tried to pull him towards her from the sea but another wave, bigger than the last, knocked her sideways and they both lay sprawling, half submerged. Pazart and Sista – who had been watching, immobilized by fear and fascination – suddenly moved forward and grabbed their clothing, heaving the dead weight of Sonna and the struggling Mobel towards the beach until they were beyond the reach of the forceful currents. Sonna coughed and spluttered as Mobel forgot her own weariness and tried to help him. Her soaking hair was matted with the sand scattered through it and her thin frock clung to her like a wrinkled skin. She knelt, holding Sonna's head against her tightly, rocking him like a mother.

'You shouldn't have run away Sonna, you shouldn't,' she said gently.

Sista and Pazart, still recovering, joined Mobel.

'You shouldn't do that, Sonna, we and you is friend now,' said Sista.

They rested on the beach feeling sad and weary. Pazart looked out to sea, thinking that it would not give up. He watched it fold itself into a long roll, gather speed and rush towards the shore with a great noise, hoping to succeed in making them run squealing as other children had always done. Pazart could hear the swish, swish, swish of breaking waves and knew the sea was saying, 'Look, I shall rush towards you once more, this time with such speed that you will be glad to run screaming with fear and laughter! I shall chase you high upon the shore and perhaps I shall catch you! I shall try to get hold of your legs so if you wish to escape, you must run like the wind! Now little-picnies-with-the-sad-eyes, wake up! Get ready to run as soon as I have rolled myself up once more. I shall not wait, so beware.'

But even when the sea returned with its rolled up waves shouting, 'Run, here I come,' Pazart and the other children remained where they were, staring with sad faces.

Pazart could tell that the sea was feeling ashamed of making such a fool of himself. Even the stones ignored him but the little gravel was always ready for a game. He tossed the eager gravel and sand now as if to show Pazart he could find other playmates whenever he liked.

Mobel was sitting with her feet stretched out in the sand disregarding the waves, for the sea was the monster who had taken her father from her, leaving nothing but his fishing canoe floating upside down. Mobel looked at Sonna who was silent and miserable. She would not have believed she could make a friend of an enemy within a few hours. He was a stranger, a country boy and he had humiliated her, yet now she wanted to comfort him. She could not understand it.

Sonna's knees were drawn up and his hands clasped around them. The dried sea water formed salty deposits on his dark face and sand clung to his clothes, neck and hair. He tried to use the short sleeve of his yellow cotton shirt to wipe his nose but failed. He hesitated for a while, hoping that a sniff would be a substitute for his handkerchief, but the trouble remained so he decided it would be less embarrassing to pull out the end of his shirt and get rid of the annoyance. Shamed by it all, he kept his head straight in front of him, as if he had seen something of importance far out to sea.

The silence began to be uncomfortable. Sonna became restless. 'I going to tell you why I run away,' he said suddenly, still gazing out to sea.

'You don't need to tell,' said Mobel, so softly that the others had to look at her to assure themselves that she had really said it.

'All the same, I want to tell,' insisted Sonna. It seemed that he couldn't find the right words to start. He licked his lips several times but no sound came. At last he managed to say hurriedly, 'My father didn't do anything bad.'

They did not know what to say so they remained silent.

'Him was taking some people at we districk to tell the gover'ment that we want land, and . . . and when him and the people go to the town, them arrest him, 'cause . . .'cause them say him talk bad things 'gainst the gover'ment.' He spoke the last words of the sentence as if they were something he had studied but not managed to understand.

His friends still did not interrupt because they could not find the right comment.

'Him get one year,' continued Sonna, 'and them say he do a thing what them call sed . . . sedition. But him didn't do a thing like that. All him do was to talk. Him say it was wrong 'cause gover'ment have so much land and wouldn't rent it or sell it to people, and them don't have anywhere to plant anything. And him said the gover'ment didn't do what them say for him and the others what go to war when them beg them to join Jamaica Contingent. But him didn't do a thing like what them say, him only talk and march to the Town Hall.'

As he continued Sonna found it easier to find the words. 'My mother and me didn't have anybody when my father go to prison, but we cousin and the people in the districk try to give we something every week. But it make my mother feel bad when we have to take it – for them didn't have much, and we couldn't get work – so my mother say we would come to Santa Lucia and she might get work and I could go back to school, and when them let out my father we would meet him, and maybe we could all live here where nobody wouldn't know that him go to prison.'

He stopped as if the story had ended and Mobel was just about to console him when he began to speak again: 'One night my mother wake up and was crying . . . and when I hear her and ask her why she cry, she . . . she say I didn't have any father any more! I ask her how she know, if somebody did tell her, but she only shake her head and cry. Nex' day we go and ask . . . and them tell we yes, it was true my father was dead.'

Sonna looked as if he might cry, so the others looked away, feeling his loss as if they had known the family. He steadied his voice and began again: 'My mother couldn't get any work and she start to say funny things after my father dead, and one day she couldn't find the street where we live, and when we go there she start to make noises and say it is not we house. She start breaking up the things and people send for the police, and them say she was mad and take her to the asylum.'

Mobel said, 'But people what get off them head can get better, Sonna. I know a man what go to asylum and come out and now him not mad any more.'

But Sonna shook his head and the gesture seemed to release his tears. 'She won't come out,' he said, 'them bury her yesterday.'

There was a long silence. The others thought of the brave way he had faced them and wondered if they could have fought a hostile gang if they'd been feeling so much sorrow.

'We understand how you feel, Sonna,' said Mobel.

'We didn't know, Sonna,' said Sista.

'We sorry, Sonna. You and we friend now,' said Pazart.

'I sorry too,' said Sonna, looking at the sand, and they knew he was apologizing for the fight in the park.

They sat in silence again in the seclusion of their own thoughts. Mobel tried to put what she was thinking into words. 'Last time I feel like you, Sonna, was when Bulla dead.'

They all turned towards her and waited for her to continue. She had lost some of the typewriter ribbon tying the ends of her many plaits and her head was covered with still tinier curls since it had come in contact with the sea.

'Bulla and me use to sleep together. Him was a good dog. I save him from the dog-catcher, and after that we always sleep together. That time I was six, my mother and father was dead, and I didn't have anywhere to sleep sometimes, but when I did have Bulla I didn't mind so much. Him was big and black and shiny.' She spoke quietly now. 'One night me and him was crossing the road. I didn't see the car, 'cause I was thinking and didn't 'member to look.' She closed her eyes. 'I wasn't hurt but the car hit Bulla. The man who was driving come out and flash a light on me and want to touch Bulla but I bawl out for him to leave me and Bulla alone, 'cause him crying and I know him was going to dead and I didn't want nobody to look. When him dead I climb over a high bank by the roadside. I feel the sand soft under me foot. I climb back over to the road and I try to lift Bulla, but him was too heavy, so I take off me father old jacket, what I use to wear, and put it under him, then I hold the sleeves and draw it along with him on top of it up the road a little way till I reach a place where the bank was low and I manage to pull him over. I find a good place near a tree what soft and I get a stick and I dig a grave. It take a long time. After I bury him I mark the place. After that, I don't know but I feel like nobody else left in the world, only me. I didn't want to live anymore.'

She suddenly stood up and began to brush the sand from her legs. 'We have to look out for Bangbelly now,' she said abruptly.

Once more the children's minds came back to their experiences with the Constable some hours before and they nodded in agreement.

'Him is a bad man and him will do anything to catch we now,' said Pazart.

'Every day we will have to watch out,' put in Sista. 'Him will hide behind cars and inside tramcars till him see one of we, then him will try to grab we.' She took Sonna's arm to emphasize the danger, in case with all the talk of hiding and tramcars he thought it was a game. 'Him don't care how much time it take so long as him get us.'

Pazart tried to change the subject. 'Where you live now Sonna?' he asked.

Sonna seemed reluctant to answer. Then at last he said defiantly, 'I don't have anywhere to sleep.' Then he added in a quieter tone, 'I sleep in the market sometimes, the big market what always open.'

Each of the children assured him they had done the same. Mobel said, 'In the market plenty people what come from the country sleep with them load till daylight and the police don't say nothing to them. And when them see a picni sleeping there, near one of the country woman, them don't say nothing for them think you is with the country woman.'

'Except Bangbelly,' said Pazart.

'You say you didn't have anywhere to sleep, Sonna?'

'I sleep in a boat up the top of the beach,' he answered with less shame in his voice.

'Whose boat?' asked Pazart.

'Don't look like it belong to anybody, 'cause from I see it, nobody touch it but me. It covered over with coconut boughs, and it on two big rollers, high up on the sand under an almond tree. You ever notice it when you pass up the beach?' Sonna asked.

The three darted startled glances at each other.

'And that is where you been sleeping?' asked Mobel in a strained voice.

'Yes, two weeks now since I been sleeping there.'

'But you didn't feel 'fraid, Sonna?' asked Sista.

The boy looked at the dying sun, big and red, going down into the sea and confessed, 'Yes, sometimes.'

'And what happen when the big rain and wind come last week, Sonna? You mean you was there that night?' asked Pazart, and the other boy nodded his head:

'I was wet and cold the whole night.'

'You mean you was there the whole night?'

'Yes.'

'And the sea was so rough?'

'I couldn't go in the market for them close it for fear we was going to have hurricane.'

'Jesus! And all the lightning and thunder?'

Sonna continued, 'I was 'fraid, but it was so dark that when I come out to see if I could come from the beach I couldn't see even the sea, except when the lightning flash, and . . . it was just like I hear somebody calling me back into the boat, saying, "Come back! . . . Come back!" So I go back and sit down in the boat though it was soaking wet, 'cause all the cover blow away from it. I double up in the bottom of the wet boat, and after a little it was just . . . just like somebody was there with me keeping me company, 'cause I didn't feel so 'fraid, even when the sea make so much noise, and the wind make the rain sting when I raise me head. So I stay there till daylight.'

The three children listened with wonder on their faces. Their imagination filled in the details of the horror the boy must have experienced. Mobel said, 'Sonna?'

'Yes?'

'The voice you . . . you think you hear that night?'

'What 'bout it?'

'Was it like the voice of a woman . . . or a man?'

'A man.'

'You think it was you father calling you?' Mobel asked.

'No, I would know my father's voice.' Sonna spoke with conviction.

Mobel sat back with a look of satisfaction on her face which all but Sonna could interpret. Sista and Pazart too seemed satisfied and convinced, as if it was the most natural thing in the world. Only Sonna had not noticed Mobel's look of pride. He said, picking up the loose end of his experience that night, 'If I didn't hear like somebody was calling me back, I would drown! For when daylight come, I find where I was going to cross that night was full up with water what would cover me!'

Sista said, 'Gawd!' in an awed whisper.

Mobel stretched out her hand, and grabbed Sonna's arm. 'You know who save you that night?' she asked excitedly.

'No. Who?'

'It was my father!' said the girl proudly.

'You father?' asked Sonna, trying hard to understand.

'Yes Sonna! That boat you was sleeping in did belong to my father!' She spoke sadly now. 'Him was a fisherman. Them didn't find him when him drown, only the boat. So the other fishermen carry the boat high up on the beach and cover it over like it is him grave. So it is him what did call you!'

Sonna said, 'Oh!' and like his three friends, was fully convinced that the voice he had heard was that of Mobel's father.

'You must come and live with us, Sonna!' said Sista.

'Yes, we will go now, we want to show you the place and it far from here!' put in Mobel.

'And Sonna, you and me will have we own room!' said Pazart.

And Sonna, now walking between them, felt lonely no longer.

CHAPTER TWO

Santa Lucia, like Kingston, has its residential areas with beautiful bungalows, well kept lawns, tennis courts and gardens. Like Kingston, it is overpopulated, with big American cars running alongside donkey carts, and powerful, streamlined buses side by side with mule carts and an occasional bullock wagon.

Women in colourful frocks and plaid handkerchiefs sit on top of hampered donkeys, while youths on bicycles ride with skill and abandon in and out of the milling crowd.

Trams with open sides clang their way along sunlit streets while American tourists enthuse over horse-drawn carriages available for hire.

Near the waterfront are the narrow lanes where, long ago, buccaneers from the Spanish Main used to sprawl and divide their doubloons and pieces of eight. Now there are only handcart men and their vehicles awaiting employment. Streets – where caballeros with spurs jingling and swords swinging from scabbards, used to quarrel and duel for the love of some mantilla-covered senorita in the days when the Spaniards ruled the Island – are now walked by dark-skinned women in colourful clothing with loads of fruit and vegetables on their heads. They smoke cigars with the lighted ends turned inside their mouths so that only occasional wreaths of smoke betray the fact that they are breaking the no-smoking law which applies to the markets. Husky-voiced, they shout out the merits of their wares.

But unlike Kingston, Santa Lucia has no port for accommodating large ships. Her harbour has treacherous breakers and only the lightest craft may come alongside the pier. And unlike Kingston, Santa Lucia has a river that cuts the city in two, from under the hill to right down to the sea. Although bridges join the two sections, they are divided still further by the disparity between the rich and the poor. For while wealth flourishes on the east side of town, right up to the foot of the hills facing the sea, the signs of poverty are visible as soon as any of the bridges going westward are crossed.

Once over Main Bridge, so named because it is the most important of the five bridges spanning the river, there are no large, white buildings to be seen; no air-conditioned stores with uniformed men to open and close the doors of chauffeur-driven cars. On the western side of town there are only hot, congested shops filled – from the doorways inwards – with pots and pans, beds and canvas cots, cheap canvas shoes, printed cotton and readymade suits known as 'reach-me-downs', purchased only by those too poor to buy cloth and hand it over to a tailor. Fried fish shops stand side by side with rum shops, where buxom women serve gills, half-pints and pints of white rum to all-male customers. Shoe repairers tap nails into soles and heels of shoes, heedless of the perspiration running down their faces. Next door stands a Chinese shop with a stock of anything from smoked herrings to rolls of tweed made in England.

Walk along the road from Main Bridge, still going westward, and the city becomes shabbier and shabbier with its uncared-for streets, its wastelands. Turn off from the main road leading to far-away Kingston and other towns, proceed with your back to the sea so that you face the plains and distant hills and sooner or later you will come upon Mango Walk.

American tourists flock from their great liners in excitement to bask in the warmth of the sun on this Island that has no winter and has never seen snow. They enjoy the colourful scenes, the laughter on every face and the palatial bungalows with their flower gardens and tennis lawns. But they never see Mango Walk.

Once it was a cemetery belonging to the Santa Lucia Corporation. Long ago, a few homeless people discovered they could make shelters from their findings in the scrap heaps. The government did not interfere. Others followed, some with ambition and a knowledge of carpentry, others with few funds. Later a variety of huts and shacks rose out of the abandoned cemetery and a few dwellings with wooden walls, wooden floors, wooden doors and galvanized roofs.

The roads to Mango Walk were rough and uneven, some made so by floodwater from tropical rain and hurricanes, others by the constant trek of feet between the heaps and clumps of cacti.

One of the early squatters wanted privacy and to conceal the shame of his abode, thought of fencing off his lot with the type of giant cactus that grew plentifully here. Others adopted the idea and in a few years every hut or shack had its seclusion behind cactus fences taller than the tallest man and so thick that there was hardly an inch between the prickly stalks.

A newsman once responded to the hostile reception he received there when he went to take photographs, by naming the place 'Cactus Village', claiming that the people were as prickly as the cacti which protected them. It remained known as such to those who could afford a morning newspaper. But to the people who lived and died there, that part of the town was always Mango Walk, even though there were only a couple of mango trees in the whole village.

The children lived in two little rooms, one facing the other. The original builders had planned to construct these rooms on a foundation about three feet from the ground, with a small verandah, a pair of windows, wooden walls, galvanized roofs and floors made of pine boards. They seemed to have discovered half-way through that funds would not allow them to continue, so they had divided their materials for the rooms in equal parts. In the end, each room had only three-quarters of its galvanized roofing, a door but no windows, only half the floor and two of the four sides were boarded up with unpainted soapboxes and newspaper with cardboard added to keep out the wind and the rain.

Each room was about twelve feet by twelve feet. There was a small pit-latrine and a lean-to for a kitchen. A large, treeless yard – with hard, uneven earth which showed cracks in the dry months and turned into a brown, slippery, treacherous place in the rainy months – was surrounded by the everlasting cactus fences on all sides, with a few feet left open as a gateway.

Sista's grandmother had lived and died there of consumption just as her parents had done. Sista had been left in isolation; no one would take her for fear of catching the disease. Alone and crying one night she had been found by Mobel, then six, who had joined her there. Later, Pazart had found a home with the two.

And now Sonna was quite settled with his new friends and they with him, as if they had known each other all their lives. There was no awkwardness between them. They said exactly what was in their minds to one another and shared everything, even the lessons in reading and writing that were given to the poor children by Captain Dimlight of the Salvation Army. Sonna showed great promise and the Captain was glad to have him as a pupil. Pazart, impressed by his friend's ability, would always back him in an argument even when he did not really understand the point that Sonna was trying to make. It was also evident that they listened to Sonna's advice and little by little he became the leader of the group, though had they been asked, they would never have admitted it. For three years, Mobel had been the self-appointed leader and had guarded the position jealously when challenged by Pazart. Now she was handing it over willingly to someone who had not even asked for the privilege.

Mobel sometimes recalled being in the park, beaten flat on her back, and the rude comment that a boy had made about her. The memory wounded her pride until she remembered that Sonna, who had been the cause of it all, had been saved by the voice of her father. Then her acceptance of him was absolute once more.

CHAPTER THREE

Living roughly on the streets had taught the children greater awareness than was usual for their age. Sonna decided that they would sell their goods more safely if two of them kept watch.

'We will tell the other children to do like we,' he said.

'We must find a name for weself,' said Mobel. 'That will make the others do like we.' The rest agreed, knowing that the children would accept the idea more readily if it had a hint of adventure in it. The four sat down and thought. Countless names were considered and rejected. Then Sista said:

'Captain Dimlight always call we "God's Little Sparrows", like the song him did compose and everybody sing now.' She sang the words for Sonna and the others joined in:

> 'I shall never fear tomorrow,
> I can banish care or sorrow
> Knowing all the while . . .
> I am God's little chile . . .
> God's little sparrow.'

Sonna knew the air; he sometimes played it on his tin mouth-organ, and all over the Island people were singing or whistling the comforting little chorus. Sista's suggestion was the best; they decided to call themselves, 'The Sparrows'.

In less than an hour they were contacting other children with their new ideas for the way the selling should be done. No one objected when Sonna outlined the rules: No giving buyers wrong change, no going away with anybody's change, no selling eleven needles for a dozen – in short, no dishonesty. But when, in addition, Sonna suggested that they should smile and say thank you, even to someone who had not troubled to buy, there were objections from all sides; even his friends were doubtful about this.

'Who you to come and tell we what to do?' said someone. 'We know Pazart and Mobel and Sista, but who know you?'

Mobel was angry. To challenge Sonna's authority was to challenge hers. She braced her chest, sprawled her legs and with her arms akimbo jeered at the children standing opposite them in the quiet lane.

'You Mister Baboo and you Mister Leslie and you two others what I don't know, you want to take me on? If you feel like it you can come.'

Those challenged shifted their weight from one foot to the other. 'We and you don't have any row, Mobel,' said one.

'We wasn't talking to you Mobel, nor Pazart, nor Sista.'

Sonna felt it was time to show everyone that he could fight his own battles. 'Any of you want to feel how a donkey can kick?' He moved forward with clenched fists, and now they recognized him as the country boy who had beaten Pazart and Mobel and had even sprawled

Bangbelly. They backed away. 'We didn't know it was you,' said one with lame truth, and the dispute was over.

By the following day it was all over the market.

'Those little picnies real smart. You know what I hear?'

'What?'

'Them make themselves into a little gang. Some will watch out for Bangbelly and police and some will sell.'

'Bless the poor little souls!'

'Them make rules. No thiefing, no begging, and thank you, even if nobody buy them goods.'

'We must look out for them, them setting good example.'

'True. Them poor little sparrows!'

'And you know? That the very name them call themself . . .'

Pazart awoke, raised himself on one elbow and listened sleepily, forgetting for a moment that Sonna was sharing his room. His old home-made cot creaked as he sat up. He thought he had been woken by a noise but he could hear nothing now. Perhaps he had been dreaming. Then, just as he was about to return to sleep, he heard the sound of crying.

'You awright, Sonna?' he whispered.

The sobbing stopped abruptly.

'Yes . . . I is awright.'

But Pazart knew something was wrong from Sonna's muffled answer.

'I was dreaming,' said Sonna.

'Oh,' said Pazart, as if the explanation satisfied him.

Then Sonna added, 'I was dreaming I was home with my mother and father.' He paused. 'I dream I was telling them that I did think them was dead but it was only a dream. I was so glad. Then I wake up and find them really dead.'

Pazart was now sorry he hadn't pretended not to hear the crying of his friend. He struggled to find words of consolation, feeling that Mobel and Sista would have been able to say the right thing. 'Why I can't think like them?' he asked himself, and the question gave him the lead he wanted.

'Sonna!'

'Eh?'

'You don't know that you is lucky?'

'How you mean?'

'You know you mother and father and have them till you big like you is.'

Sonna knew what Pazart was saying; he had already heard that his

23

parents had died when he was just a baby and his grandmother, who had raised him, had died when he was five.

'I sorry Pazart,' said Sonna, shamed by Pazart's words.

'I don't mind now,' said Pazart, trying to seem cheerful.

'Sonna?'

'What?'

'You won't feel frighten' if I tell you something?'

'Feel frighten'? What you mean Pazart?'

'It's 'bout me Sonna. I know you going to feel frighten'.'

'I won't feel frighten' Pazart.'

'But if you don't want sleep with me no more, you will tell me the truth?'

'Yes.'

'Promise?'

'Yes I promise. Tell me what it is now.'

The darkness around them suddenly seemed to come down heavily on Pazart making his chest contract, while the silence of the night outside made the telling of his secret the most difficult thing he had ever tried to say.

'Sometimes I have fits Sonna, have it bad. Now you know.'

He spoke quickly and defiantly, yet Sonna sensed that his answer would mean a lot to Pazart. 'That all?' he asked, imitating the way his father had used to reassure others.

'You mean you don't think it bad?'

'I think it was something bad you was going to tell me.'

The cot creaked as Pazart raised himself further. 'You mean you not frighten', Sonna?' he asked in disbelief.

'Fit is nothing, nothing bad I mean.'

'But the children always run from me when I have it.'

'Them foolish to run,' said Sonna fiercely.

'Pazart?'

'Eh?'

'Mobel and Sista, them know?'

'Yes I tell them but them never see me when I have it.'

'You think them would frighten' if them see you?'

'I don't know,' answered Pazart, and then said, 'Mobel wouldn't run. Even if she 'fraid.'

Sonna remembered how able she had been at the park and inwardly agreed with Pazart.

'Maybe Sista would frighten bad but I don't think she would run away either,' said Pazart thoughtfully.

24

'Pazart?' said Sonna after a pause.

'Eh?'

'The fits . . . when you grow big you won't have it any more you know.'

'True Sonna? You think so?'

'It is true, my father tell me and him always know.'

'Gawd. Wish I could grow big now! Sonna?'

'What?'

'If I have fits you won't make anybody throw water on me?'

'Awright, I won't make anybody do that.'

'Promise?'

'Yes I promise.'

Pazart sighed contentedly and soon his deep breathing could be heard in the darkness. But Sonna lay on his back and it was nearly daylight before he fell asleep.

CHAPTER FOUR

It was not yet midday. The sun beat down on the almost deserted street. Bangbelly, stick in hand, waited at the bus stop. His cloth cap was pulled down over his bloodshot eyes, and his ashbrown chin was unshaven. He wore a brown jacket that was a little short and would not meet over his protruding stomach. He was not on duty, his badge of authority was tucked away in his pocket. But his ungainly appearance was deceptive; it concealed a man who was quick in mind and body.

The news that the street children were now calling themselves The Sparrows and had been organized by Sonna, the boy who had humiliated him in the park, had not taken long to reach him. He was still sore over the incident, which had marked a change in the attitude of the people towards him. In the past they had feared him, perhaps even given him grudging respect, but since it had become known that a few children had got the better of him he had become a figure more ridiculed than held in awe.

He had noticed this change when he had walked through the streets near the market place a few hours after the incident. He had not been treated with quite the usual care or deference. Some of the market traders had answered his questions in a tone that had bordered on insolence. He had seen the little smiles on the faces of the market women as he had approached, which they had not even troubled to conceal.

Next day when he had returned there, everything had carried on as before at first. He had seen the usual lads with boxes held by straps around their necks displaying all types of trinkets and the little, shed-like carts where young women sold combs, reels of cotton, socks and cups and saucers. Further along he had noticed the sharp-tongued *higgler** women with baskets of bananas and other fruit in their hands; they had called out their wares, creating a bedlam of voices.

Then as Bangbelly had walked among them their voices had fallen silent. All heads had turned towards him and they had stood in line like a crowd of disciplined spectators awaiting a royal visit.

Bangbelly had felt apprehensive but he had concealed his fear behind impassive features, gripping his baton more tightly. As he had passed the rows of faces, he had heard the low hum of a once popular American song from unmoving lips. He might almost have been imagining the rhythmic rumble that had seemed to grow up around him, louder and louder. He had remembered the words:

> 'I'm flying high,
> But I gotta feeling I'm falling,
> Falling for nobody else but you!'

He had begun to grow hot. The song had been revived especially for him because of what had happened in the park. No one had needed to speak the words; they had known he would grasp their significance. Some pedlars had pretended to strum their trinket boxes while others had drummed on theirs. Hard-faced higglers had put down the hands of bananas they had been offering for sale to clap the beat of the tune. Pretty black-skinned shopgirls had peered out through single doors of stuffy little stores to see what the sound was about. Passers-by had realized that the humming had had something to do with the incident that had embarrassed him and had grinned in appreciation.

Bangbelly had marched through the mocking throng with his face set in a rigid mask, looking neither left nor right until at last he had reached the end of the lines.

Bangbelly could not recall that incident without feeling afraid. The boy called Sonna and his friends had, with one stupid little action,

higgler: market or street trader, usually a woman.

undermined all his authority, and in doing so had diminished an aspect of his life that he had prized. He was angry that a few children could have made him feel so weak and foolish. He wanted to come up against them again in order to show that he could not be held in contempt a second time. He looked out for the children, but they were organizing themselves so well now that he found no opportunity for reasserting himself.

A tiny old woman shuffled across the street with the carelessness of one who thinks little of life. Her tall stick tapped as each wrinkled foot made its way before the other. She wore a loose-fitting frock made from half a dozen different materials. The waist was tied tightly and gave the bodice the appearance of a half-filled sack.

Her face was small, round and wrinkled and her lips looked as if they had never known the company of teeth. Her head was tied with plaid. Despite her evident poverty, her clothing had none of the frowsy, dirty odour of the homeless aged.

The Constable, deep in thought, did not notice that the old woman had crossed the street and was now at his side, so when she whispered hoarsely to him he jumped, startled for a moment.

'Cross me palm wid a piece of silver Massa an' I will tell you fortune. Jus' a piece of silver Massa an' I will tell you Gawd's truth 'bout you past, present an' future.'

Bangbelly recognized her as the woman he had often seen selling herbs, named Ma Kuskus after the sweet-smelling roots of a weed of that name, renowned as a moth repellent. For a moment he wondered if he should take out his badge and arrest her but his experience in the park had made him curious. He was not taken in by her, but it would be interesting to see what particular tales she would spin for him. He was sure they would be founded on the general opinion of him and it would be useful to know how people saw him.

She stood by his side, palm outstretched, the other hand resting heavily on her stick.

He thrust his hand in his pocket, searching for a silver coin. Unable to find what he wanted, he drew out all the money and finally held out a small silver threepenny piece between two heavy fingers. 'None of you damn lies now, ole woman, tell me God's truth or you will be sorry.'

The woman rested the stick on her body and took the money. Then she took the Constable's hand and pressed the silver into his palm, peered down and with startling swiftness brought the hand she was holding close to her face. Then with a hoarse cry she dropped it as if it had stung her. The sudden release caused the silver to fall to the ground

27

but she did not seem to notice. Bangbelly moved towards her but she jerked aside as if he were a leper and shouted, 'Don't you come near me! Keep away you hear me? Keep away!' He was startled by the genuine terror on her face.

A couple of people were now coming closer, drawn perhaps by the scene, but Bangbelly needed no witnesses, he only wanted to know what had frightened the woman.

'Stop woman, I want to speak to you!' he said authoritatively.

'Go away, go away,' she said, still backing away from him. Her bare feet missed the level of the sidewalk and she fell. He went to assist her, not wanting any suggestion from the witnesses that he had been responsible. He wished he had followed his first impulse and arrested her. But as he moved to touch her she hissed, 'Don't dare come any closer! Don't touch me wid dem bloody han's! Stan' where you is! You stink, you hear me? Stink wid de smell of blood!'

The woman heaved herself up with surprising speed and hastened away, disappearing from view as the road curved, leaving Bangbelly gazing after her. He became aware that passers-by were eyeing him curiously and he turned to walk to the bus-stop, irritated with himself for being drawn into the old woman's madness. Yet as he went he was troubled by what she had said, and the occurrence seemed to emphasize the ground he had lost since those children had scorned him. Before that had happened, no old woman would have dared to behave towards him in such a way.

At last the bus came. Bangbelly sat at the back and began to relax again. When the conductor came up to him, he handed over a sixpence for a threepenny fare. The conductor was about to place the change in his outstretched hand, when the Constable moved back with a jerk, causing the money to roll to the floor. The sight of his own palm, the silver threepence and the gesture of the conductor had made him remember Ma Kuskus.

For a few days Bangbelly's duties had taken him away from the market and he had not been sorry. He felt that his absence might allow the business with the children to fade from people's minds. But as soon as he entered the gate of the great open-air market he realized that this was not the case. He could hear hurried whispers and saw children scuttling to and fro, apparently passing on the news of his arrival.

He considered turning back on some pretext but he knew he could not stay away forever. It was better to face whatever demonstration they might be plotting against him and get it over with.

As he passed the stalls he could feel the eyes of everyone upon him and he was afraid. He had experienced the same feeling as a boy when he had been sent on an errand in the country on a dark night. He remembered how he had imagined that the spirits from the white-washed graves in the cemetery along the lane were just behind him, ready to put their cold, white hands on his shoulders. It would have taken only the rushing wings of a bat or a frightened bird to make him run, sobbing. The re-emergence of these irrational thoughts disturbed him deeply.

He reached the market office without betraying his anxiety and wiped the perspiration from his brow. Nothing had happened – perhaps nothing would happen. Like the graveyard ghosts, the hostility of the crowd was probably only the product of his imagination. When the time came for him to go off duty he prepared to leave in a better frame of mind.

But as he re-entered the market he realized his mistake. Every man, woman and child seemed to have left their wares and had converged in two solid lines from the office door to the main gate. It was as if their apparent success with the humming a few days earlier had given them courage and they were preparing to repeat the exercise with even greater enthusiasm.

Bangbelly knew there was no turning back, for they would wait as long as he was there. He began to walk between them. At first, nothing happened beyond some whispering but then a voice that was unmistak-ably female, imbued with the hoarseness that came from shouting wares all day, cried out:

'God proteck de Sparrows!'

Half a dozen voices took up the chant:

'God proteck de Sparrows!'

And the long line before him, and those behind joined in:

'God proteck de Sparrows!'

'God proteck de Sparrows!'

'God proteck de Sparrows!'

They clapped their hands to the chant in a one, two, three, one, two, three timing, and it seemed that the echo of their voices was all over the city.

Frightened and raging he walked, trying to keep his head up, and looking straight before him.

'God proteck de Sparrows!'

'God proteck de Sparrows!'

It came from the little ones clinging to their mothers' aprons. It came from the old toothless ones who sold herbs in bundles at a penny a time. It came from the bass voices of the men who sold yams, those who sold corn by the bushel and even from the men and boys who pushed handcarts loaded with goods for a few pennies.

Bangbelly could see how well they had planned the demonstration. The lines consisted of women and children while the men stood back. The police would not readily charge them with batons even if they were summoned.

He seemed to have been walking for hours, yet he was barely half-way to the gate. The chanting was now more urgent and stamping feet kept time with the clapping hands.

'God proteck de Sparrows!'

'God proteck de Sparrows!'

Even his own heart was beating to the chant.

'God proteck de Sparrows!'

'God proteck de Sparrows!'

He stopped and the crowd stopped abruptly too, the last chant abandoned mid-sentence. Even their clapping hands seemed to have frozen with him.

He put his hands on his hips and looked at their faces. The sun shining overhead cast shadows, making the scene eerie and unreal. Though the crowd was clothed European-style, each of its members suddenly seemed to lose frocks, trousers and shirts to stand wild and naked before him, just as they would have appeared in a Tarzan film. The blood pounded in his ears and created the beating of a drum. As he swiftly passed his hand across his forehead he was startled to see that he was the same colour as his tormentors. He looked again. The illusion vanished; the faces were no longer wild and the bodies were clothed. Bangbelly started towards the gate once more and the chant began as before:

'God proteck de Sparrows!'

'God proteck de Sparrows!'

'God proteck de Sparrows!'

His own feet seemed to mock him as he walked between the taunting people; every step kept time with the chant.

Suddenly he stopped again with such fury that those nearest to him cowered momentarily, expecting a blow from his baton. Again the chanting ceased. The crowd waited, hostile and hard-faced. With his right hand he lifted his baton high, as though pointing to the skies. He spoke with difficulty.

'Awright, awright. You say God proteck the Sparrows? Well, see if God can proteck them from me.'

A gasp went up from the crowd that made Bangbelly realize the awfulness of his blasphemous challenge. He stood in total stillness for a moment and then he brought his baton down with a sharp movement and started 'through the avenue of people once again.

'God proteck de Sparrows!'

'God proteck de Sparrows!'

'God proteck de Sparrows!'

Now there was a new note in the chant, a defiance in the higher pitch of the tone which told Bangbelly that the crowd had accepted his challenge; that they were sure God had accepted it.

Bangbelly reached the gate where the line of people ended, his legs numb. He staggered across the street to the nearest bar. The barwoman produced the half-pint of rum he ordered without taking her eyes off his face and the other customers watched in silence as he poured and drank until the bottle stood empty. Without looking at anyone, Bangbelly slammed the cost of the drink on the counter and left.

'If ever there was a man ready for murder, that man is him,' said the barwoman to no one in particular and the customers nodded in silent agreement.

The rum caused Bangbelly to walk even more unsteadily than he had done before, but inside he felt strengthened and calmed. He was no longer afraid, just angry that he could have been so humiliated.

He passed a cookshop and heard laughter from inside. He wondered if the news of his confrontation with the market people had reached there yet. Perhaps they were laughing about that.

He paused outside for a moment and felt the strange mixture of feelings he could not identify that always touched him when he saw the place. The rum had sharpened these emotions. Bangbelly took out his handkerchief and wiped his forehead, still gazing at the cookshop, a poor, run down place, which provided cheap food. Bangbelly suspected gambling too, but he had never caught them at it. Ironman ran the place. Bangbelly knew him well. He was large and brawny. When he had been arrested on a charge of theft, it had taken umpteen constables to hold him down. The laughter sounded again and Bangbelly moved on, not wishing to be seen there in his weakened state. He could not push Joseph Cawley – Ironman's real name, that few people had ever heard –

from his mind and the feelings that the rum had heightened still remained. Suddenly Bangbelly knew what it was that the cookshop and Ironman aroused in him. It was hate. He hated the man. He was both surprised and relieved. Surprised because the most he usually felt for people was indifference, and relieved because loathing was not a feeling to be ashamed of, not like fear, or regret or loneliness . . .

Bangbelly walked faster now, buoyed up by his thoughts. There had always been enmity between himself and Ironman. They were probably the most talked about men on the Island. People compared their strength and speed and pitted them against one another in imaginary fights. He had fought Ironman once and lost . . . The memory of that still rankled. Ironman was poor but he was liked. He had no head for business. Sometimes he even gave away food for nothing, yet he was respected for it. In spite of his position as Constable and the money he earned, recent events had proved to Bangbelly that he did not have respect.

He reached his house, angry and tired. He went inside but did not merely close the door behind him, he bolted and locked it as an extra precaution against the world outside.

News of the way the market people had mocked the District Constable and the challenge he had made against God swept through the city of Santa Lucia and beyond into the country parts. Soon they had even heard it fifty miles away in Kingston.

The story was quickly condensed into a code. Handcart men began tapping the sides of their carts with three long and three short taps, which even Bangbelly was able to recognize as 'God proteck de Sparrows!' Fast-pedalling cyclists rang their bells as they passed him to imitate the six-syllabled slogan. Taxi drivers tooted their horns accordingly whenever the Constable was in sight. Tram motormen gonged six times, long and short, just for him. Children shouted, 'God proteck de Sparrows' from a safe distance.

One Sunday night when he was on special duty, Bangbelly heard a preacher telling his flock about a man who had recently challenged God. He assured them that God was not mocked: that God had promised that even the lowly sparrows were looked after, not by man but by God Himself and that in spite of the humble position they held in the eyes of man, God would not let a single one fall to the ground from hunger nor cold, though the lands where they dwelt were covered with ice and snow for many months of the year. Afterwards he asked the crowd of worshippers to kneel and pray that the evil words of this blasphemer would fall on his own head.

CHAPTER FIVE

The Sparrows found great pleasure in being on the beaches of Santa Lucia that stretched along the edge of town some three miles from their home at Mango Walk. Half the beach to the east was closed to them. Here, starting from the point at which the Santa Lucia river merged with the sea, were warehouses, wharves, private bathing beaches, yacht clubs and the palatial bungalows that had been built a few yards from the white sand.

On the other side of the beach the poverty was as great as it was in the west of the city. The five miles of beach and swamp which stretched and curved from this part of the town were strewn with ragged fishermen's huts. There were nets and canoes hewn from huge cottonwood trees and only the poor in search of a bath, driftwood, fishing or solitude came here.

When there was a wind, whiffs of foul air drifted from the swamp and the town's sewer. When there was no wind, there were gnats, sandflies and mosquitoes. But to Sonna and his friends, none of this mattered.

Equipped with little balls of fishing lines and tiny hooks in old Vaseline tins, with a few worms as bait, the two boys would wade knee-deep into the sea until they were able to climb on one of the many rocks to be found near the shore. When the girls were with them, they would walk along the beach until they reached the broadleaf wild grape trees that grew profusely there.

One day, after they had finished selling their wares, the four arrived there as usual and the boys decided they wanted to bathe and splash about in the warm sea.

'Mobel and Sista, we don't want you to watch we!' they shouted, though the girls were about a quarter of a mile away, searching for wild grapes.

'You fancy youself Mister Sonna and Mister Pazart. Who want to see you?' Sista shouted.

'We don't want to get blind,' said Mobel and her mocking laughter infuriated the boys.

'Wait till we come out the water Sonna, we going to make them cry the way we going to tease them,' promised Pazart.

'Just wait till we come out and put on we clothes,' agreed Sonna.

Their swim completed, the two boys walked sulkily ahead of the girls. Mobel and Sista seemed to be enjoying some secret joke which Sonna and Pazart felt concerned them, so they walked on with their hands in their pockets, their bare feet kicking at the sand, seeking inspiration for revenge. The girls continued to giggle stupidly. Sonna's face lit up.

'Pazart,' he said loudly, though his friend was right by his elbow.

'Yes Sonna,' said Pazart with equal loudness, sensing that Sonna had found something to help them get back at the girls.

'Don't you glad you is a man and not a woman?'

'Yes Sonna, me glad. Women chat and chat and giggle like them is foolish.'

There was a sudden silence which the boys registered with pleasure, though they were careful not to show it and kept their eyes in front as if they were only interested in the mangroves and the few wind-battered coconut trees on the swampy part of the beach which they were now approaching.

'Do you know why them talk and talk and giggle and giggle like them don't have any sense Pazart?' asked Sonna innocently.

'No I don't know why. You know?'

'Yes Pazart, I know.'

Not a sound came from the girls walking close behind but the boys could feel how hard they were listening.

'It is because of what Captain tell we 'bout Adam and Eve. You 'member how God didn't have any more ribs to make them foolish woman with, and Him cut out one of Adam own and lend it to Eve?'

'Oh yes Sonna, I 'member.'

'Well that is why woman so foolish; God didn't bother to make all the thing for them like Him make for we. And if it wasn't for we man, them woman couldn't live at all, at all!'

'You right Sonna, you right! Gawd, me glad we is man!'

The boys guffawed at their own joke as they swung back from the swampy beach ahead and went towards the town. Now the girls turned back also, but Mobel, burning with indignation, was not satisfied to walk with Sista behind the boys any more. She came up abreast of the laughing two, and Sista, not to be outdone, went to the other side, so that now they were walking four abreast.

'Sista!' said Mobel loudly.

'Yes Mobel?' said Sista, taking the hint.

'You see any *man* anywhere?'

Sista pretended to look all around the beach and towards the sleeping sea.

'I don't see any man, except one out there fishing in a boat.'

Sista pointed seawards to a boatman.

'You sure that the only man you see, Sista?'

'Yes Mobel, the only man.'

'What 'bout them two *something* what call themself man?'

'Them *something*, Mobel? It's because them have hands and feet and *mouth* them think them is man.'

'We is man too,' blurted Pazart, now unable to keep silent.

'You hear Mobel?' called Sista. 'Them is right! Them is not man, them is *mantoo*!'

Pazart could not control his temper any longer. 'You want me to show you with me fist if I is "Mantoo" or not?' he shouted, jumping in front of Sista, but in a second Mobel had pushed Sista to one side and was facing him instead.

'It is me you must challenge, Mister Pazart,' she said softly, but before Pazart could reply or pass on the challenge to Mobel, Sonna intervened. Looking Pazart in the eye he said, ''Member what we decide, Pazart? We decide we won't fight with girls anymore. 'Member?'

'Yes Sonna, I 'member,' replied Pazart with relief in his voice.

'We will fight them when them give we back we ribs what God lend them, eh Pazart?'

'Yes Sonna! If them have shame them would give we back we ribs! Make you and me run away and leave them Sonna, then we can take a freshwater bath in the river,' suggested Pazart.

'Good idea!' replied Sonna, and started to run ahead.

'You need it!' shouted Mobel after them, inviting a shower of pebbles from the indignant boys.

They were nearly home now and had slowed down to a walk, the girls strolling ahead this time. They had stopped teasing one another and were deep in earnest discussion.

'. . . Captain say we mustn't say "him" when we mean "his".'

'Yes and we mustn't say "we", we must say "our".'

'Sometime I 'member, but not all the time.'

'You say "him" and "we" all the time Pazart.'

'Awright what 'bout "dead" instead of "death", don't you say that all the time Miss Mobel?'

'Everybody say that, even Sonna, just like "thief" 'stead of "steal" like what Captain tell we to say, and "stole" and all them hard words to 'member.'

'Them is not so hard to 'member, Mobel, for sometimes I 'member them.'

'Oh, so Miss Sista, you think you can 'member to say everything?'

'I didn't say so Mobel, but me and Sonna 'member to say some of them sometimes, specially when we talking to strangers.'

'Mister Sonna so please to hear Sista praise him that him just sit down with a grin on him face. You feel proud, eh, Mister Sonna?'

'You don't start on me, Mobel, for I didn't say anything.'

'No, but you look like you was laughing in you mind 'cause Sista and you think you can talk better than me and Pazart.'

'See how she foolish Pazart? She think we care if one talk a little better than the other. My father say it's nothing to shame of if we can't speak good English, for we not English, we is Jamaican what come from Africa, so really African language belong to we, but we don't know it any more.'

'You right Sonna. Me not shame 'cause me can't speak English good.'

'Me not shame either,' concluded Mobel and peace returned.

CHAPTER SIX

It was serial night and Sonna's first moving picture. There must have been over two hundred children, sitting mostly in the front seats by themselves, away from the adults. They had ages to wait until the first show started and they would not sit quietly. They squeezed in and out of the benches in excitement.

'Keep me seat Speedie, I soon come back.'

'Awright.'

There was so much to show off by walking along the front seats close to the stage: a new shirt or pants, an organdie frock; perhaps a pair of shoes; yet no one considered the shoed one half dressed because he had no socks, or thought the worst of someone with bare feet as long as the legs, face and hands were clean and hair was combed. To be inside, having raised the mighty sum of sixpence, was enough.

Sonna and Pazart were sitting in front of Mobel and Sista. Every now and then, Mobel would kneel on the hard, unpainted bench, her back to the screen, to scan the faces behind them. Now and again she would touch Pazart's shoulder and point to some old acquaintance among the crowd.

'Pazart, look, Chinaman!'

'Where?'

'Look, upside that woman with the big hat. See him waving?'

'Hi Pazart.'

'Hi Chinaman.'

'Can't see you at all, man. T'ink you stow to 'Merica.'

'Think you gone to Hong Kong,' replied Pazart.

There was laughter, then the half-Chinese eyes grew sad as he said softly, 'Maybe one day . . .' and those around him laughed no longer.

'Him father is Chinese,' Pazart explained to Sonna. 'Him mother Jamaican. Him father go back to Hong Kong and don't come back and him mother sick with consumption. Him clean cars and carry people basket in him little cart.'

Saddened for a moment, Sonna said nothing in reply, but then his attention was caught by Mobel who had seen a friend parading a pair of khaki trousers. He was calling out to another boy.

'Hi Boysie, you get in!'

'Must!'

'Want a seat?'

'No! Me and Speedie sit down together. Him keeping me seat.'

'Where him is?'

'See him right in the middle, side a that girl with the red ribbon in her head?'

'Ah yes, I see him, I going tease him. Listen! Hi Speedie.'

'Hi Baboo.'

'See you get a girl at last!'

'Yes, I done with you sister!'

The roars of laughter made Baboo furious. 'Awright Mister Speedie, I going to mash up you mouth soon as picture over. You wait!'

'Come! Me and you go outside now Mister Baboo, and see who face will mash up.'

'It's 'cause I don't want to miss the serial why I don't go outside with you now.'

'You right Baboo, 'cause I would black up you eye so bad, you couldn't see the picture at all, at all!'

'You jus' showing off, Mister Speedie, you jus' . . .'

A man's voice shouted: 'If you goddam picnies won't shut you goddam mouth, I take off me belt and lace you behind good and plenty, and if you father come, I lace him behind as well! Man pay them sixpence and can't rest 'cause o' these picnies!'

Silence from the children.

'You talk true my friend, these picnies won't sit down and behave themselves. Every minute them get up, every minute them mash me 'pon me foot and don't even say pardon! Don't know why the hell them let them in!'

The children sulked and glared and grumbled at the spoil-sport, but there was still an hour to go before the lights were to be cut off, for the rule in the small, open-air cinemas was: Be here as early as you can – first come, first served!

Pazart was talking to Sonna: 'Really true – it's the first time you come to pictures?'

'Yes, first time!'

'We come umpteen time . . . I mean sometime when we get the money. Last time we see Tom Mix and him horse! Gawd him good Sonna! Him and him horse! Him can ride and shoot.'

And Mobel leaned over their shoulders and added, 'Sonna, that horse, him understand more than some people!'

Suddenly a gush of music seemed to come out of the screen and a voice started to sing:

'When there are grey skies,
I don't mind the grey skies,
You'll make them blue, Sonny Boy . . .'

Pazart saw Sonna's surprise and whispered, 'Them got 'lectric gramophone hidden back there.' It was only a guess but Pazart knew it was near enough and he was proud to be able to show Sonna something. All three were waiting impatiently for the lights to go out. They wanted to see Sonna's face when the film started and people came on the screen and began to move and talk. Pazart explained that once it was dark they would see the beam which projected the film shine like the searchlight they had once seen from a warship in the harbour.

The older boys began to join in the song.

> 'Blue moon, you see me standing alone,
> Without a dream in my heart,
> Without a love of my own . . .'

They sang and whistled. Barefoot young men held the hands of the girls beside them and forgot the troubles they would face tomorrow.

Sonna looked at the radiant faces around him. He had never seen so many happy children and adults. The lights went out and the show began and everything else was forgotten.

CHAPTER SEVEN

It was Sunday afternoon. The Salvation Army Captain, commonly known as Dimlight, walked past the wharves and the market towards Ironman's Yard and Cookshop.

He was tall and well-built and though his face was dark, he looked more Indian than African, an inheritance from a European grandfather and a West Indian grandmother. He was thought to have been the son of a rich landowner who was now *custos* of a neighbouring parish but he neither admitted nor denied it. Few people knew that he had quarrelled with his father ten years before at eighteen when his passage to Cambridge in England was being arranged. He had joined the Salvation Army to the deep anger of his father whose hopes for his only son had been destroyed.

He wore the well-tailored white uniform of his calling with a white sun helmet at a jaunty angle. As he walked, he was greeted warmly by those he met. He was liked and admired, partly through his efforts to teach the children of the streets to read and write and partly because he allowed himself to be called Dimlight to his face. His sense of humour was such that he enjoyed explaining the origin of the name. It seemed that one night, although his storm lantern had gone out under the strong wind, he had kept the meeting going, and just before the end in the middle of a prayer, a boy had shouted, 'Captain you light dim! I going call you Dimlight!' After that it was forgotten that he had ever been Captain Stanmore.

Of all the children that the Captain taught, he had the greatest hopes for Sonna. He wanted to help him to become a Salvation Army Officer, saving souls for God. He was largely satisfied with his own achievements. He filled the hall whenever he had meetings and he had encouraged many recruits. Headquarters had even congratulated him on his zeal. Eventually there would be a promotion but he often prayed he would not be sent away. Without him, the children would return to roaming the streets untutored.

He reached Ironman's gate and pulled the string that released the latch and looked across the yard. In one corner there was a large handcart where a man was sleeping with his legs hanging over the side. In another corner stood the house, which had four rooms with doors, side by side and a verandah which ran parallel. Two young children were playing a game here and were too absorbed to notice him. There were several men sitting around the tables that were positioned all over the yard. They also seemed engrossed, and like the children, were unaware of him. It seemed they were playing dominoes. He could hear money clinking on the tables as they prepared to start another game. Undaunted, Dimlight surveyed the robust-looking players wondering which was Ironman.

He said 'Good evening' to them, but there was nothing in his voice to show that he wished them this. They nodded, scarcely looking at him, clearly anxious to get on with the game. 'I would like to speak to the gentleman,' he stressed the last word, 'who owns the restaurant here.'

'Oh you want Ironman,' said one and added, 'Never knew him was a gentleman till now!' amid much laughter.

'Ironman, Gineral Bood come to see you!' shouted the comic and the laughter was louder still.

'Who you say want me?' a deep voice came from one of the back rooms.

'I tell you! It's Gineral Bood himself, man; don't keep the gineral waiting or else you might get court martial!'

Ironman came out and said, 'Yes Cap'n what I can do for you?' He seemed neither interested nor disinterested; barely polite.

It angered the Captain that this man made no attempt to cover up the sinful affair once more being continued at the tables.

'Your name is Ironman?'

'That's what them call me.'

Dimlight took a deep breath before speaking. 'It is like this. I have some children who are very poor, mostly orphans. I encourage them to come to me often, so that I can do my little to help them to grow up to love and fear God.' He paused and looked pointedly at the men at the

40

tables. 'It is a difficult task, for as I said before, these children are poor and almost live on the streets, but that does not prevent them from being sensitive about such things as clothes. For instance, I discovered that though I invited them time and time again to come to our Sunday schools regardless of their lack of clothes and shoes, they would not come. When I discovered that they stayed away because they did not wish to sit with others more fortunate than themselves, I arranged to have a class for them alone. I not only tell them of the goodness of God, but I also assist them, in my poor way, to take an interest in reading and writing. Being short of helpers I have been forced to change the time of the meeting. Most of the children have come to me and said they would rather come another time because they have to go down to Ironman's Yard. Consequently I have made enquiries and I am greatly disturbed by what I have learnt. What I have seen since entering your gate has confirmed my fears.' Dimlight pointed dramatically to the men gambling at the tables.

Ironman had stood with his hands deep in his pockets while Dimlight was speaking. Now he looked at him and asked, 'What do you want me to do?'

'To leave my children alone.'

'Didn't know them was you picnies.'

'I am their father in a spiritual sense.'

'That all?'

'That's a great deal.'

'Think them picnies can live on that?'

'What would you recommend? Gambling? Or would it be stealing?'

Their voices were now raised, and the men who had been steadily playing dominoes looked up.

'What you mean, Cap'n what-you-name? That I encourage the picnies to thief?'

'I did not say that, but you cannot blame me if the appearance seems far from respectable,' replied Dimlight.

'Stretch you muscle 'pon him,' advised one of the men, but Ironman was holding himself in check.

'You don't have any right to judge me, Cap'n Dimlight.'

'I have every right to protect young children from evil.'

'I going to ask you something, Cap'n.'

'I am listening.'

'You think what you call saving souls is the most important thing?'

'Of course.'

'What 'bout them body, Cap'n?'

'Our bodies are of little consequence. The soul lives long after the body perishes. Indeed, endlessly. I thought even you would know that. Perhaps you are unfamiliar with the Bible?'

The men left off playing, sitting with the dominoes and cards still collected in front of them. There was resentment in their eyes, and the tension could be felt.

'It happen that I can't read, Cap'n, but I know a little 'bout the Bible.'

The mild answer embarrassed the Captain momentarily and took the crowd by surprise.

'Let us get back to the cause of my coming. I want you to promise not to encourage the children to come here, especially on a Sunday. If you promise, I shall take it you will keep your word, and there the matter will end.'

'You threatening me, Cap'n?'

'I am not threatening you. I merely wish to make myself understood.'

'Make him understand you fist, Ironman!' called someone.

'We are living in civilized times, remember that, please. Brute force should be left to primitive people who can do nothing else,' said the Captain.

'Gimme a chance with him, Ironman! Cap'n, I want to ask you a question,' said the man who had been sleeping in the handcart. He was short and stocky, with broad shoulders and a round face.

'If you must, then please make it brief; I am not a man of leisure,' said the Captain pointedly.

'That one gone right over me head, Cap'n,' said the man getting out of the handcart and stretching himself so that his merino vest parted company with the waist of his blue jeans. 'As I say, Cap'n, that one pass right over me head. Them always say, don't waste you shot on birds what you can't eat!'

The men guffawed at the quotation, and this eased the tension. Ironman leaned against the side of the house with one of his hands fingering his cheeks as if he wanted to discover if he needed a shave.

The man from the handcart took the butt of a cigarette from the back of his ear, put it to his mouth and walked over to one of the others for a light. When he had the stub going, he sauntered back to the Captain, half dragging his bare feet as if they were serving as brakes for his body which wanted to go forward with haste.

Dimlight watched him angrily. 'As I said a moment ago, Mister whatever-your-name-happens-to-be, I am not a man of leisure.'

'Don't worry 'bout the *Mister* Cap'n and you can call me Noname, for I don't know what me name is.'

'How unfortunate! I do hope you do not hold it against your parents, whoever they might be!'

Aware of the sarcasm, the man who called himself Noname looked as if he might lose his temper, but when he spoke again, it was in his usual slow drawl.

'I don't mean what you mean, Cap'n, thank you all the same for the way you say you sorry for me. But what *I* mean is this . . . most of we don't know what we real name is. For when them bring we people to this Island, them ask them: "What is you name?" When we ancestors say, "Cudjoe Anwasa", them masters say, "From now on you name is John Brown." That was to prevent them finding them mother, them father, them brother, them sister, and any of them relation, Cap'n; so now according to the name on me age paper, me name is Campbell, and that fella standing beside you name MacDonald and the other one Atkins, though we face black like them ace of spades 'pon the table, and according to what I use to read, me Campbell and him MacDonald, should be full of Scotch blood. But we don't even have Scotch whisky in we blood.'

The men roared and even the Captain smiled.

'So, since I don't know me right name Cap'n, I call meself Noname. Now then, me and you going talk in a civilize' way 'bout this civilization, but before I go into that, I want to take you up on what you say to me friend Ironman 'bout body and soul.'

'Go ahead,' said Captain Dimlight, resigned.

'You believe God make people to suffer, Cap'n?'

'Not originally, but the first man sinned in spite of God's caution, and as a result of this, suffering and sin came into the world.'

The Captain felt sure of his ground. The men left their tables to draw around them. Ironman continued to lean on the wall of the house and looked on with remote politeness when the Captain spoke but with marked interest when his friend did.

'Cap'n in the Ten Commandments, part of it say: "The iniquities of the fathers would fall on the children to the third and fourth generation." You think that is right?'

'Ah, Mr. Noname, but you conveniently left out the rest of the words: "And showing mercy unto thousands of them that love Me and keep My commandments." That is an important promise.'

'You score, Cap'n! I will 'member that later!' said Noname with a smile. 'Now Cap'n, what would you say if you great grandfather do something wrong and them arrest him, try him, find him guilty, send him to prison, or even let him off, for it don't matter either way? Now you, what born long after you great grandfather dead, get arrested. The judge find you not guilty, then the clerk of the court say: "My Honour", or "You Honour", anyway, "My Honour" sound more right to me. As I was saying, Cap'n, the Clerk of the Court say, "My Honour, though this man is not guilty we can't let him off, for him great grandfather, who dead before him was born, was guilty of an offence." And so the judge tell the man that though him is not guilty, him great grandfather was found guilty so him must go to prison! What would you say 'bout that Cap'n?'

The men eagerly turned their eyes to the Captain.

'God did not mean those words in the way you interpret them. God meant that when one does evil, it does not only injure the person concerned, but may also affect the future generations who follow him, just as the good he may do is to the benefit of his children and his children's children.'

Noname nodded his head as if he was quite convinced the answer was the right one. 'Cap'n,' he said.

'Yes?'

'God is just and full of mercy. Don't you agree?'

'If I did not, then I would not be standing here in the uniform of one dedicated to serve Him!'

'Right, Cap'n! When the Children of Israel was in Egypt and Pharaoh wouldn't let them go, do you think it was mercy and justice to kill all the first-born innocent when later on all God need to do to wipe out Pharaoh and him army was to tell Moses to stretch out him hand over the water? Why couldn't Moses get the power to kill all Pharaoh soldiers and Pharaoh himself, since him must kill at all, and leave the poor innocent first-born babies alone?'

The crowd of men looked approvingly at Noname.

'The Egyptians were a nation of idol-worshipping people, full of evil,' began the Captain. 'They kept the Children of Israel in slavery . . .'

'Somebody keep we in slavery too, Cap'n, but God didn't kill them first-born!' interrupted Noname.

'Will you let me finish?'

'Yes, Cap'n, you can finish, but I couldn't make that one pass! Now you talk on,' said Noname coolly.

The Captain gave the man a piercing look and then went on. 'God wanted to give these people a lesson. We are not in a position to sit in judgement on His ways of chastizing those who would not heed Him.'

'But Cap'n, them Egyptian was heathen as you say, so them didn't know any better, specially the young little babies what don't even know how to talk yet. But make we forget the Egyptians, Cap'n, and go to God Chosen People. You 'member what happen to forty poor foolish picnies what laugh after the stranger because him bald head look funny? That is something you and me would do when we was small, Cap'n. I 'member one bald head man who use' to come to the Baptist church when I was a good boy. The man must have use to rub something on him bald head, for every Sunday soon as him sit down, we picnies use to watch him head, and the same thing happen every time. One or two flies come and pitch right on top of the bald head. No matter how we try not to see it, we couldn't keep we eye off it. And every time the man feel it and brush it off, and the flies come back, we giggle like hell . . . beg pardon, Cap'n, we giggle like the devil! But Elisha or Elijah, I can't 'member rightly which man of God it was, get mad with little picnies 'cause them laugh and call him bald head, and God make the bears eat up forty-two of them on the spot for something what any picni would do! It is in the Bible, Cap'n, look up Second Kings, Chapter two, Verse twenty-four. And at the same time, you look up Second Samuel, twenty-fourth Chapter, and you will see that 'cause King David, the man after God's own heart, count the people, God vex with him, but him didn't touch David, Cap'n, but him decide to punish him for this sin by bringing pestilence and famine on the people, destroying seventy thousand of them in three days. Yet it was David and not the people what do wrong. Cap'n, before I make you talk again, I want to say right now that I is not atheist or what you call people what don't believe in God. I feel there is a God, but not in the way you and all you umpteen religion teach it. Now you can make we hear what you have to say, Cap'n.'

The Captain looked uncomfortable. The men, he knew, were on the side of this Noname. 'You have given examples from the Bible which, I agree, are correct. But you seem to have overlooked the fact that every one of your examples was directly, or indirectly, punished because of what they or their leaders had done that was contrary to God's wishes. None of these were punished because of the good they or their people had done.'

Noname laughed, showing strong white teeth and seeming younger than thirty as the Captain judged him to be. 'All you need to do now, Cap'n, is to say like my poor dead mother, when I ask her how God manage to make himself when him didn't have any hands to make himself with. She use to say, "Chile, don't go into God's business, don't talk blaspheme words." And she use to make me kiss the Bible and say, "God forgive", though I was only five at that time. Anyway, Cap'n, you say I didn't give you any example of good people bringing suffering and death to themselves on them own?'

'I did!' confirmed the Captain.

'Job, Cap'n! Job! Him was a good man, Cap'n, the goodest man in the Bible. God want to show the devil how good the man was. Him make the man, beg pardon Cap'n, him allow the devil to make Job lose him health, lose him riches . . . and Cap'n, Job innocent children and servant, God make them get killed without any other cause than to show that them father was a good man. After that, God reward him by giving him back all what him lost. But him didn't give him back him dead sons and daughters Cap'n, for if even me, a poor sinful man, should lose one of my three picnies I have in me house, nobody could tell me I get the one what dead back because I happen to have some more. Picnies not like shilling and sixpence, Cap'n. When you lose one, even if you have a million more, you still lose that life what you help bring into the world. So no need to say God pay for what him lost. And it is no use you tell me what a parson try to tell me that the Old Testament is quite different from the New, and kinda hint that Jehovah in the Israelites' day was different from God in the New Testament. For we either have to take the whole thing as it stand or rejeck it from Genesis to Revelation. If you say God changes so much from Moses' day till Christ come, then you would be saying God make himself full of fault and only grow out of it later, and even me would say that was wrong. For, as I say, I believe there is a God. Call him Allah, like the Moslem, call him Nyankupon, like some of me people before Christianity go there and kill it. Call him Nature like them what can tell you how much fish in the sea and star in the sky. It is only different name to me, Cap'n, but it mean the same thing. What I hate is the Smart Aleck what will never understand 'bout God tell you them know all the answer and them way of thinking 'bout God is the only right one. All of you fighting against each other to say you religion is the right one.

'You looking at me, Cap'n, and saying in you mind, what a hell of a chatterbox this man is! And you wondering why we use we time to sit down and play card and domino, eh Cap'n? Well, this is we game of golf and tennis. It is we club and cocktail party. But best of all it get we together so that we can talk. Talk and see if we can find a way to get the wind out of we picni belly. Well it can't, but so long as we can meet and talk, we might find a way.'

'I think it would have been far better if you men spent your Sundays praying to God to help you out of your difficulties.'

'Cap'n, if it was prayers we need to make we get work and feed we families, Jamaica would be the world richest place! But it look like we pray so much that God get tired of hearing we!

'If you want to know what put me off you Christian world, Cap'n, when you passed a shop window full of nice things to eat, watch the little boy or girl what stand there with them nose pressing 'pon the window, and only the piece of glass and something you and civilization call money standing between the child and the food. Ask youself what the little one must be saying in him mind, Cap'n. Ask youself if when we was "primitive" this could happen. Ask youself 'bout Christianity and civilization. After that think how these picnies' fathers march to the Kingston prison gate and make history by asking the superintendent to take them inside the prison so that them won't eat the food what them wives manage to scrape together by some kinda miracle.'

'You forget that we heard recently that thousands in England marched from Jarrow to London for the same reason?' asked the Captain.

'Yes, Cap'n, but it is them own gover'ment. Them vote for it. We don't have no say. Cap'n, bet you saying to youself: but how a handcart man, the lowest of people in this Island, can try to argue with you? What you don't realize, Cap'n, is that we black people starting to think. And we starting to see the holes in you religion, and you democracy, and you civilization.'

The Captain felt unprepared to give a convincing answer to the questions Noname had brought before him and was angry. He felt he was letting down the religion and civilization he represented. Most of all he had ruined his argument when he had overlooked Job, and said that Noname had no example of the good and their kin suffering because of their goodness. The men were looking pityingly at him and it galled him so much that he lost his temper.

'You condemn everything. Religion, civilization, democracy. What would you have in their place?'

'What you don't understand, Cap'n, is whatever the religion, the politic, or the organization is from now on, as long as the black man didn't organize it himself, him will always look on it with suspicion. For we black people find that almost everything what the white people organize have a catch to it, and is always a catch against we!' said Noname.

The crowd nodded.

'After Ethiopia, Cap'n, think we going to think much of *justice*, *democracy* and *civilization*, and even Christianity? Look at the bitches –

excuse me Cap'n – bombing women and picnies, and all the other nations only talk and talk for show sake!'

'You talking sense, Noname!'

'Not a nation woulda help Ethiopia because she is black man country!'

'Same thing Marcus Garvey say: blackman must stand together and don't depend on any other nation.'

For the first time the Captain looked as if he agreed with what they were saying. 'I still think that civilization is almost if not perfect,' he said.

Noname looked at the Captain strangely and then said softly in a voice tinged with bitterness, 'I know a man, Cap'n . . .' He paused, looking only at his bare feet. 'I know a man,' he repeated as if he was trying to pick up the loose end of a half forgotten story. 'Him was what you would call a good Christian, Cap'n. Believe God would give him anything him pray for. Go down on bended knees all the time. The Bible was him life.' Noname sucked his breath loudly through his nostrils and the men around looked embarrassed.

'This man had a wife . . . a pretty wife. But bad. Him was a small fella, smaller than any of we in this yard, Cap'n. There was a man living over the road. Big fella, like Ironman here in size. Strong like bull too. Well this big man and the little man wife was carrying on. Everybody know and cry shame at them. But the big man was a bully. And him like to make people talk 'bout him. Him wouldn't leave the little man wife alone. The little fella quarrel with him wife because of it. When the big fella hear, him catch hold of the little man and beat hell . . . beg pardon, Cap'n, him beat the little man bottom.'

There was subdued laughter as Noname changed the wording to accommodate the Captain, but he ignored it and continued. 'Yes, Cap'n, beat him good and plenty. Five times him beat the little man. The little man go the police. Police say, "Sue the man for trespass or assault. We didn't see him beat you, furthermore, it was inside you place!" The little man go to a lawyer. Lawyer tell him: "Divorce the woman, but you must have witness or witnesses to prove that the woman had been committing adultery. You must see them in the act." The lawyer say again: "And it will take time. How could you expect otherwise my dear sir? Law in a civilized country is quite different from jungle law."

'The lawyer bid the little man goodbye after him collect the one guinea fee for advice. The little man go home. Him and him wife quarrel after him come and find the big man cap in him house. Little man go to

48

Clerk of Court office with the cap. "Not enough evidence in law, my man, not in law."

'The little man go home. When the big man come and start to beat the little fella again, the little fella pull out a revolver and shoot the big man dead. Him turn the gun on himself and pull the trigger, but him wasn't dead. Them rush him to hospital. When the little man find him wasn't dead, him cry and beg them to finish him off or make him finish himself off. Them say, "No! You can't do that! You say you is guilty but that don't cut no ice! We can't allow you to kill youself. We can't even allow you to dead because of the wound what you have. We going to get the best doctor to save you life! We send to another island for the best surgeon we have in the West Indies . . . We sending a motor boat for him right now. We can't allow you to dead. And no need you refuse to eat. We going to get you well even if we have to force food down you throat! And when you is quite well and strong again, we try you and we will broke you neck. We can't allow you to broke you own neck, that would be uncivilized!"

'So them try the little man and find him guilty, Cap'n, and according to civilize' law, him must pay the penalty; an eye for an eye, a tooth for a tooth. You know that part, Cap'n, for it is in the Bible.'

Noname stopped, and the Captain, who did not know all the facts, thought the story had exhausted the man. Noname looked up from contemplating his toes and asked:

'Cap'n, you ever go near the Santa Lucia prison, or even the prison at Spanish Town when them hanging a man?'

'No,' replied the Captain, a little sharply.

'I go, Cap'n . . . only one time. I hear in the old days them use to hang people in the square so everybody can see. But them more civilize' now, Cap'n. Them build the gallows as close as possible to the prison wall, so that if you stand in the street you can hear every single thing from the condemn' cell open across the yard, right to the gallows. You can hear even them footsteps, Cap'n, when them coming to the gallows near the gate, both at Santa Lucia prison and at Spanish Town. And if you climb any of the umpteen coconut tree over the road both here and at Spanish Town, you can see them when them come out of the condemn' cell coming across the yard near the gate and the wall, into the shed where them have the gallows. You can hear every single word what the condemn' man say if him just raise him voice a little, and when them fly the trapdoor, Cap'n, if you stand outside the wall near the gate, whether Santa Lucia or Spanish Town prison, you hear the sound like when you drop a big barrel full with something from the top of a cart! Yes, Cap'n, civilization say we must hang the man, eye for eye, and tooth for tooth, but we are too civilize' to make you look! You can listen when the man bawl for mercy when we take him out, strong and fit at half-past seven in the morning. Must be half-past seven, and it must be Tuesday morning. You can hear when him bawl, "Lord have mercy!" and him feet get weak under him, so them have to half-drag him across the yard. And when them broke the poor bugga neck, you can know not only by the boom of the trapdoor, but them haul a black flag half-mast; it must be a black flag, like black day, and blackmail, and black devil, and black look, and black sin, and the black cap the judge put on, and all the umpteen black what signify badness according to you civilization rules, Cap'n.

'Don't look at me like you vex', for I don't make the rules. Yes, Cap'n, as I was saying . . . not a red flag to signify blood them just shed, but a black flag. And little after a man come out of the gate and stick up a paper to say civilize' justice was done, for the little man was not allow to dead when him was poorly, nor when him beg them to leave him and make him dead, and them did not allow him to starve for them feed him by force, so that him was well and strong when them hang him!'

Noname looked as if the long talk had sapped his strength. He went to the side of the house, accepted a cigarette with a nod from Ironman and calmed himself with a couple of puffs. Captain Dimlight stood watching him, not knowing what to say. He wanted to argue with him on point of law and order, and on crime and its punishment, but somehow he could not begin. He wanted to ask him why he was so bitter. Yet he held his tongue.

Suddenly Noname raised himself from the wall on which he was leaning, put out the rest of the cigarette, and walked right out through the gate while the rest stood in silence.

Ironman looked at the Captain. 'Don't think him don't have any manners why him walk out like that,' he said. Dimlight opened his mouth and was about to say something but Ironman continued:

'The little man him tell you 'bout . . . the one what them hang . . . it happen when Noname was only nine year old. The woman – she was Noname stepmother – and the little man was Noname father.'

'I am sorry,' said the Captain with embarrassment. He wanted to change the subject. 'Now, Mr. Ironman, am I going to get that promise that you will co-operate with me?' he asked.

'What you can do for them picnies might be good, Cap'n, but them picnies need something stronger than that: food for instance,' said Ironman.

'It is unfair to tempt the poor children with your left-overs,' said the Captain.

'What you tempt them with, Cap'n . . . heaven?'

'They would not starve without your aid, I am sure. I am teaching the little ones to have faith. That is the most important thing in life, faith in God. If one had faith as little as a mustard seed, one could work miracles,' said Captain Dimlight with fervour.

'How much faith you think you have, Cap'n?' asked Ironman softly.

'Enough to convince me that if I go on my knees to God and ask him sincerely to grant me what I know is right and good, my prayers will be answered.'

'And what you would do, Cap'n, if you go down on you knee and pray and pray for the one thing you ever want more than anything and nothing happen?'

'Then I would have to search my heart. But I have no doubt in my mind whatsoever, that God would grant me my request.'

The spectators looked impressed by the Captain's sincerity; few had ever seen a man so confident in God. Only Ironman looked as an aged man might look on an inexperienced child who was predicting future wealth.

Dimlight looked at his watch, and prepared to go.

'I am hoping you will think over what I am asking you to do for the sake of the children's souls,' he said.

'The Bible say something 'bout render to Caesar what belong to Caesar, Cap'n. You look after the soul and leave me to the body,' said Ironman.

The Captain turned and left without comment.

CHAPTER EIGHT

The Sparrows were sitting on the beach, drowsy in the heat.

'Sonna?' said Sista suddenly.

'What?'

'I going to tell you something what Mobel said.'

'S'elp me Gawd, Sista, if you tell any lie on me, I beat you till you sick!'

'It is not lie I going to tell Mobel.'

'I know you, Miss Sista. You always get something to tell somebody, and it is always lie.'

'You listen Sonna and Pazart, I going to tell you the truth.'

'And I shall bust you mouth, soon as you finish Miss Sista, you see!'

'Me and Pazart don't want to be in any girl talk, what you say 'bout that, Pazart?'

'You right, Sonna. We is man. We don't care anything 'bout girl talk. Them don't talk sensible.'

'Only you can talk sensible, Mister Pazart, and Mister Sonna? You fancy youself!'

'Leave we alone Mobel. Me and Pazart want we ears to eat grass!'

'We know you and Pazart is donkey, Sonna, is not you ears you eat grass with!'

'Go away, girl. You and Sista is bigger donkey than we.'

'But Sonna, you don't give me a chance to tell you what Mobel said. Me and she was talking 'bout . . .'bout . . . married . . .'

'Lawd, Sista, me and you going to fight like puss and dawg! You wait and see!'

'I will fight you back, Mobel! You listen Sonna and Pazart. We was talking 'bout married, and Mobel ask me, when I grow big if I would get married, and I say, yes, and she ask me, like who I would married to, and . . . and I say . . . but I was only making fun . . . I say Captain Dimlight, and she say that by the time I grow up to get married, Captain would get married long time and have plenty children nearly big like me. And I say to her: "When you grow big Mobel, you would married?" and she say "no" first, but afterwards she say "yes". And I ask her who she would married, and she say . . .'

'Sista, I going to broke you mouth sure as faith if you tell any more lie on me!'

'You saying so because you don't want me to tell, Mobel.'

'That's because you is telling lie!'

'It is true, Mobel, and you know it. You say you would married Marse Ironman, and I say time you grow up him would have grand-picnies, and you say "Awright then, I going to married to Sonna!" '

Mobel sprang at Sista even before she had quite finished bringing out Sonna's name, and both girls fell, rolling in the sand. Sista put up a good fight, but she was no match for Mobel, and she was too busy trying to keep her frock over her legs. The boys could see that although Mobel was very angry, she had no real intention of hurting Sista. At last she was sitting on Sista's chest.

'Awright Mobel, get up off me. I tired.'

Pazart, who was looking across the beach, suddenly became alarmed. 'Mobel, Bugsie and him gang coming. Make we go before them see we.'

Mobel looked up anxiously, 'Yes, come, make we go before them see we,' she said, echoing Pazart.

Sista looked puzzled. Sonna voiced her thoughts. 'You mean it's four of them and four of we and you want to run from them, Mobel?' he said.

'Bugsie is bad, real bad and them is bigger than we,' she answered, not looking at Sonna.

'I know Bugsie thief, but since when you run away from people because them say them is bad?'

'Think I want to fight every day? Cap'n don't like we to fight either.'

'Make we go now!' urged Pazart and he and Mobel began to walk away, Sonna stood still, and Sista hovered somewhere between them. Mobel glanced back and said almost pleadingly, 'Come Sonna, come before them find out is we.'

'I not running away from any boy or girl,' said Sonna. Pazart stopped, uncertain and anxious. As they hesitated, Bugsie and his friends recognized them. They stopped to talk in conclave and then came forward. Suddenly they began to sing:

> 'I shall never fear tomorrow,
> I can banish care or sorrow,
> Knowing all the while
> I am God's little chile,
> God's little Sparrow!'

They sang mockingly. Now they stood waiting to see how the Sparrows would respond, but Sonna and his friends were silent.

Addressing Sonna, Bugsie said, 'You Mister Sparrow, me and my friends want to join you gang.'

'Don't answer him,' said Mobel.

'Oh, Miss Mobel, you don't want to talk to we now eh? You think you too good to talk to we, you and Mister Pazart?'

Mobel bit her lip and looked out to sea.

'I say I want to join you Sparrow gang, Mister Man,' repeated Bugsie.

'We don't have any thief in we gang!' replied Sonna and he waited for Bugsie to attack. But Bugsie merely relaxed and suddenly began to laugh. His companions joined him. Sonna looked at Mobel who seemed tearful and then at Pazart who was moving from one foot to the other with his eyes down. Sista just looked puzzled.

'You don't have thief in you gang, Mister Sparrow?' said Bugsie mockingly.

'No, 'cause I don't like a thief.'

'Sonna,' said Mobel with such feeling that he looked round expecting to see she had hurt herself, but she only looked back at him saying something with her eyes that he could not understand.

'Ask Miss Mobel if she never thief yet, Mister Sparrow, and ask Pazart as well. Ask Mobel 'bout the ten shilling week before Christmas. Ask Mister Pazart 'bout the loaf of bread out of the breadvan.'

Sonna waited for Mobel and Pazart to deny the charges but they said nothing. Then suddenly Mobel sprang on Bugsie, pulling him towards her by the collar and crashing her head into his face three successive times. Then she fell upon him with her hands on his neck as if she would strangle him. His friends did not help Bugsie. Sonna, Pazart and Sista pulled Mobel from him and she stumbled towards the sea. There she scooped up the salt water in her hands and threw it over her face. Bugsie and the others fled. Mobel returned in a silence which no one broke as they wandered home.

At last, unable to bear it any longer, Pazart said, 'Sonna?'

'What?'

'You vex'?'

Sonna did not answer.

Sista butted in with the same question.

'You vex', Sonna?'

'Don't bother me,' he said roughly and then added more gently, 'What you expeck? You make I feel shame before Bugsie.'

'You never thief yet Mister Sonna?' said Mobel with a hardness of an adult.

'I never thief from people!' declared Sonna.

Mobel recognized the word 'people' as a qualification of the statement and pounced.

'But you thief from you mother and father?' she asked triumphantly.

'I don't have any mother or father,' parried Sonna.

'You just trying to get out of it, Mister Sonna, but you can't get out,' said Mobel aggressively.

Sonna looked trapped. 'I take piece of bread and little sugar and piece of coconut sometimes from my mother's cupboard but it is not the same as thiefing from people 'cause she would give me if I ask.'

'That's thiefing just the same, Mister Sonna.'

'It is not, Miss Mobel, but I don't need to quarrel with you now.'

The word 'now' alarmed them. 'What you mean, Sonna?' asked Sista anxiously. Mobel moved away to the other side of the street.

'I not staying.'

Pazart moved closer looking at Sonna to see if he meant it, but Mobel merely climbed on the grass bank opposite, where she sat with her dress high above her knees and her feet dangling carelessly.

'But you don't have anywhere to go,' said Sista.

'I going just the same.'

'Suppose . . . suppose me and Mobel say we won't do it again? . . .'

'Talk for youself, Mister Pazart, don't talk for me!' interrupted Mobel angrily from the other side of the street. 'If Mister Sonna want to go, think I would beg him to stay? Mister Goody Goody Sonna, 'fraid him will catch the thiefing from me and Pazart. Don't know how him never catch the thiefing from me and Pazart all this time!'

Mobel had hardly finished speaking when Sista crossed the street to face her angrily. 'You don't have no right to talk to Sonna like that Miss Mobel!'

'I talk like that if I like Miss Sista, and I thief if I like as well.' Mobel stopped swinging her feet.

'You know Sonna is right Mobel, thiefing is a bad thing and I didn't know you and Pazart ever . . . ever . . .'

'What you stopping for Miss Sista? Why you don't finish what you was going to say? Me and Pazart thief. Pazart can beg you and Mister Sonna pardon and say him won't do it again, but not me! Furthermore, Miss Sista, you might catch the thiefing as well from me and Pazart, for you is a goody goody. You and Mister Sonna can go together. Me and Pazart will stay.'

Sonna was moving away.

'Don't go Sonna,' called Sista as she saw him walking off, while Pazart looked towards him in bewilderment.

'Make him go! I don't care!' cried Mobel loudly as if she wanted him to hear. 'Why you don't follow him Miss Sista?'

Sista hesitated and then ran after him.

Pazart turned angrily towards Mobel and then saw the look on her face. He bit his lip and took her arm, expecting her to throw off his hand but she did nothing.

Sista had caught up with Sonna now and was trotting to stay beside him.

'What you going to do?' she said.

'I going home.'

'To stay?'

'I going for my things.'

'Mobel say I must come with you.'

'She didn't mean it.'

'And she didn't mean it with you either, Sonna. Mobel have a good heart but she don't show it.'

'Sista, you not coming with me.'

'Why?'

''Cause . . . 'cause . . .' Sonna could not provide an answer but Sista said, 'It's 'cause I is a girl and you is a boy. Same thing as why we don't sleep together.' Sista began to cry but no sounds came from her.

They reached the house in Mango Walk. Sonna gathered up his things and left.

He took the long road going away from the city. He walked determinedly and had soon covered more than two miles. A little way ahead there was a man sitting under a tree with a bicycle. As Sonna approached, the man looked up from the repairs he had been doing to an inner tube. Each recognized the other at the same instant. Both looked surprised.

'Hello, Sonna.'

'Hello Marse Ironman.'

Ironman liked the proud boy who had brought something new to the children of the streets by his example. He guessed that Sonna had influenced Pazart and the others to insist on paying for their meal whenever they came to his cookshop. Although he regretted this, because it meant that they often went hungry, he could not help but admire his spirit. He guessed that Sonna was leaving and was saddened by it. His own son might have been like Sonna, had he lived. But all he said was, 'Glad you come. Maybe you can give me a hand with this inner tube. Can't find the hole where it puncture and don't have no water to try it.'

Sonna was glad to have an excuse for stopping. His heart was back there with his friends. But they had done one of the things he had learnt to despise from babyhood. Without a word, he rested his bag on the ground and he and Ironman began to work in silence, each feeling the bond between them and wanting the repair to take as long as possible. But they were soon finished, so they sat quietly side by side and Sonna slowly realized that he no longer had to work out his problems alone. He had not felt like this since his father had said goodbye to him.

'Marse Ironman?'

'Yes Sonna?'

'Suppose . . . suppose you was to find out that somebody what you know do something bad, and you never know all the time till somebody else tell you . . . What you would do?'

Ironman thought for a while, guessing that this was his reason for leaving. Then he said, 'Sometimes we do something we know is bad because we couldn't do better. And because we know is a bad thing, we feel shame and later when we have a good friend we don't know how to tell this friend, for we might say to weself, "If I tell him what I do him won't want to friend with me anymore."'

'But Marse Ironman, him do a bad, bad thing . . . like thief.'

Ironman looked distant, as if he no longer had any interest in the conversation. Then he said, 'Sonna!'

The boy looked up in surprise at hearing his name spoken so sharply.

'Yes Marse Ironman?'

'Suppose I tell you I was a thief?'

'But you wouldn't thief, Marse Ironman.'

There was no doubt in his voice and Ironman drew back for a moment, recognizing that he was in danger of losing both Sonna's friendship and his respect. Then he said, 'I thief Sonna,' and he told the story while Sonna listened in silence. When he had finished he stood up to go, and Sonna noticed with regret that Marse Ironman was no longer looking at him or treating him with affection. There was another long silence. Then Ironman said:

'Sonna, you can ride?'

'Yes, Marse Ironman.'

'Then take this. I hardly ever use it and it is a twenty-six inch frame, too small for a big man like me. I give you as a present to 'member we all with, and you must have a little money, boy. Take this ten shilling: later on when you reach where you going and you broke, don't be 'fraid to sell the bicycle. Here, take it boy. Make I strap you bag on the carrier. Now! Take the money out of me hand, and you better start now before night ketch you on the road where you not near any house.'

Sonna looked at the money and at the bicycle, the dream of his life, and shook his head. 'You know Marse Ironman, you is just like my father. Tell you what Marse Ironman, you play I is you son what you tell me 'bout, and I will play you is my father what come back too.' And then with a look of mischief Sonna added, 'Marse Ironman, the bicycle, is it strong?'

'Course it strong. Why?'

' 'Cause if you put me on the crossbar we can reach home quicker.'

CHAPTER NINE

After Sonna's return, the four Sparrows became closer than ever, seldom out of each other's sight. Daily, they followed Sonna's plan for selling and Pazart and Mobel kept watch while the other two sold the goods. Sista always looked round anxiously, her fear of the police preventing her from approaching many customers, but Sonna's fearless manner and his polite confidence ensured that he always sold at least twice as much.

One afternoon, the children were sitting at the side entrance steps of the Salvation Army hall, waiting for Captain Dimlight. It was early closing day. The lane was quiet, and there was only an occasional truck or bus or a lad on a bicycle.

They sat with their boxes between them – only two since they had been pooling their goods. Sonna had charge of one and Sista the other. They were watching the water in the gutter running speedily into the drains when Pazart had an idea. 'Make we race matchsticks,' he said. The suggestion met with Sonna's approval. The boys left the boxes with the girls and each took a discarded matchstick, named them Neddy and Gee Gee and declared them water-horses. They followed the stream of water towards the bottom of the lane, each calling eagerly for their particular horse as they neared the winning post. Caught in the excitement, the girls ran after them. Then Sonna looked back anxiously for no reason that he knew and shouted, 'Bangbelly!'

The name caused them to sprint ahead in panic. They could hear the sound of his boots behind them. Mobel and Sonna dropped back a little, like protective parents, to keep pace with the slower Sista and Pazart but gradually they realized that the Constable's boots did not sound so close now, and eventually Sonna dared to look behind him. Bangbelly was walking in the opposite direction. It seemed that the children had had too good a start and he was not wasting time in fruitless efforts to capture them. The four halted in relief, Pazart and Sista looking winded.

'Where the box?' said Sonna.

His question brought consternation as they each realized they had left the boxes behind.

'Mobel and Sista, you mean me and Sonna just leave you to look after we box and you leave it same place and come to watch we? You mean you so careless? Now Bangbelly sure to grab them. What we going do?'

Sista looked at the boys tearfully. 'We couldn't help it! We didn't mean to leave the box far,' she cried.

Mobel, mortified at being responsible for such a catastrophe, took refuge in anger. 'Awright Mister Pazart, I leave the box on purpose! What you going to do 'bout it now?' She took up her usual fighting stance and stood before the boy. Pazart also felt ready for a fight, but then Sonna passed between the two and began to walk back up the lane without a word.

'Where you going Sonna?' asked Mobel in alarm, remembering the last time he had walked away from them.

'I going to see if him take we box,' he said.

Mobel ran after him, caught up and blocked his path. 'You not going up there Sonna.'

'Why?' said Sonna, trying to pass her.

''Cause him might be hiding behind any one of them gate or fence up the lane to ketch we, that why.'

'Get out of my way Mobel, or I will push you down!' Mobel realized that he was really angry and stood aside, though as he walked up the lane she walked beside him, closely followed by the other two. Warily, they approached the steps, their knees trembling and their mouths dry. There was no Bangbelly and no boxes.

'God! And I got all my money in a matchbox inside the box,' whispered Sista.

'I put what Sonna give me to hold in the other box, too,' blurted Mobel, too anxious to try to disguise what she had done.

'I have only threepence in me pocket,' said Pazart.

'And I have fivepence in my pocket,' said Sonna, after a search.

They were too worried to face Captain Dimlight now, so they began to walk home. Mobel wished that Sonna would quarrel with her and blame her for their loss. But instead of telling her off, he smiled sadly at her as if to say never mind. She had to look away and found that she wanted to cry. She was getting soft and foolish like Sista. Anger was easier to bear, so she said to Sonna, trying to provoke him:

'Why you won't say what you think, Mister Sonna?'

'What I think 'bout what?' said Sonna in surprise.

'Why you don't say is me what make we don't have anything to sell now?'

'But I lose my box as well,' reminded Sista loyally.

'You didn't do it on purpose,' said Sonna shortly, and the girls knew that he not only wanted to stop them blaming themselves but also to prevent Pazart from blaming them. Mobel walked on, more mad with herself than ever, though Sista was thinking more about Sonna and his kind words than about the loss of the boxes.

Five days had gone by since the children had lost their stock. Mobel had taken charge of the eightpence and had walked the two miles and back to the bakery to get a penny's worth of stale bread to serve them for breakfast and lunch. She had gone further afield to find wild spinach which she had cooked with a couple of pounds of cornmeal bought with three more of the pennies. She had also purchased coconuts and grated them to use as cooking fat for their almost inedible meals and had dished out and divided the portions like a mother, taking less for herself than she gave others, who for the first time had not questioned her authority. They scarcely went out, fearing equally the sympathetic words of the adults – who had nothing else to give – and the jeers of the other children.

Now, neither money nor food remained and they were hungry. As time passed the hunger intensified until they felt they could no longer endure the gnawing emptiness without distractions. They decided to go for a walk.

It seemed that wherever they went, the smell of food surrounded them. Everywhere, shop windows displayed corn pone or fried dumplings. Talk of food was taboo, it only increased their hunger – but food was all they could think of. Therefore they walked mainly in silence, trying not to look at the displays of food but all the while imagining the feast they could buy with a few shillings: red or *gungo* peas* soup with dumplings; shrimps cooked with rice; ackee, yellow as an egg yolk cooked with codfish and coconut oil; yams and corned pork; spiced meat patties; vanilla ice-cream.

They moved away from the shopping centre and took one of the lanes to the beach, walking silently in single file with light heads and knees that trembled. They made for the wild grape trees but found none that were ripe; wherever they searched the fruit was small and green. Sonna picked a few of the best ones and they ate them with difficulty, but they were something to chew and to swallow. Sonna could see that Mobel looked ill – worse than the rest – but he could do nothing. For the first time he began to see what made people thieve. If his friends were to become ill, what other choice would be open to him? They sat in the sand, Sonna supporting Mobel as she leaned against his shoulder. And then they saw Ironman coming towards them.

'Hell of a job I have to find you picnies,' he grumbled.

gungo peas: commonly used pea plant, sometimes called Pigeon or Congo peas, widely used with soup or cooked with rice.

'Marse Ironman!' they said together and felt a mixture of hope and shame.

Anxious not to hurt their pride, Ironman began to speak with haste. 'Is Noname what cause me to look all over the place for you. Wouldn't make me ears eat grass! "Ironman, them picnies mighta sick for all we know. Mighta even dead," him say to me. And when I say I go and look to see how you all do, him help fix this basket with little something in it. "Tell them we miss them, Ironman," so Noname say. "Tell them to come and visit we, and when them coming them can bring back the carrier what we send the things in." Now I must run. When you come I will have something for you.'

The children were as surprised by the length of Ironman's speech as they were by the basket he thrust in Sonna's hands. They had never heard him say so much before. He went quickly, obviously wanting to avoid their thanks, but they shouted their gratitude after him. They opened the basket hurriedly; there was a four-tier enamel carrier packed with stewed goat's mutton, rice, yam, potatoes, and dumplings made of mixed cornmeal and flour. A couple of loaves of bread lay to one side of the basket with a bottle of cool ginger beer. There was a packet of cornmeal, sugar, a tin of fresh herrings, dried codfish, cocoa, condensed milk, dried coconut and cooking fat. There was even a box of matches, a tightly corked bottle of kerosene for their oil lamps and a packet of salt. Right at the bottom of the basket lay five shiny shilling pieces.

Sonna remembered the bond that had been forged between himself and Ironman. The sense of warmth and security he felt almost overwhelmed him. Like the others, he began to eat, taking as much comfort from the friendship as from the food itself.

CHAPTER TEN

A few days later the Sparrows were sitting with a number of tattered magazines between them. They were the gift of the aged man on the dunghill who collected old newspapers and were greatly treasured by the four. All their favourites were included: *Magnet*, *Union Jack*, *Sexton Blake Library*, and *Peg's Paper*.

To the children, the best of the magazines were those with the Sexton Blake stories. Next came Billy Bunter, though they were all prized. The moon was full that night; they could read with ease in its silvery glow but they wanted to enjoy the moonlight with something they could not do in the confines of their tiny rooms.

'Make we play Ring,' suggested Mobel, and the others readily agreed. Within minutes the four were running about the village, and adults of all ages were walking along the lanes behind hordes of children, momentarily forgetting their hardship. Lads went in search of long neglected drums, hoping the children's play might give them scope to show their skill, and began the rhythm.

'Little Sally Water,
Sprinkle in de saucer,
Rise Sally rise, an' wipe you eyes . . .'
'London Bridge is fallin' down, fallin' down, fallin' down . . .'

The deported men and women who had brought these songs from overseas must have been homesick – like those from Africa.

The children now turned to the songs of their ancestors and Sonna's heart started to beat a bit wildly. He remembered that only the night before, he and his friends had been speaking of ring plays and dances. He had boasted of his father's prowess as a singer and dancer in these rings and Mobel had proclaimed the fame of hers. Each child had argued hotly on the merits of their fathers' interpretation of the songs and dances from the land of their forefathers. Now Sonna felt sure that Mobel would, sooner or later, ask for something which could give her the chance of showing what she had learnt from her father, and he would be forced to do likewise to prove his boast. He kept his eyes on Mobel all through the pieces they played and sang, wondering how long it would be before she found some way of showing off and bringing him into it as well. He realized that whatever song and dance she might choose, she had to play the part of the female dancer which was rarely as difficult as that of the male.

'*Look Under De Bed You See Two Coco Deh*' sang out a childish voice, and the crowd of singers answered: '*Take One Leave One Till A Morning*!' The six drummers grinned broadly as they made their goatskin-covered drums speak in a language which had once belonged exclusively to Africa, but which was now the basic theme of West Indian music. The drummers leaned their heads to one side, as if they wished to listen only to the beats of their own drums. Men shook maracas and old people remembered when they were young and full of hopes and dreams. The policemen at the nearest station a couple of miles away, heard the sound of the drums faintly, and secretly wished they could have been near, for the music of Africa went deep.

An interval, then: 'Give we *DUN-DO-WAH* now!'

Even without looking Sonna knew who was standing in the centre of the great circle asking for a song and dance, difficult even for the adults who usually performed it. The crowd, delighted at the boldness of the girl, echoed the call.

The drummers began tapping and she began to move her hips. Her print frock was high above her knees and her face damp with sweat. Her hair, now without the typewriter ribbon of old, stood in little mounds with ends pointing upwards as well as outwards like tiny horns. Her lips were slightly parted as if she were enjoying a secret joke.

It was almost time to choose a partner. As he looked apprehensively at Mobel, Sonna started to remember the story of the dance. The original Dundowah, a West African Cleopatra, had a lover who adored her, but knew how fickle she was and thought that by threats, coaxing, and promises of gifts, he could manage to keep her faithful to him until he returned from his hunting. But as soon as he disappeared into the forest, the beautiful but faithless girl went around the village, taunting men with her charms and daring them to make love to her. They, knowing that her lover was a brave warrior, were not easily tempted, but the dances and promises of the girl were too much to ignore, and one man was persuaded. But as soon as he had accepted her invitation to love her, the wrathful warrior returned and discovered her unfaithfulness. After beating her lover, the warrior turned on Dundowah, but as she begged him with her hands for mercy she danced such a dance that the warrior was charmed and he gave her the gifts he had brought her instead and was hers once more.

Sonna knew that Mobel would ask him to partner her and could not see how to refuse. Every country child knew the play – the excuse that it was for adults would sound lame. Mobel was waiting for the singing and drums to warm up. Sonna's ears burned, he trembled at the knees and wondered if he could do it. He got angrier and angrier as he saw Mobel standing in the bright moonlight slightly swaying to the quickening tempo of the drums. She was not yet looking at him but he knew she was getting ready to challenge him before all those people. He made up his mind. He would show her that he was not afraid of the crowd if she was not, and he would dance Dundowah just as his father used to do, and his father was the best dancer of his village. Mobel turned towards him and danced like a true daughter of Africa.

Sonna came out of the circle to face her in the centre of the ring, without knowing how he did so. He forgot the packed yard and the faces round him. His strong, tuneful voice started the opening lines, which were promptly answered by the adults and children with the title of the song, Dundowah.

'Don't make nobody come ya!' threatened Sonna and the crowd roared:

'Dundowah!'

'Don't make nobody come ya!'

'Dundowah!'

He danced with elbows bent and flapping to his sides while his feet made indescribable patterns to the music.

'I will give you pretty somet'ing!' the boy promised and the crowd answered, 'Dundowah!'

'I will give you pretty somet'ing, Dundowah.'

The men, exhilarated by the performance of the two in the ring, urged Sonna to greater efforts while the women encouraged Mobel.

'Show her boy!'

'Good gal, vamp him!'

'You good, picni, you good!'

'Make her see you is man, picni!'

The high-pitched notes of the small drums weaved themselves into faultless rhythm, while the heartbeat tempo of the big drums took hold of the enthusiastic crowd, heightening the excitement.

Sonna met the hip-moving Mobel with both improvisation and the traditional movements as he continued to sing his lines:

'I will give you pretty bangle!'

'Dundowah!'

'I will give you pretty earrings!'

'Dundowah!'

'I will bring you two big earrings!'

'Dundowah!'

'I will bring you pretty somet'ing!'

'Dundowah!'

No words of the song were necessary from the girl. But she had to dance the interpretations to his appeal in the most seductive manner, and Mobel danced sideways and backways, always using the curve of her back and the suppleness of her body to play the irresistible vamp. The crowd, watching the two, could not agree who was the greater, but all were certain that they had never seen adults perform as wonderfully as the children did that night.

At last Sonna danced his way out of the ring, and no sooner had he disappeared than the fickle girl started going around the ring dancing temptingly before each of the boys, to the singing of the drums and the laughter and banter of the great crowd. At last the invitation was too much for one of the boys to ignore, and he shyly danced out to face the triumphant Mobel, and the drums spoke more powerfully than before. In the midst of the romantic dance, Sonna burst into the ring, and with mock actions beat off the intruder to the tempo of the music. Then he turned to Mobel:

'Gal, what make you bad so?'

'Dundowah!'

'I good mind to kill you!'

'Dundowah!'

'I feel I could kill you!'

'Dundowah!'

'I good mind to beat you!'

'Dundowah!'

The boy seemed to waver as the girl danced before him until at last he pretended to take something from his pocket and give it to her as a peace offering, and they moved silently in front of each other until the song and the drumbeats came to a stop.

'Damn good picni boy!'

'Damn good gal!'

'Never see any big people do it so good, much less picni . . .'

'It make me 'member when I was a young man . . .'

'Ah laugh an' laugh till me belly ache to watch them.'

Mobel glowed inside as the crowd dispersed, and she realized that she was happy because in her heart she knew that Sonna was the better performer. At home, Sonna said of Mobel to Pazart, 'Look like Mobel can dance more than anybody.' And Pazart replied glowingly, 'You and Mobel can do everything better than anybody else. Me and Sista feel good when we hear what the people said.'

Then Pazart blew out the little kerosene oil lamp.

CHAPTER ELEVEN

It was early in the evening, and a roll of notes lay snugly in Bangbelly's pocket. Through the 'payment by results' system, which the District Constables on the Island enjoyed, his earnings were always way above average. Over ten years he had salted away five hundred pounds. No one knew of it. He wondered if they would have mocked him so readily had they known . . .

He had always intended to retire once he reached his target of eight hundred pounds, but events of the past weeks had made him consider leaving sooner. With far less than five hundred, one could live well in the country. Perhaps he would only wait another year. He could buy a piece of land, have poultry, pigs, a few head of cattle, a small banana cultivation, even a country woman to share his mountain life with him, far up in the hills where he was unknown.

'Just a minute *Inspecta*!'

The unexpected interruption to his thoughts made the Constable start. A figure emerged from under a tree by the roadside and stood in his path. Surprised, Bangbelly could see that the man stood at ease with both hands thrust in the pockets of his blue trousers. He wore no shirt, just a sleeveless merino vest and he had a soft cap, the type ship's firemen and engine oilers normally wore, but with the shiny peak turned towards the back of his neck.

He recognized him as Ironman.

'What . . . what you want with me?' he asked, his voice betraying the unease he tried to hide.

'Business, Inspecta, business,' said Ironman, sounding calm, even friendly, though Bangbelly's uneasiness remained. As the men faced each other a small crowd began to assemble. Bangbelly recognized the one they called Paperman, Noname and several others. It seemed they were going to make a show of it.

'Something I have to ask you, Inspecta,' said Ironman.

'I ask the question,' said Bangbelly coldly. 'And you know well I is not any Inspector.'

'I did think you would rather Inspecta than Bangbelly.'

'Ah, now I see the play, Mister Ironman. You come and stop me to provoke me and make you and me have a fight, and I get myself into trouble. But I won't lose my temper. If you want to know, my name is Jasper Power, you shoulda know my name, them call it out all the time.'

Ironman chose to ignore the meaning of the remark. 'Please to meet you, Mister Jasper Power. My name is Ironman, hope you and me won't be any more strangers. Now to cut a long story short, I going to ask you to give me four pound for the goods you take from the Sparrows, and then me and you can kiss one another good-night.'

'Four *what?*' asked the Constable unable to believe what he heard.

'Four of them paper money, Mister Jasper Power, only four!'

'Jesus! Man, you gone stark staring mad?'

Around him the small crowd was becoming larger. Someone jeered derisively. The Constable decided to play for time.

'Them picnies you call Sparrows don't have no right to sell anything without licence. Them don't have no right to be on the street at all, but I tell you what . . .'

'I is all ears-hole Constable,' said Ironman, sarcastically.

'. . . I will give you back the things to give them,' he ended lamely.

Ironman laughed and Bangbelly felt the sting of anger and humiliation. His old enemy was unnerving him and he was babbling like a boy. The realization spurred him into action; he lunged at Ironman with his baton with the intention of crashing it on his head, but Ironman had gripped his wrist as the weapon descended and with a jerking, twisting movement, wrenched the Constable's hand. Bangbelly gasped with the pain and the baton clattered loudly to the ground. He tried to release himself but only managed to increase the pressure. Ironman walked him over to the nearest tree and amid the gibes and laughter of the spectators, fixed him there, securing him with his own handcuffs.

The Constable looked at him. 'I will go to the gallows for you one day, Mister Ironman,' he said in a low voice.

'You take the words right out of me mouth, Mister Bangbelly, right out of me mouth,' replied Ironman.

He reached into the imprisoned man's pocket and drew out the roll of notes. He peeled off four pounds and threw the rest to the ground in a gesture of contempt.

'Thief!' said Bangbelly harshly, and Ironman seemed to flinch at the taunt.

'Thief,' he said again, louder than before. 'You know you is a thief, Mister Ironman,' he added with such cold insistence that the listening crowd sensed that he referred to more than the four pounds that Ironman had just extracted from the bankroll. Bangbelly pressed home his advantage. 'Tell everybody it is not true, Mister Ironman. Tell them I is telling lie if you can.'

'Tell him, him is a damn liar, Ironman!'

'Ironman going to half kill him, you watch!'

The crowd was angry. Bangbelly, helpless against the tree, knew he would be powerless to defend himself should they choose to attack him. He needed to demonstrate the truth of his words.

'You all say I is a liar? Well ask him – ask him now.'

The crowd looked towards Ironman, hardly needing the denial. They were convinced that he was not a thief.

'Tell the bugga him damn lie, Ironman!'

'Yes Ironman, tell him before we face, then beat him backside!'

Only Noname remained silent. He stood back a little from the crowd, watching Ironman's face and knowing he was suffering. Slowly the others began to notice too and they fell silent.

'You wrong, people,' said Ironman. 'Him not telling a lie this time.' He began to walk away.

'Ironman, you must tell them why!' said Noname.

'No, leave it at that,' he answered

But Noname, whose own life had been so affected by a similar injustice said, 'If you don't tell them, I will.' And as Ironman remained silent, Noname began to tell the story.

As he spoke, Ironman began to remember the events of ten years before in painful detail, and though the sun had fallen below the top of the highest trees, there was a wetness on his brow. His child had been sick. He and his wife had taken him to a European doctor, who had warned them that the baby was dying of malnutrition and that he would hold them responsible if his condition had not changed in one month's time. Ironman had seen no point in saying that he had not worked in nine months and that they had even sold their wedding ring. He and his wife had gone home with little hope. Ironman had searched again for work, trying in far away cornfields and plantations but had found nothing. Finally he had taken the list the doctor had provided to the grocery store: Glaxo, Virol, milk, oats – all large tins.

The Chinaman had taken the list and put the items in the basket. Ironman had tried to grab it from the counter but the Chinaman had held on with one hand while searching rapidly under the counter with the other. Expecting him to produce a gun, Ironman had reached forward and struck him hard enough to knock him back behind the counter. Then he had snatched the basket and run.

The child had been fed and its life preserved for three more months but Ironman had been arrested and given two years penal servitude, extended to three when he had tried to escape. He had been lashed for that but he had not cried out. In this way he had gained the name of

Ironman. No one had known that his strength had been the strength of despair; he had discovered that morning, from a new inmate, that his wife had committed suicide. It was not until he had returned home that he was able to read the note she had left for him. It told of daily hardships; how Bangbelly had confiscated the little they had and then ensured through constant searches and other forms of harrying that there should be nothing more. No one was permitted to help her. Bangbelly's constant vigilance had kept her in isolation. Now the world shared the secret which Sonna had already learnt.

Noname stopped speaking. The crowd became acutely aware that Bangbelly was there among them, handcuffed and helpless.

'Give him hell, Ironman!'

'Only leave the bare breath in him, Ironman!'

'Give me a chance with him, Ironman!'

'Man like him shoulda dead!'

'Half kill him Ironman! But don't take him life. Don't get hang for a thing like him,' they shouted.

The loathing Ironman had felt for Bangbelly for so many years had been intensified beyond endurance through Noname's speech and the memories it had aroused. As he moved towards Bangbelly, the Constable thought quickly:

'You always say you like a fair fight. Give me a chance. Take off the handcuffs! Then we will fight man to man.'

'Ask him who him ever give a chance, Ironman.'

But Ironman stopped and Bangbelly knew that he would be released. For a moment they stared in each other's eyes, then, without a word, Ironman bent down and unlocked the handcuffs.

The Constable stood up painfully as he was freed and rubbed his wrists. He faced Ironman and said, as if he had been asked to choose the weapon, 'I will fight you man to man with stick.'

'Don't fight him with no stick, Ironman!'

'That's all him good with, everybody know that!'

'Them say nobody can beat him with stick, for him don't fight fair, him poke with the point when him see him can't win.'

'Tell him to go to hell Ironman! Make him fight with him fists!'

An old man detached himself from the crowd and approached them. 'You know that I teach every single man who can fight with stick in this town, Ironman?'

'You teach me as well Tahta, 'member?' said Ironman, speaking for the first time since Noname had told of his past.

'Yes, Ironman, I teach you and you was a good pupil, you would have done credit to we ancestors who bring this fighting from Africa, so what I going to tell you, don't take offence, you hear me?'

Ironman looked at him affectionately. 'I hear you Tahta,' he said.

'Well, what I want to say is this. A couple of years ago when me sight was still good, this man come and ask me to practise him stickfight, this same District Constable.'

The old man paused as if waiting for a denial, but the Constable said nothing.

'I practise with him and I won't tell no lie, him is better than me.'

There was a murmur of astonishment from the crowd.

'Don't fight him with stick my son, him better than you an' me.'

His warning finished, he began to return to his place in the crowd.

Ironman said, 'Thank you kindly for telling we.' Then he added, as if it were an afterthought, 'Ole master, think you can fetch a good pair of them sticks from you house?'

Again, a murmur went up from the crowd. The old man shook his head slowly but went to fetch the sticks.

They waited in silence. At last the man returned with two staffs of pimento, one of the hardest of hardwoods, about three foot six inches in length and one and a half inches thick.

Bangbelly was given first choice of weapon. He studied both sticks for some time, his confidence fully restored. At Tahta's signal they held their sticks before them, poised in readiness. Both ends were planted deep in the palms of their hands, and their fingers were stretched out stiffly until a split second before they were ready to strike; then whichever hand they intended to use would quickly close on the end of the stick for the blow. If they were to keep their fingers bent round the stick they could be smashed with a single stroke.

Bangbelly struck first, but Ironman anticipated his move and blocked the blow aimed at the side of his head. They began to move swiftly on their feet, shifting sticks from one side to the other, over their heads and at times almost behind their backs. Bangbelly started to show how quick he could be despite his size. He hit out almost too fast for the eye to follow at every possible angle, and Ironman had to block the rain of blows as fast as they came. Once he was not quick enough and suffered a searing pain in his right shoulder.

The crowd was always with Ironman, although they could not help but admire the skill of the Constable. The man drove Ironman back to the edge of the crowd by striking high and low. Only the cracking sounds as stick met stick could be heard and a slight groan came from the watchers as the thigh on which Ironman received the attack became almost numb with pain so that he had to limp as he tried to defend himself.

Bangbelly moved in for the final blows. One of his specialities seemed to be a kind of underarm upstroke followed by one struck from overhead and aimed at Ironman's skull. Twice he followed this pattern then he fooled Ironman with the opposite sequences and this time nearly felled him when one of the down-sweeps caught him partly on the side of his head and partly on his stick.

Blood trickled down the side of Ironman's face, but he was not ready for defeat. Suddenly he was fighting back and began to drive his opponent from place to place and it was the Constable's turn to defend himself. The crowd began to suspect a strategy; Ironman had anticipated that Bangbelly would tire first and had held himself back until that time. The Constable's breathing was now harsh and uneven. Ironman struck twice, hitting him high on the hip and even Bangbelly was growing aware of the soundness of Ironman's tactics. Now the crowd began to roar encouragement.

'Beat him Ironman!'

'Lick him to the ground Ironman!'

'Pull the shame out of me eyes Ironman!'

This last shout came from Tahta.

Ironman drove Bangbelly further and further back, giving him no respite. Cornered, the Constable lunged at his enemy's face with the point of his stick. The crowd gave a cry of anger as Ironman staggered back with his hand held over one eye. Heeding no one, Bangbelly moved forward to strike again, desperation making him careless. Ironman blocked the wild blow so that it glanced off his stick and Bangbelly, now completely off balance, was struck sharply on his head as Ironman instantly retaliated. He fell heavily, dropping his stick, and when he heard the voices of the exultant crowd, they seemed far away.

'Get up!'

He heard the cold voice of Ironman above him and obeyed. He saw that his blow with the point of his stick had caught the other just above the right eye leaving a nasty gash and blood still coming from it. He stood like a prisoner waiting for a sentence to be passed. The crowd bawled:

'Finish him off, Ironman!'

'Him trickify, Ironman! Don't take any chance with him!'

71

'Pick up you stick,' said Ironman, and Bangbelly complied with relief and surprise. Their sticks clashed again but this time Ironman was in complete control. Not a single blow was delivered hard enough to knock Bangbelly out completely. Lumps appeared over his head; his legs were stiff with pain. His arms were so numb that he scarcely knew he was holding a stick. He had long passed the stage of aggression; Ironman could tap him wherever and whenever he liked. When for the sixth time Ironman raised another bump and ordered him to defend himself, he stood up without obeying.

'Take up you stick and hold guard,' commanded Ironman relentlessly.

'No,' said Bangbelly, shaking his head to confirm his resolution, 'you can kill me now and finish with it.'

The crowd shouted in jubilation.

'What you going to do with him now, Ironman?' said someone.

'Let him go.'

There was a murmur of dissatisfaction but Ironman merely walked away.

Bangbelly felt the crowd's resentment and knew that any sign of aggression in him would goad them into violence. Slowly he took the first painful steps forward, his jacket held over his arm and his cap tenderly resting on top of his sore head, when he felt a tug on his shirt. As he looked round another hand tugged from the opposite side, this time with such force that there was a ripping sound.

Now the crowd found their voices. They grabbed at him seizing handfuls of his clothing and ripping it from him. He tried to struggle free of them whilst retaining his hold on the jacket, and soon it was almost all the clothing he had left.

He could not afterwards remember how he walked amidst the noise and laughter of the crowd until suddenly someone shouted, 'Police' and they fled. Two uniformed policemen, coming to investigate, put him into a passing taxi, and through the homeward journey his one consolation was that he still had his money – less four pounds – his badge and his handcuffs. For he did not want the story to reach the ears of the authorities.

CHAPTER TWELVE

The headlines screamed that the wedding of the exiled Duke and the Hollywood star would be the biggest occasion Santa Lucia had ever seen.

The Duke had promised to bring ten thousand children together from all over the Island to Santa Lucia Municipal Park the day before the celebration for a two-day treat. There would be plenty to eat. The army undertook to erect tents. Special trains were to be run. There would even be fireworks.

The Island was set to be full of cameramen. Several film companies would be sending their own newsreel reporters. There was a sudden cry for the cities to be cleaned up. Santa Lucia must get rid of all eyesores . . . Get rid of street-sellers . . . of those little pests who roamed the streets with a few postcards, bootlaces and safety pins . . . Round up those who should have been at school. Voters were urged to bring pressure to bear on the legislative council members to get some kind of law passed against such occurrences. There was compulsory education but parents would omit to send the children to school until they were hauled into court. The orphans? We have the reformatories . . . Children's prison? Nonsense! Better than their living conditions at present . . . far better . . .

The Sparrows heard the news in fear. The poor of the city heard it and were frightened too.

'We must go on we knee an' pray to God to soften them heart,' they said.

'Yes, we can't do nothing but trust God.'

'If we stop selling we little fruit at street corner we will dead for want.'

'We not landowner, we can't vote, we can only pray.'

'That's what Shepherd say at church last night. Fast an' pray. God will hear we . . .'

Sonna and his companions talked together for several hours, after which they separated to call a meeting of all the poor children on the Dunghill the following day.

At the appointed time, they waited and had almost given up hope when the first group of children was sighted coming up the rise of the Dunghill. Soon others began to appear. There were little boys hauling handcarts made from soapboxes which they used to carry surprisingly large loads to and from the markets. Others came with tins of car polish in their hands and cloths in their pockets. Girls arrived with small boxes from which they sold little red onions at a halfpenny each and garlic at perhaps two pegs for a farthing. The boys who sold postcards to visitors converged with others who dived for pennies thrown from liners by American tourists. There followed the sellers of pins and needles and boys who sold bootlaces, combs and razor blades. Their ages ranged from five to thirteen. They were mostly black but here and there among them were those bearing European or Asian features.

A few, knowing they were not welcome, stood with Bugsie on the outskirts of the crowd.

Sonna and his three friends were nervous but only Pazart and Sista showed it. Mobel seemed to care about nothing while Sonna looked as if he cared about everything but was full of confidence.

The children, now numbering nearly two hundred, became noisy and quarrelsome, impatient and excited.

'What you call we for Mister Sonna?'

'When you going tell we what you call we for?'

'We have to work! Think we got all day?'

'Miss Mobel, what . . .?'

A piercing whistle shrilled across the Dunghill, and with screams and cries of 'Police!' the crowd of children scattered in all directions.

Sonna and his three companions made ready to run, but unlike the others, looked for the uniform of the regular policemen, or any adult in plain clothes who might look like a district constable. They saw no such person, only some half a dozen boys who were holding their sides and shaking with laughter.

'It's them boys what do it!' said Sonna angrily. By this time the scattered children had halted their terrified dash, realizing that they had been fooled. Two hundred wrathful children began to bear down on Bugsie and the other culprits and when at last the six were released, they had not a stitch of clothing between them. The crowd laughed at the disgraced boys, until they disappeared in the bushes on the opposite side of the Dunghill.

'Awright!' said Sonna. 'I going to talk now!' he cried clearly, and the chatter stopped as they all turned towards the speaker and his friends.

'It say in the papers that police going to clean we off the streets!' said Sonna. Now that he was actually speaking his nervousness disappeared.

A young cynic shouted: 'Is that you call we for? We know all 'bout that without you tell we!'

Mobel was instantly on the attack. 'If me was you Mister Man, me

74

would shut me mouth, fear fly make mistake and make him nest inside!' she shouted, standing ready for a fight. The crowd of children roared their appreciation of Mobel's cutting words, seeing that the unfortunate boy had rotting front teeth.

'Just to show how you is a fool, Miss Mobel, fly don't make nest!' he answered.

'You will find out what I mean when the fly get inside!' replied Mobel amidst renewed laughter. The boy closed his mouth tightly after that.

Sonna began again as soon as the laughter subsided. 'Them call we all kind of bad name in the paper! Them want to put we in famitary just like we thief or do bad things! Them say today is we last day on the street!'

The mention of the reformatory brought fear as well as anger. 'But we not thief an' bad. Why them want to put we in prison?'

Sonna spoke again: 'The big people too 'fraid,' he said. 'Only Marse Ironman don't feel 'fraid, but him alone can't do anything.'

'You right, Sonna! All the big people do is pray!' The anger of the children was now aimed solely at their elders.

'We going to the place where the gover'ment is and talk to them!' continued Sonna, but most of the children began to doubt their ability to do something even adults feared.

'Think them going to listen to we?' asked one.

'Them will ketch we an' put we all in famitary if we go!' said another.

'What we going to say to them when we go?'

Mobel stepped forward angrily. 'You all 'fraid just like the big people?' she asked scornfully. 'If you all 'fraid, run go and hide under you bed. When you all gone, me and Sonna and Pazart and Sista will go at the Town Hall!'

Shamed, the doubtful became silent, and Sonna took over again.

'We will go and say to the man what is one of the gover'ment: "Please Sir, we poor – some of we don't have no mother or father, and some of we only have mother and them can't get anything to do, so we have to try to sell something, or clean cars or carry load and sell onion and garlic. We can't pay licence for we don't have five pound!" And after, we will go to the people what make the newspaper, and we will say: "Please Sir, we is not all the bad things you call we. We is not hooligan and tout and all them funny name what you write 'bout we. We only poor." '

'Yes Sonna! Make we go an' tell them that!' shouted one who had been against the whole thing before.

'Yes! Make we march to the Town Hall as Sonna say!' roared the children.

Feeling secure in their numbers, the few who were afraid when Sonna had first suggested the march now seemed bent on being in the forefront of it all. But there was grimness on the faces of the four, which made those who were inclined to look upon the thing as a great adventure, sober up quickly. And as they made ready to march from the comparatively safe Dunghill to the streets of adults and policemen, and the monster who lived in the Town Hall whose name was 'gover'ment', they were all a little afraid.

They started off eight abreast, until they reached the entrance to the streets, where they were halted by Sonna who explained his plans. His leadership was unchallenged, though there were some who were older.

'We can't full up the whole street, for we have to make things pass,' he said. 'So only four of we can walk side by side. And we mustn't make any noise. Mobel and Sista will go and look every time we reach a cross street, so cars and things won't run into we.'

The children said nothing, but quickly began forming themselves into lines, four abreast. A number of adults, curious to know what brought the crowd of children together, whispered among themselves, as they stood watching.

Mobel jumped over an open drain which ran between the Dunghill and the beginning of the street, and slipped, giving her weak ankle another twist. Sonna and Sista were concerned, but she assured her friends it was nothing. But Sonna noticed that she limped slightly as she went forward with Sista into the street so as to give the marching children warning of the traffic.

Now they were in the city streets. Mobel reached the first crossroads and marched into the centre where she raised her hands to halt the vehicles which screeched to a standstill. To the amazement of the drivers, the children began to march across the street, silent with fear and determination.

'Them infants make I feel blasted shame,' said one of the onlookers as the last of them disappeared from view. Two uniformed policemen who saw them pass, discreetly scratched the sides of their helmets and did nothing. Sonna and Pazart, still leading, grinned at each other and felt cheered. Sonna dropped from the head of the line and moved back to see that the children were keeping to the side of the street and to ensure that the youngest among them were holding their own. Then, as he returned to the front, Sonna saw Bangbelly emerge, unseen by the rest, from a nearby shop.

'Mobel!' he shouted as the Constable sprang into the road, baton in hand. Knowing that Sonna's shout could only mean police, Mobel ran forward, guessing that the danger was behind, and the thumping boots confirmed it.

Sonna cried, 'Bangbelly!' and without waiting to see the children scatter, followed Mobel and her pursuer as they darted in and out of shop-doors and between the traffic, while the crowd looked on.

Mobel came to an abrupt halt. As she had anticipated, Bangbelly slid past, merely brushing her clothing as he went. The crowd cheered, but Bangbelly recovered quickly and was chasing Mobel once again. Sonna could see that Mobel was limping. The two retraced their steps and came dashing back towards Sonna. As they came close, he jumped into the middle of the street shouting, 'Run Mobel, run!' Bangbelly, recognizing him as the instigator of so much recent trouble, did just as Sonna had hoped – he left Mobel to pursue him. Sonna ran, leading the Constable through a maze of traffic and headed for the square. Realizing that the boy was increasing the distance between them, Bangbelly aimed his heavy baton at Sonna's legs. The blow brought him down. The Constable lunged forward, grabbed his baton and dragged Sonna to his feet, shaking him with all his strength. Mobel screamed, causing Bangbelly to look towards her, and in that moment Sonna broke away. Again, Bangbelly used the baton and it struck the boy, glancing off the back of his leg just before he took the turn in the street leading to the square. He stumbled and almost recovered, but the long leather loop at the handle of the baton entangled him and the crowd watched with horror as a rickety little T-Ford van swung into his path and he fell underneath its high chassis.

The crowd surged towards him. People were calling for a doctor and someone shouted for stout planks of wood in the hope of raising the van. Then suddenly Ironman was there. He ripped off the partly loose bumper and with knees bent and head thrown back, as if he were pleading with God to help him, he began to pull. The front wheels of the van came slowly off the earth. 'God A'mighty,' said someone, and his low cry brought the petrified crowd to awareness. Three or four men rushed forward and they joined in holding the vehicle erect. Mobel dived underneath and listened for Sonna's breathing while Sista and Pazart crouched beside her. The word went up that Sonna was alive, and the news penetrated deep into the crowd.

'Him is 'live!'

'God be praised!'

'God hear we prayer!'

Ironman lifted the boy and bore him through the crowd.

Slowly there came the awareness that Bangbelly was still among them. He had remained, fearing to draw attention to himself by taking flight. The people began to draw round him closing in from all sides.

'Kill him,' screamed the voice of a woman.

'Kill him!'

'Kill him!'

'Kill him!'

Every cry came from a different voice. Bangbelly stood cornered, alive to the danger of mob anger. But as the crowd moved towards him in a body they heard someone say:

'Don't touch him! Don't put you han' on him!'

It was an old rasping voice but there was something in it which caused the people to obey. They turned. A woman walked towards them as if she had all eternity at her disposal. The crowd parted for her with respect. She passed through them, glancing neither right nor left, her bare feet peeping through a wide patchwork skirt with each step, her stick looking like the shepherd's staff from a Bible illustration.

'Ma Kuskus,' someone whispered.

She halted before Bangbelly and turned to face the people. 'So you want to kill him!' she mocked in a pitying tone. 'You want to get youself put 'pon de gallows for a man what good as dead a'ready?' She turned back to the Constable, forcing him to look at her with the strength of her gaze.

'Ah! I can see by you face, you 'member me,' she said softly. 'Dat day I *did* tell you, you smell of blood an' dere was blood in you han' . . . *Look!*' She pointed to the hand in which Bangbelly was holding the baton he had retrieved after the accident. The man looked as he was bidden, unconsciously displaying his palm before the crowd. It was deeply stained with blood. He held it away from his body as if wishing to disown it. The old woman laughed mirthlessly. Bangbelly's mouth moved but no words came.

'Now I going to read you future, Mista Constable, an' I not going to charge you a penny. But, Mista Constable, you can say you don't want to hear an' I will shut me mout'. Jus' say de word. You don't say nuttin' Mista Bangbelly. Dat mean you want to hear you future?' She laughed once more. The people at the back of the crowd began to push forward so as not to miss anything the herb-seller might utter.

'Now hear de firs' one,' she said, and no one seemed to breathe.

'You will know how it feel to be bury 'live.'

The crowd gasped. Bangbelly's head jerked to one side as if he had been dealt a blow, but he was still silent.

'De secon' one is you will make a knot for you own neck, Mista Constable.'

He began to breathe heavily.

'An' de t'ird one Mista Constable? You youself goin' beg dem to hang you!' The old woman spat out the last prediction with such hatred that those who were near to her shrunk back.

Bangbelly appeared unable to respond. Then something seemed to give him hope. He almost managed a smile and found his tongue for the first time.

'You can't frighten me, ole woman. Furthermore, what you say is nonsense, it don't make sense.' Hearing his own voice again gave Bangbelly strength. He faced the crowd as if he wanted them to note his reasoning. 'I will tell you what make you prediction foolish, ole woman. First you say I will know what it feel like to be buried 'live. Then you say I will make rope for my own neck! And then you say the third one will be begging them to hang me. I ask you: if the first was to happen to me as you say, or even the second, how the third would come in? For if I was to believe what you said, I would be dead man from the first one happening!'

The old woman cocked her head to one side and looked up at him.

'Dem have a sayin' dat t'ird time is lucky Mista Constable!' She spoke mockingly and smiled.

'Awright ole woman, that's enough. I have a good mind to put you on a charge!' He paused. 'In fact, I going to show you what I think 'bout you witchcraft talk.' He moved forward intending to make an arrest.

Then Ma Kuskus spat. Her spittle appeared in the centre of the Constable's forehead and slid down between his eyes.

Bangbelly stood there staring, without even blinking, his gaze fixed on the withered face of the old woman.

'Dem say dere was a man what spit on Jesus,' her voice was nearly a whisper. 'Him couldn' dead!'

The man still had his eyes focused on hers.

'You will know how him feel befo' long!'

The crowd stood awed and silent. The herb-seller raised her arm and pointed over their heads.

'Go, Judas!' she hissed and the venom in her voice made the people afraid.

Bangbelly began to step backwards with his baton in one hand, while the other, bloodstained, still hung a little way from his side. The crowd parted for him as if fearful of contamination. No one called after him; no one tried to stop him. He was overwhelmed by his own isolation. He lifted his hand and passed it over his eyes as if he had been dreaming and then he stumbled on through the still, endless figures of the crowd who conveyed a pitiless contempt in their eerie silence.

Bangbelly's cottage was the last at the end of a narrow lane; his nearest neighbour was over a quarter of a mile away. It was several chains from the road, surrounded by trees. He pushed the gate, walked up the narrow path and opened the door. It was only when he was inside that he became aware of the heat. He removed his jacket and shirt, breathing heavily. Then he reached in the cupboard for a large bottle of rum. He took several mouthfuls neat and sat on the single iron bed with the bottle in his hand. Under its influence, he began to feel calmer, but his mind was still confused and it seemed he could hear the crowd, no longer silent, coming along the lane. He swallowed more rum but it only intensified his fear. He went to the door and listened; though he could hear nothing now he closed the door and bolted it. He also checked the wooden windows, though he knew he had bolted them that morning. It was suddenly dark. He lit the oil lamp but turned the wick down low, listening all the while. He began to pace up and down thinking, sometimes aloud.

'If the boy dead them would charge me with manslaughter or even murder. Murder! Nobody going to believe I didn't mean to kill him . . . not after what I said in the market that day.' He stood still for a while as if working out some sort of plan. Then he returned to the cupboard and took out a large biscuit tin, putting its contents on the table so that he could reach the bottom. Next, he removed an automatic revolver and a bulging foolscap envelope from which he drew a wad of notes secured together neatly with elastic bands. The sight of the money restored a little of his self-esteem. He returned it to the envelope and took a piece of black oilskin which he tore into four strips. He wrapped each portion round the envelope until it was totally concealed. Working feverishly now, he found a smaller biscuit tin, pressed the bundle, together with the revolver, into it and covered it tightly. Then he put the whole into the larger tin, sealing that also. He had been too occupied to listen but now he paused for a while and then prized up two of the floorboards using a small cutlass. With its point, he began to dig a hole. Once it was deep enough, he buried the money, taking care to put the floorboards back exactly as before.

He flung himself on his bed in the hope of getting some rest but the tension he felt was too great. He lay in thought for a while, and then jumped to his feet. He would go to the hills some five miles from the town. There were government forest reserve lands up there. He could make plans, without danger, in solitude. He packed rum, biscuits, all the silver he had, his baton, handcuffs and badge. Then he blew out the light, and, after listening for sounds, walked out into the darkness.

CHAPTER THIRTEEN

As soon as he opened his eyes, Sonna's attention was caught again by the whiteness of the ceiling. He gazed at it as if he were wondering how it could possibly have been made so white and smooth.

He looked across the room. The Sparrows were sitting on the edges of their seats as though preparing to race forward at a signal from the nurse who stood close by.

'Pazart, Sista, Mobel!' cried Sonna.

They came to him, only just managing to contain themselves and not excite him as they had been instructed. Such unaccustomed reserve made them all uneasy and an embarrassed silence followed.

'Them put me in a nice room,' he said.

The nurse had told him that it was through the generosity of a wealthy widow whose conscience had been pricked by the procession of children and the injury to himself that he had been put in such a room.

He spoke so cheerfully that the others were convinced he would be well soon. Relief loosened their tongues. They told him that prayers were being said for him everywhere and many had sent messages and gifts. The poorest children had gathered wild flowers to send to him and Ironman never left the waiting room.

When the nurse informed them it was time to go, they could scarcely believe that half an hour had passed. Now they remembered so many things they'd been hoping to tell him. They got up resentfully.

'We will come back to see you tomorrow,' said Sista, trying to be cheerful.

'Tomorrow,' said Mobel and kissed him.

Sista followed her example, glad that Mobel had taken the initiative. She would not be laughed at now. When it was Pazart's turn he and Sonna acted like the 'men' they were and shook hands. Sonna clutched him tightly and whispered, 'Take my mouth-organ, it under my pillow . . . take it with you.'

Pazart shook his head but Sonna insisted. 'Awright then, since you want me to, I will keep it for you,' said Pazart reaching under his friend's pillow for it.

Sonna watched them carefully as they followed the nurse, taking in each of them.

'Till tomorrow,' they called.

'Till tomorrow,' he answered, but when they were out of sight, he turned his face to the wall.

On the following Sunday people gathered in the poorer quarter to pray for Sonna. They believed that God would not turn a deaf ear to so many.

Shepherd Peter, who modelled his life after his biblical name-sake, to the extent of becoming a fisherman after he was called to serve his Master, looked at the congregation in front of his small chapel, most of whom were strangers, and rubbed his bony hands together.

He felt the issue which had brought all these people to his church was a personal challenge. He was God's servant and God had been mocked. He and all the other true servants of Christ must pray and fast, asking God to save the child and to strike the evil man down. Perhaps God would even appoint him as the avenger, and send him to strike the ungodly, as in the days of old.

> 'God work in a mysterious way,
> His wonders to perform . . .
> He plant his footsteps in the sea,
> And ride upon the storm!'

So says the hymn, thought Shepherd, and as if the people had read his thoughts they began to sing those words.

In another part of the town, Captain Dimlight also led his congregation in prayers for Sonna's recovery. When the meeting was over, Pazart, Sista and Mobel went with him to his cottage at the back of the hall and shared the sandwiches his housekeeper had provided.

He phoned the hospital again and although Sonna was said to be improving the three were still anxious and restless. Recognizing that they would not sleep that night, and feeling that they should not be left alone, Dimlight sat up with them and they listened as the rain hammered on the low tin roof.

Each time he looked up, the Captain saw that the eyes of the children were on him. The atmosphere was oppressive.

'Cap'n, you sure him going to be awright, don't you Cap'n?' said Pazart.

'Of course. I know he will,' he answered.

Mobel, looking down at her hands as they rested in her lap said, 'Cap'n, them tell you at the hospital if the doctor come, sir?'

'The schooner has not arrived yet, as far as I know, but there are many good doctors already at the hospital. Don't worry, if God needed this man to save Sonna's life, He would give that schooner wings so that it would be here. Perhaps this is to show us that the skill of men is not necessary for His miracles.'

He felt comforted and pleased with his speech; it showed in his face and the children were reassured. They went into the hall and sat behind the first row of pews from the platform. Dimlight took his Bible and searched for passages that told of the goodness of God and His promises. He began to read:

'Behold the fowls of the air: for they sow not, neither do they reap, nor gather into barns; yet your Heavenly Father feedeth them. Are ye not much better than they?

'Consider the lilies of the field how they grow; they toil not, neither do they spin; and yet I say unto you, that even Solomon in all his glory was not arrayed like one of these . . .

'Wherefore, God so clothed the grass of the field, which today is, and tomorrow is cast into the oven, shall He not much more clothe you, O ye of little faith? . . .

'Are not five sparrows sold for two farthings, and not one of them is forgotten before God? . . .'

He read promise after promise until the children's hearts were stilled. He closed the Bible and told them how, overseas, in places like England, and in some parts of America, the winter comes, and the people must have fireplaces built in all their houses so that they can make fires to keep themselves warm; how the trees lose their leaves, and the grass is gone from the earth. How the strange whiteness called snow comes with the cold, so that people must wear many pieces of clothing; how this same whiteness makes it impossible for the birds to find anything on the ground, especially the tiny sparrows. But God would not see them die of cold and hunger, though they could provide nothing for themselves. He put it in people's hearts to feed them and He found ways of guiding them to some cosy place away from the cold so that they would not freeze to death. Dimlight had never been to England, or any of the cold countries where they had winter, but he knew of the goodness of God, and how He kept His Word to His people, for is it not a wonderful example of His love for even the little sparrows? . . .

Pazart heard the story and his mind wandered to the sparrows and the place where they lived. He and Sonna had always promised themselves that when they grew up they would become seamen and travel to England, where these birds lived, and where they would see real snow, and hold it in their hands to find out if it was really cold as ice from the ice factory. They would go to see the street where Sexton Blake and Tinker lived, and remember all the stories they had read in the old magazines the man on the Dunghill had given them. He thought again of his friend, and his heart filled with gratitude to God, who promised so faithfully to help the orphans, and even the birds, and he felt a warm feeling towards the Captain.

Mobel and Sista also felt comforted by the Captain's quotations, and the certainty of God's love. They felt they owed a great debt to this man who brought them the comfort they had not had since they lost their parents.

The Captain closed the book and turned his back to the children and knelt, silently communing with God, while the Sparrows sat side by side with hands folded in supplication. One of the double doors stood open, wide enough for a child to squeeze through. The rain poured overhead, making splashing sounds as it overflowed the gutters around the hall. The thunder threatened, and every now and again a flash of lightning came through the partly opened door.

They could not tell when the feeling started, they only knew that it came; that something was happening to them, making them frightened and wanting to shout. Pazart looked at Mobel's face and saw that cold, clammy sweat was appearing on her brow, as it was on his. He looked at Sista, and saw that she too was afraid.

Only Captain Dimlight remained steady and confident on his knees, pleading with God. The children remained tense, waiting and listening.

Then it came. There was a flutter of wings as a pigeon flew straight from the open door, over their upturned faces, straight into the wall beyond, hitting it with a thud. Amidst a flurry of feathers it nearly fell to the ground but made one last effort to gain its wings. It succeeded just long enough to bring it over the head of the praying Captain. Then it fell in the aisle beside them where they knelt.

The Sparrows looked incredulously at the dead bird. The Captain had scarcely heard it for he was far from his temporal surroundings, pleading with God. But now it seemed that something had come between him and the prayers he was sending. He opened his eyes and turned towards the children. They were looking at something, frightened and dazed. He stared on the ground and saw the dead pigeon. 'Tch, tch, tch,' he said and was sorry for the death of the bird, guessing how it had happened, though nothing like it had happened before. He began to comfort them with whispered reassurances when Pazart looked up and said:

'Sonna dead.'

It was not the statement alone nor the conviction it carried that startled Dimlight but the voice which said it. For it was not the voice of a child, nor a man, nor any human. He would have expected the Blue Mountain to sound like that had it possessed the power of speech. It was ageless, cold, hard and pitiless.

'Sonna dead.'

Again it came from Pazart, but this time it was a boy's voice. He had repeated his own words as if to convince himself that he had heard them properly. His eyes became those of a boy again; a boy who had been told an unbelievable thing but was beginning to realize what it would mean if it were true.

Dimlight felt he was allowing himself to be drawn into the fantasy of three tired, overwrought children.

'What nonsense is this?' he asked. 'Sonna is alive right now and doing fine, I have no doubt. I should not have allowed you to stay up, it is too much for you and this accident with the bird . . .'

'You said God would hear we prayers!' said Sista harshly.

'Children, children, can't you understand? Our little friend is alright.'

'You say God wouldn't make him dead,' continued Sista.

The Captain ignored her. 'I arranged that if there was any change the Sister at the hospital would telephone me right away, no matter how late. The phone has not rung. We would have heard it.'

'You lie, Cap'n Dimlight!'

The voice of Mobel came harsh and strong, echoing round the empty hall.

'Stop it!' shouted the Captain, outraged, not only because of the insult but also because it had been uttered in the house of God. 'Have you no respect for God, if not for man?'

'You lie! You lie! You l . . .'

The Captain struck her hard with the back of his hand and she staggered back, but her eyes never left his face.

'God forget the Sparrows, Captain,' mocked Sista softly.

The telephone rang. Mobel began to giggle and then to laugh. The Captain put his arm on her shoulder in order to calm her, but she shunned his outstretched hand. 'I am going to answer the telephone,' he said. 'Come, we will all go.' He tried to be cheerful but they stood their ground, watching him with eyes that seemed to mock. Mobel stopped laughing suddenly. The Captain walked towards the phone without a word and picked it up.

'Yes? . . . yes, the Captain speaking . . . Oh my God! . . . Oh my God! Yes, I understand. One moment, could you tell me the exact time he . . .? Thank you. Yes, of course. Yes. Goodbye.'

Dimlight walked back to the hall like a blind man, feeling his way along the wall. He did not know what he would say when he faced the children. He went through the connecting door without knowing it, and passed the Penitent Form. Then he looked up.

They stood at the door, their faces turned towards him. He knew that they were not waiting for confirmation. They did not even wish to see his humiliation. They had been sure of the facts long before. They had made certain that he would suffer long after they had gone. 'Thou art weighed in the Balances and found wanting,' just as the hand wrote over the head of Belshazzar.

The children began to walk through the door without a word. 'Wait, wait!' he said and hurried after them but the sudden darkness outside blinded him and he could not see them. He went down the half dozen steps and called, 'Sonna! . . . Sonna! . . .' before he realized he was calling the name of the dead, not the living. His call echoed round the building and came back to him, 'Sonna' . . . 'Sonna' . . . until it died.

He returned to the place where the pigeon had fallen. He turned his face towards heaven and closed his eyes.

'God hear me!' he shouted and clenched his fists. 'I give you a challenge God! A challenge, do you hear? I challenge you to strike me dead here and now!'

He waited for the vengeance of God to reach him but nothing came. There was only the noise of the rain on the roof and the sound of the echo that had somehow returned . . . 'Sonna' . . . 'Sonna' . . . 'Sonna'.

CHAPTER FOURTEEN

Ironman had been with Sonna in the moments before his death, and their love had bound them close to one another in the hospital room. Sonna had exacted a promise which Ironman knew he had to keep; the awareness of that promise intensified his anguish as he walked along the dark streets in the rain. He would have to tell the children. The realization fuelled his rage against the man who had done this; it welled in him until he feared that it would crush and overwhelm him. Yet he had to keep his promise. He walked on barely able to recognize the familiar streets around him. An hour passed, then two . . . it was still dark but the rain had ceased. Suddenly he bumped into something and fell to one side of the track. He picked himself up, feeling for the little torch he always carried at night. Its light showed what looked like a man, muddy, wearing only one boot. Pushing aside his own sorrow, he raised the half helpless man thinking he was hurt. He played the light on the bowed head of the stranger and as the rainsoaked face with bloodshot eyes was raised and brought into the glare, Ironman recognized Bangbelly. He cried out as if in pain and hurled himself upon the drunken Constable and they crashed to the ground. Suddenly Ironman shouted, 'You shouldn't make me promise Sonna, you shouldn't, you shouldn't.' Then he tore himself away from the defence-less Bangbelly and ran, whimpering like a child along the path.

Bangbelly sat up and looked after him. He started to shake with laughter. 'Is true what you say Ma Kuskus, I want to dead and I can't dead.' He could not control his laughter and it rang round the wooded track. Its incongruity frightened him. He struggled to his feet and continued on his journey to the hills.

The sun was so low that it seemed it might sink into the sea – or beyond it. Bangbelly had spent the whole day in the rugged hills and valleys. He had not intended to stay so long but events of the previous day had overcome him. It was as if Ma Kuskus had bewitched him.

In the empty forests he had raged against the God who had permitted his sufferings using verses from the Bible, and despairing because he knew that if the child died, even the authorities would be against him. Now his voice was hoarse. In his agitation he had lost his bearings. He did not know the way out of the forest, there were no landmarks, no tracks to guide him. As a child he had learnt that evil things lurked there, waiting for darkness to free them from their hiding places. He recalled tales of white horses with three legs who breathed flames through mouths and nostrils and whose hooves flashed fire and brimstone as they galloped. He drained the flask of the last of its contents and flung it away. An image rose in his mind of the bulls known as Rolling Calves. They too breathed fire and dragged their chains behind them. No grass for them; they feasted on blood and reeked of it. *Blood!* Bangbelly rubbed his palm, remembering the words of Ma Kuskus. He examined his hand with inflamed eyes and could almost see the stain there. He thought he smelt it as well. He wrenched the baton from his shoulder where it hung on its leather loop and threw it with all his might among the trees. Still the word 'blood' rang in his ears. He began to run, catching himself on thorn bushes, stumbling over boulders while his breath came painfully in heavy gasps.

Suddenly he was in a grassy clearing. As he dashed across, he caught a glimpse of what appeared to be a black, shiny body almost upright in the long grass. He could not stop so he tried to jump over it. As he took the next stride, he felt something clinging to his ankle. He cried out in horror, fearing snakes, as the thing tried to tie his legs while he ran. He moved in circles, trying to break its hold, then he tripped and fell, screaming in fright and kicking out. As he jumped up and tried to run again, he fell a second time, crashing his head against a boulder which knocked him unconscious.

When he came round, Bangbelly could not, at first, remember where he was. It was dark now. There was something on his ankle. Forgetting his earlier fright, he touched it with his hand and found that it was leather. He pulled and found something else he could identify by touch: a polished piece of wood. It was his baton. Now he remembered in full the terrors he had felt some time before and connected this with the baton and its leather strap. He began to giggle and the sound rose until it was a roar of mirth and he could hardly remember what he was laughing about. Yet he still laughed. He began to walk forward, running in little spurts as if each burst of laughter was the force which propelled him. Then blindly he stepped forward into nothingness.

His fall was broken by the shrubs and bushes that grew above a great bed of boulders. He was in a pitch black ravine, strewn with rocks. He felt around on hands and knees and discovered a thin opening. He followed this though it became narrower still and lower and lower until he was forced to lie flat to go further. When the space above and around him was no greater than a few inches, he abandoned his exploration. Exhaustion wrought by the rum and the intensity of his emotions now overcame him and he fell asleep.

A night, a day, and half another night had passed before Bangbelly awoke from a dream. A great mob had been chasing him and had beaten him until they thought him dead. Then they had begun to bury him, just as the old woman had predicted. God, he was glad he was awake.

He moved one of his hands and met a solid wall. He brought his left hand out slowly and again he came up against another hard surface. He tried to raise himself to a sitting position. His head cracked hard against the stone.

'Them bury me 'live!' he cried in panic as his hands on each side tried in vain to find an opening. He began to claw the rocks with his nails as the terror of the situation took full hold of him. 'I not dead!' he shouted. 'Take me out, I still 'live!' He began to realize that his voice would not reach beyond the place of his confinement. His panic increased but still he clawed on until his fingertips were raw and he lay exhausted and bleeding.

A flash of lightning and a peal of thunder roused him to full awareness again. Despite the chaos inside him, he was able to tell from the flash of light that in order to leave his tomb, he only had to gauge the point through which the light had come and push himself feet first towards it.

He emerged in the ghost-filled hills. It was raining and the thunder and lightning around him seemed to be portents of his terrible end. Swaying in the darkness that alternated with angry streaks of light, he tried to read the signs. All the verses from the Bible that he had learnt as a child came to him now.

'Whither shall I go from Thy Spirit?' he asked. 'Or whither shall I flee from Thy Presence?' A clap of thunder reverberated over the hills.

'If I ascend unto Heaven, Thou art there,' he shouted. 'If I descend into Hell, Thou art present.' And still the rain poured, splashing his upturned face.

Now his voice rose to a higher pitch: 'If I take the wings of the morning and dwell in the utmost part of the sea, even there shall Thy Hand lead me, and Thy Right Hand hold me.' He raised his hands high, standing solidly on both feet like some prophet of the Bible shouting to a multitude. But only the trees laden with water from above were there as witnesses.

'Yea, the darkness hideth not from Thee, but the night shineth as the day, the darkness and the light are both alike to Thee.'

He paused, then: 'You hear that, Ma Kuskus? I know my Bible. A hundred and thirty-nine psalms! I not afraid of you!' He began to cry, just as another peal of thunder rolled over the hills. 'He was despised and rejected of men. A Man of Sorrow and acquainted with grief.' The aptness of his quotation overwhelmed him and he could not continue. After a while he said: 'He is brought as a lamb to the slaughter, and as a sheep before his shearer is dumb, so He open not His Mouth.'

Bangbelly shook his head as he uttered each of these words, unable to understand how one could allow oneself to be sacrificed without protest. He covered his face with his hands and spoke in a low, hoarse voice: 'Are not five sparrows sold for two farthings, and not one of them is forgotten before God?

'The Sparrow!' he cried, remembering why he was there. 'Oh God, and I did blaspheme that day!'

These last words silenced him. He began to walk, undoing the belt that was tied twice around his thick waist. He found a tree and began to climb. When he reached a branch that would support his weight, he fixed the belt around his neck and secured it to the tree. For a while he just sat there, thinking about his life. Then he spoke to God as if He were sitting beside him.

'I didn't want to do what I done to the child, oh God, I did just want to ketch him, mostly because of revenge. I didn't mean to say what I say that day in the market either! I didn't know how I manage to say such a thing, or why I say it. Maybe I don't need to tell you all this for you know everything.' He paused, and the rain coming down from the leaves above on to his face made it seem as if he was crying.

'If I had my life to live over again, I would be a different man, but now it is too late.' He pushed himself forward.

As Bangbelly came to, he found he was clawing at his neck. The belt, his desperate substitute for a rope, had not been fit for the task he had set it.

And so he had fulfilled two of the prophecies of Ma Kuskus.

CHAPTER FIFTEEN

'You hear?'

'I hear him dead.'

'So is really true! With all the pray we pray . . .'

'Coming from town?'

'Yes.'

'How the Sparrow?'

'You don't hear? Him dead! Burial today!'

'Jesus Christ! You sure?'

'Sure-sure, Ironman tell me himself!'

'God never hear we prayer!'

'True. Everybody so shock them can't believe it . . .'

'What happen?'

'Damn truck shut down man, can't get the blasted thing to start!'

'I will give you a hand. Hear 'bout the Sparrow?'

'No . . . him not . . .'

'Yes! Burial this afternoon.'

'Christ A'mighty! I must go back in time!'

'Me too, soon as ah pull six load of sand.'

'Look like God don't business with we! Look how we pray!'

'Man when I hear, me head grow big . . .'

The sun was barely up, but nearly a hundred children stood on the spot where they had listened to Sonna before their march.

The three remaining Sparrows stood before them, their eyes red from grief and lack of sleep.

'Sonna dead,' Mobel told them in a toneless voice. 'This afternoon is the funeral. Marse Ironman will help. We don't want any more big people . . . them can only pray. We will make a cart and carry him weself to the burying ground. We will get plenty flowers. Everybody must wash them clothes and patch them and bathe and comb them hair. Anybody what got any money to give, even a farthing can bring it and we will give it to Marse Ironman to buy the things.'

As Mobel finished her cold, brief outline, anger swept through the crowd. 'We will bury him weself Mobel! You right, big people can't do a thing but pray!'

There were only about two hundred of them at the start, but as they walked along in silence, hauling and pushing their burden towards the city, others came to join them.

The hearse was a roughly made handcart with four wheels instead of two and ropes attached to the front instead of shafts. A well made cedar coffin lay amidst a collection of wild flowers and dwarf palm branches.

Sista, Pazart and Mobel each had one of the three looped ropes attached to the front of the improvised hearse. A number of children walked beside it and behind, helping to push or hold back the vehicle.

Even the weak and disabled had gathered to take part. There were Indian, European and Chinese children walking beside their black-skinned friends. It seemed that all the world's children wanted to be represented on this march. From out of lean-to huts and houses made of cardboard and tarred paper they joined the procession as it came in sight. The only sounds were the crunching of wheels on the rough, dusty road and the shuffling feet of the marchers.

The 'big people' knowing they were out of favour with the children kept back, not joining the line until a gap had been made. Youths became the guardians of the march and walked on both sides of the smaller children. By the time the main road was reached, there were about five hundred children aged between three and twelve, shuffling quietly behind the bier, flanked by the same number of older ones and followed by a couple of hundred adults.

It had been well noted by the authorities that the funeral procession was taking place at the same time as the wedding of the Duke. In the Municipal Park, ten thousand children had gathered for the special treat that had been arranged. Then someone saw a dusty band of children coming down the road pushing a cart that bore a coffin.

The word went round: 'It is the Sparrow what dead. Them picnies going to bury him themselves.'

On hearing the news every child went to the fence to watch the coming procession. Slowly, silently and wearily they came. Their faces, hands and feet, so clean at the start of the march, were now covered in dust and sweat. The children in the park also fell silent as the procession drew near. Then, as if it had all been pre-arranged, the ten thousand children started to hasten past the adults, in spite of attempts to stop them, and respectfully began to take up their places beside their less fortunate brothers and sisters. One of the newcomers, wanting to identify himself more closely with the ragged, barefoot mourners, stepped to one side, and took off his shoes and socks before rejoining the line.

In the city, the officials heard of this new development and decided that the children must be turned off the route at all costs. If they reached Cathedral Square where the wedding service was taking place, there would be hell to pay.

Pazart saw the little park where they had first met Sonna but it was becoming blurred. The trembling was not yet apparent but he knew it would soon come. He held the rope over his shoulder tightly and said to himself, 'Oh God, don't make I have fits now! Please God, don't make I have it! . . . Please God . . .' He bent forward to keep the rope taut. Mobel caught sight of his vacant face. She called softly, 'Pazart,' but he did not seem to hear. He walked along mechanically and put his hand in his pocket without knowing what he did. He felt something solid in his palm. It was Sonna's mouth-organ. The hand in Pazart's pocket welded itself to the piece of wood and tin. It was the link between them, it could not be broken. Then Sonna was walking beside him. They were talking together, remembering all the things they'd done, all the plans they'd made. ' 'Member the day when you and me go fishing 'pon flat rock? And when all four of we did go one night with crocus bag and tin lamp out at the swamp to ketch land-crab? 'Member Sonna? And me was running with you and me killing meself with laugh . . .'

The procession was right in the heart of the city now and Main Bridge could be seen ahead. Two hours had passed since the three had taken the lead with the ropes. Pazart did not feel the soreness of his hands, nor the blisters.

'Sonna! 'Member how you say when you and me grow big we would drive train? And we would go on a big ship and see snow and them sparrows Cap'n tell we 'bout and see where Sexton Blake and Tinker live in Baker Street? Sonna . . . Sonna . . . 'Member when you tell me when you miss you father, you mother tell you to say, "For Thou art with me. Thy Rod, and Thy Staff they comfort me." '

'Pazart! Pazart you awright?' Mobel whispered. Her voice reached him and suddenly it was as if he had been pushed out of a soundproofed room into a sea of scraping and shuffling noises. His eyes began to function again; the crowds of faces on both sides of the street came into focus. He clutched the hard mouth-organ firmly in his pocket.

In order to ensure that the children did not disrupt the wedding and so draw the attention of the media to their plight, it had been arranged that a van would be placed across the start of Main Bridge, thereby blocking the route and forcing them to make a detour through the narrow side streets.

A Sergeant sat in a patrol wagon beside his driver waiting for reinforcements to arrive for the blocking of the bridge. They could hear some kind of ball game being played around them. 'Gimme my ball,' shouted a young voice. 'You don't have no right to take my ball 'cause it just barely knock you 'pon you foot. Gimme my ball, is just 'cause you bigger than me!'

The Sergeant turned but the hood of his wagon prevented him from seeing whoever was involved in the dispute.

'Gimme my ball!' came the voice of the child.

'You shouldn' make it knock me,' and through his voice the Sergeant judged the speaker to be approaching manhood.

'Don't kick my ball! You will kick it under the wagon!' There was a pause and then the same voice said, 'You see that? Same thing I say! You gone and kick my good ball under the wagon.'

'Why the hell you don't stop this noise, you hooligans?' shouted the Sergeant, unable to keep his peace any longer. He heard the two talking more quietly now.

'You see now? Is a policeman in there and the ball is under the wagon, and I want it.' The young voice seemed to be sobbing.

'Get the child's ball from wherever it is and get the hell out of here!' roared the Sergeant. He tried to catch sight of them but only saw the younger one, a ragged boy of about ten, rubbing his eyes with the back of his hand.

The youth called: 'I just getting the ball to give it back to him sir, it run under you wagon.'

'Then be quick and get out of here or you will get a boot where it will hurt,' said the driver.

The threat seemed to take effect; the two boys darted off.

A moment later, the first of eighteen policemen detailed for duty at the bridge started to get into the wagon. It was calculated that the children would reach the point of diversion in roughly ten minutes. A dispatch rider would give the police the signal to move in and effect the blockade and in this way action would be taken only at the last moment, giving no time for the news to spread and exacerbate the already tense situation. Traffic, except that which had a V.I.P. label on the windscreen, was also obliged to use other routes.

A dilapidated lorry towing another in a similar condition, was now avoiding Main Bridge by moving into the lane the children were to be directed into. The first was loaded with gravel and sand and four or five workmen stood in the hoodless body of the other. They laboured through, spluttering and backfiring. At that moment the signal came and a policeman on a motor cycle immediately headed for the patrol wagon.

The vehicles by this time had come to a halt. Exasperated, the traffic policeman left his stand and went over to the driver who was saying:

'Noname, get to hell out of the truck, and see if you can crank it man. Don't you see the motor shut down?'

Someone hauled himself out of the truck and moved lethargically towards the engine.

'Hurry up and crank the thing man!' urged the driver.

'Don't you see I hurrying man?' replied Noname, without the least sign of doing so. At last he took the crank handle in his hand and reluctantly gave it half a dozen turns but no sound came from the engine. 'Blasted truck won't start man! It look like it will never start till Kindom Come!'

By now an Inspector had appeared feeling he must take a hand. He looked anxiously up the street. The children were approaching. 'Get your men in the other truck to help you to move both these vehicles out of the way.' Even as he spoke he knew it was pointless. Nothing would get them moving and there was nowhere in the narrow lane in which to park them and still leave room for the procession to pass by.

The marchers were now almost upon them. The Inspector looked towards Main Bridge, expecting to see his Sergeant with the wagon effecting the blockade, but there was no sign. The children could not be prevented from crossing Main Bridge.

As the last of them passed over it, the two lorries miraculously came to life again and moved away. Shortly after, the Sergeant and his eighteen men arrived. The youngsters with the ball had immobilized his vehicle; when the signal had come, he had been unable to start.

The children were out of sight again now, but a contingency plan had been devised. The dispatch rider was sent to set it in motion, but he quickly returned with the news:

'Sergeant Major instructs me to report, Sir, that it is not possible to turn the procession into St Andrews Lane, for this lane is under repairs.'

'Under what?'

'Under repairs, Sir,' answered the rider. 'I saw it myself as I passed. There was heaps of sand and gravel with the notice up, "Road Under Repairs", and a number of men standing around in working clothes with picks and shovels.'

At the 'Road Closed' barrier, a lad drew up on a bicycle.

'Everything work 'cording to plan,' he said to the men leaning on their picks.

Not long afterwards, Mobel, Pazart and Sista came into view. They were still hauling the knotted rope. Ironman stood upright and still as the bier passed him. Then he turned to his friends and they all began to dismantle the bogus barrier.

The children passed under the palm-covered arches of the entrance to Cathedral Square just as the wedding ceremony was at its height. Silent until now a few at the front of the line began to sing:

> 'Now the day is over
> Night is drawing nigh . . .'

Sista remembered the hymn; Sonna had often played it on his mouth-organ. The children behind picked up the words and they were repeated along the line, back and further back like an echo in a cavern, until the furthest point was reached and then the song swelled and returned, filling everything around the square with sound:

> 'Shadows of the evening
> Steal across the sky . . .'

Many of the spectators, who had at first been outraged by the arrival of the barefooted urchins, were now deeply moved by their singing. The cameras of the world clicked and whirred, prying into the souls of the marchers, capturing their misery, their frustration, their bewilderment.

> 'Jesus gives the weary
> Calm and sweet repose . . .'

So sang the children, and the adults around them were disquieted by the irony they seemed to detect in their voices. Mockingly, one of the smaller ones began the song that Captain Dimlight had composed:

> 'I shall never fear tomorrow . . .
> I shall banish care or sorrow,
> Knowing all the while
> I am God's little chile
> God's little sparrow . . .'

96

Mobel's feet dragged as she bent forward to keep the rope taut. Her hands like Pazart's were full of blisters. Her lips were dry and scaly. She had no eyes for the spectators. Perspiration caused her clothes to cling to her and her hair, neatly combed some hours before, looked grey with dust.

Pazart still held tightly to the mouth-organ. There were cuts on his feet but he did not appear to notice them. His eyes were red and he did not join in the singing nor look at anyone. Sista was aware of nothing but Sonna. Before the setting of the sun they had reached the place in the cemetery.

The Minister, always on hand for administering the last rites for those who had no minister of their own, pushed his way through the people around the grave of the child. He had never, in his long years, seen such a great gathering. When at last he reached the graveside, he was breathless and his hands trembled. He opened the book and was about to read it, when a hand took it gently but firmly from him. Surprised, he was about to protest but Sista looked down on the pages before her, and began to read haltingly:

'I am the Resurrection and the Life, saith the Lord . . .'

She could not continue. Mobel quickly took the book from her and read:

'He that believeth in Me, though he were dead, yet shall he live.'

She passed the book to Pazart but before he could say the words they heard the voice of Captain Dimlight repeating the passage from memory as he looked down on the coffin covered with wild flowers. His trousers and white buckskin shoes were mud-caked and his face bore the stubble of a beard.

'I know My Redeemer liveth, and that He shall stand at the latter day upon the earth . . .' And so he continued in a dull voice, while the crowd marvelled at his ability to recite the entire Order of the Burial of the Dead without once consulting the book. At last it was finished. As he looked up from the coffin, even the Sparrows pitied him; his suffering showed in his eyes. Everyone waited for him to address them, sensing that he would have something more than the usual words of comfort to give them, but not quite knowing what to expect.

Then he began to speak in a voice that carried to almost every member of the crowd: 'I have suddenly found that I am a teacher who does not know what he has taught. I have just repeated the ceremony of the Burial of the Dead, in the way a parrot would if it had been taught the very same words. How can I explain, except in parrot-fashion, the incident in the Book of Job where the righteous are allowed to be punished? How can I explain the reason why a good and just God should make a man, because of the colour of his skin, be the hewer of wood, and the drawer of water, a servant, a slave for the rest of the world? We are made to understand that all that is black is evil, so we can take it for granted that God, being good, cannot be black, nor could Christ, if we go by the teachings of those who gave us the Christian religion. And yet I have been going on blindly, trusting, believing, winning souls for a cause which I myself do not truly comprehend.' Dimlight paused, not sure how to make them see that he had denounced religion for the black man as it was interpreted by the religious bodies. He bowed his head and continued:

'We look down on the last remains of this child, purer in soul than most of us now standing around his grave. We remember how thousands of us prayed to God to save him. How, by mere chance, the doctor who might have saved him lay becalmed in the sailing boat some few hundred miles away. God did not hear our prayer. Was this boy less than one of the birds of the air whom God promised to protect? Was this innocent child counted less than one of the sparrows in God's sight? The same which God promised to provide for so they may not fall to the ground?'

Dimlight raised his eyes over the heads of the people, and said, in a voice that reverberated around Cathedral Square, 'If this is the promise of God to His people, if we are only to be the hewers of wood and drawers of water, we cannot be His people, and if He promised to look after the sparrows, then there are no *black* sparrows.

'This day I have resigned from the Salvation Army. I can no longer teach what I do not understand. But I shall live among you, trying to undo what wrong I have done; trying to find the answer – not from the Bible, but from my experience and from life. Perhaps I shall find God in this way, perhaps I shall not, but I will try to love my neighbour, as a Man who lived nearly two thousand years ago once taught.'

As he ended, people whispered to one another trying to find the meaning of the Captain's strange words. The Sparrows stood in silence, looking dry-eyed at the mound that hid Sonna from view. When they looked towards Dimlight again, he had gone.

Slowly the mourners began to disperse. Now only the Sparrows remained, fighting their anger and their bewilderment, silently talking to Sonna, promising to punish the person who had done this to him. And for a while it was as if the mound of earth, strewn with wild flowers, did not exist as a wall between themselves and their friend.

CHAPTER SIXTEEN

It was Shepherd Peter, leader of the religious sect, who had found Bangbelly. Like many others, he had been in search of him since Sonna's death. Bangbelly's house had been found empty. Afterwards Shepherd had seen it in flames.

Then, by sheer chance, he had come upon Bangbelly sleeping, dirty and unshaven, and had struck him with a heavy stick. He had dragged him to a small clump of bushes and had put the Constable's own handcuffs on his wrists. Then he had struck with the stick once more, this time at one of Bangbelly's ankles, ensuring that he was completely immobilized. Lastly he had gagged him and hurried away towards the town.

After Sonna's funeral, Shepherd and one of his aides loaded a cart with hessian bags and returned to the spot . . .

It was past midnight when the cart rumbled past what resembled a bundle of clothing crowned on the top with the head of a broomstick tied with a plaid cloth and seated on a donkey. The men glanced in its direction. They knew it was a woman, but could not tell if she had seen them, for her head remained bowed as they passed. Shepherd tried to recall a story he had heard recently about someone who fitted her description but at that moment there was a muffled groan from the back of the cart and he proceeded to silence it, forgetting the woman in the process.

Two hours later, the cart with Shepherd and his companion was returning to the city without the burden it had been carrying earlier beneath the hessian bags. Once more, they saw the old woman on the slow-moving donkey. Briefly, as they approached, the lights from a late-night market lorry illuminated the road and the bundle looked up, startling them with a piercing look from her sharp black eyes. The men drew back as they recognized her, and the donkey and rider merged into blackness.

Shepherd's companion said, 'Dat ole woman . . . she know it is we . . . maybe she know what we jus' done! Dem say she know every-t'ing.'

Although he was disquieted, Shepherd tried to reassure his friend. 'Don't you worry 'bout her. I hear she did curse him an' even spit on him out at de square dat day.'

'Is true, my sister was dere, only . . .'

'Only what?'

'Only de ole woman say dat him would want to dead an' can't an' dat him would hang.'

There was a thoughtful pause. Then Shepherd roused himself. 'Well de ole woman guess wrong. De only drop him will get is de one we jus' give him over de precipice.'

But they continued the journey along the darkened road in an uneasy silence.

BOOK TWO

CHAPTER SEVENTEEN

Ma Kuskus gave a grunt as she looked down on the body at her feet. It had taken her all morning to reach the ledge where she and her donkey Ginny were now standing.

Above her towered two hundred feet of cliff, sheer in places, not too steep in others. The hardy shrubs and weeds that grew there concealed her totally from view. Below was another two hundred feet or more of rock, ending in a gorge. A track had been formed along the more gentle slope of the cliff by the flow of rainwater which ran regularly into a noisy stream via a gutter-like curve. Although it was dangerous in places, Ma Kuskus had used this path to reach the body. Now she bent over it and listened for a long time. Then she squatted on her haunches, her great patchwork frock spreading round her. She brought a pipe from somewhere in its folds which had a stem about an inch long. She felt inside a cloth bag, attached by a string around her neck, and drew out some finely cut tobacco and a box of matches. She struck one of the matches and put it to the bowl of the chalk pipe. Her cheeks contracted each time she inhaled until she released the smoke with a gentle 'phut'.

She looked at the swollen, battered face of Bangbelly with blood sealing one of the eyes, the nose almost clogged, the half-dry crusts around the mouth. She looked at the twisted, bootless foot and the tattered clothes caked in mud. But her face registered nothing.

The sun rose higher and a couple of flies came from nowhere to circle and land on his face. These flies seemed to help Ma Kuskus to come to a decision. She went to Ginny's hamper and returned with a bottle marked 'Bay Rum'. Tearing off a small piece of cloth from her underskirt she began to apply the liquid to his features. Only a slight movement of the chest showed that the body still had life. Ma Kuskus called Ginny, who stopped eating grass and approached like an intelligent dog. From her hampers Ma Kuskus brought some hessian bags and small bundles of rope.

With surprising strength, she managed to wrap every piece of hessian around the body of Bangbelly, confining most of her effort to his chest and waist.

Using the rainwater path, Ma Kuskus coaxed Ginny on to a second ledge that lay beneath the first. The route was narrow and perilous, but Ma Kuskus was there with her whispering words of encouragement. Once she clasped her hands around Ginny's head as if to say, 'Ef you go Ginny, den you ole mistress an' frien' will go wid you.' This seemed to calm the donkey and at last she halted beneath a piece of rope which had been hung from the ledge above as a guide to where the unconscious man lay.

There was a difference of nearly two feet between Ginny's pack-saddle and the ledge above. Ma Kuskus bridged this by leaving Ginny and returning to the hillside where she uprooted some of the shrubs and bushes that grew between the rocks with her cutlass and bound them into a great loose bundle which she tied expertly to the pack-saddle and hamper. Then she went back to the upper ledge.

She tied a rope around Bangbelly's leg, leaving the other end free and another to his wrist. Slowly she rolled him to the edge of the platform and taking the ropes, pushed him gently with her foot on to the donkey below. Bangbelly fell on top of the bundles and for a moment it seemed he would overbalance. Ma Kuskus steadied him with a pull on the ropes, and then came down again to tie him securely on Ginny's back. Bangbelly's head was pointed towards the donkey's rump, with his arms spread out on each side as if he were embracing her in a topsy-turvy manner. Ma Kuskus sealed the gesture by tying both hands in this position, running the rope under the donkey's belly. The legs were divided, one to each side of Ginny's long neck, then securely tied. She worked for an hour using the rest of the ropes in a series of knots and lashings until it looked as if the body was caught in a large net from which it could not escape. Then they began the journey down to the gorge.

Half a dozen times, Ginny slipped on the wet surface of the track and a quarter of her body hung in space. Ma Kuskus herself slipped and rolled and but for her rope, would have fallen. But at last they reached the base of the cliff and began the five-mile trek through woodland and rough tracks.

The sun was going down when Ma Kuskus, bruised and exhausted, reached the door of a roughly constructed hut. She began to untie the knots.

CHAPTER EIGHTEEN

The people who had flocked to the various meeting houses and local churches to pray for Sonna more than a week before now turned out to praise God for avenging his death. Did not the Bible say, 'An eye for an eye, a tooth for a tooth'? The law with its prisons and gallows also upheld such action.

They sang hymns of praise, picked out by the shepherds of the zealous home-founded sects, fashioned after the old fire and brimstone missionaries which had once claimed the souls of the people. Bibles – the cheapest reading matter available for many years after slavery and even in the thirties, the biggest buy at one shilling for an approved Genesis to Revelation edition – had helped to create a people more orthodox even than those for whom it had originally been intended. Only the young questioned the rigidity of their elders' interpretation.

Shepherd Peter, sharing his secret with his congregation and considering himself a hero who had defended God, walked through them like 'a father among his children, while they swayed gently to the singing of the hymns with eyes closed.

The police knew it was a 'Ninth Night' for a departed person, for it proceeded like all other Ninth Nights, with the singing of hymns, refreshments at midnight, then more singing until dawn. But they could think of no one who had died nine days before and could be worthy of such memorials from the poor. And then they detected a variation in the wording of the last spiritual:

> 'He is gone! He is gone!
> He is gone to a silent home
> An' forever wid de devil . . .
> Amen, so let it be!'

The hymn was usually sung, 'Forever with the Lord'. And so they were able to discover the reason for the Ninth Night by deducing who was 'with the devil' and secretly they were relieved; at least the matter was closed.

Since Sonna's death, the three children seemed to have become adults. They no longer quarrelled over childish things and there was no laughter in their home. When they went out to sell their goods, they no longer tried to conceal what they were doing from the police. Many times, they might have been caught but it seemed that Sonna's death and the publicity surrounding it had given them immunity for now at least.

After the funeral, several poor market women who could scarcely look after their own, had offered one or two of them a home. The children had declined courteously, and Mobel had conveyed the impression that someone had promised to help them, while leaving them free to live together as before.

But even Ironman had been unsuccessful in trying to assist the children. Although he loved them as his own, their meetings were now so painful for them all that he had no wish to be with them more than he could help. Sonna's death, far from uniting them, was pushing them far apart. They could not share their grief and could find no comfort, not even in each other.

CHAPTER NINETEEN

He looked up and saw a rough roof of palm leaves, perhaps a little higher than a tall man, constructed flat and ridgeless.

He felt himself on some kind of a bed, and he could see the trees through the open door which revealed the only light. Slowly he managed to turn his head, and discerned that the bundle of clothes in the corner was a woman sitting watching him.

He tried to identify the place he was in, failed and gave up.

'Where I is?' he asked weakly. The woman in the corner got up and took a clay bowl from a barely-glowing, charcoal fire he had not noticed before. She came over slowly, holding the bowl with both hands.

'You?' he gasped, shrinking back on the rough bed. She did not answer. He tried to raise himself on one elbow, but could not manage it.

'What you going to do with me?' he asked hoarsely.

'Drink!' commanded Ma Kuskus, bringing the bowl towards his lips. He moved his head back from the vessel as if there were a snake inside it.

'Drink, fool!' said the woman angrily. This time he watched her face, and in a half-resigned, half-fascinated manner, allowed the proffered bowl to reach his lips. With one bony hand helping his head off the pillow, Ma Kuskus began to feed him slowly. When he had swallowed the contents, she released his head, as if she wished to show that the task was unpleasant and she was glad it was over. She returned to the corner of the hut.

There was silence for about half an hour. To his surprise, far from killing him, the drink actually made him feel stronger. He had managed to piece together a little of what had happened to him but there was much he could not remember or did not know. Now he wondered how to break the silence and how his words would be received.

'Thank you for the drink,' he said at last.

'Don't t'ank me yet!' said Ma Kuskus ominously.

'Can you tell me where I is?'

'Far from town.'

'Can you tell me what happen yesterday?'

'*Yeste'day?* You mean two month ago!'

'Two month?' he said in disbelief. She did not answer. Again there was silence. Again, the sick man spoke first. 'Sorry, I have to ask you couple more question.' He waited, but she did not invite him to speak so he took her silence as consent.

'Me eye . . . The one what have the bandage . . . what's wrong with it?'

'Blind,' said Ma Kuskus, as if she were happy to inform him of his loss.

He began to tremble. 'And me foot, it feel like it bandage at the ankle as well. It gone too Ma Kuskus?' He tried to conceal his despair with a careless tone.

'Cripple' at de ankle!' replied the old woman. He was sure she was enjoying herself. He lay on his back digesting the information while Ma Kuskus sat like a stone in the corner. Then he turned over on his side to face her, forcing himself up on one elbow, while his uncovered eye tried to pierce the half-dark corner of the hut.

'I have to ask you one more question, Ma Kuskus.'

'You said it was a couple question you did want to ask!' she reminded him.

'I don't mind what I did say! What I want to ask you is: Why you didn't make I stay where I was . . . and dead?' The question came fierce and bitter, and he panted as he waited for a reply.

'Maybe I is one of dem Good Samaritan in de Bible!'

'You want me to believe that?'

'What de hell I care what *you* want to believe *Mista Bangbelly?*'

The man lowered himself off his elbow on to his pillow, then without another word, buried himself in his blanket.

By the following day he was able to sit up, though he felt weak and giddy. Ma Kuskus sat by the door of the palm-thatched hut, tying together bundles of herbs and fibres, sweet smelling kuskus roots, noted for keeping moths from clothes as well as imparting its fragrance on whatever lay amongst it. Long ago, someone had called the old woman by the name of the famous root, and it had stuck. No one could remember hearing her called by any other name.

The Constable sat on the low wooden bed with the old blanket covering the lower part of his body, waiting, it seemed, for the old woman to say something. But she went on with the tying of her herbs and roots.

'Ma Kuskus.'

'What?'

She did not look up. Because of his bandaged eye and the bright sunlight, only her silhouette was visible.

'I want to ask you something.'

'What?'

'The child . . .'

Cruelly she waited. She knew what he had been wanting to ask but she would not help him.

Realizing this, he braced himself. 'The boy, I mean . . . him dead?'

'Yes.' Her answer was abrupt but full of enmity.

'Then I didn't dream it!' he said to himself.

'Ef you t'ink you dream it, I can take you to town an' show you de grave!'

She kept on with her work, never glancing once in his direction.

'Why you didn't let me dead?' he asked bitterly, his hands clenched under the blanket.

'As easy as dat?' she said quietly.

'So you save me because you don't think I suffer enough!' There was no question in his tone; it was a statement of fact. He waited in case she wished to admit or deny his charge, but she went on making her heaps of herbs and roots grow larger.

Slowly he lowered himself back on to his pillow and pulled the brown blanket up to his chest. He stared at the thatched roof with his uncovered eye and remained quiet for a long time, while Ma Kuskus stopped her binding, and started puffing at her short-stemmed pipe.

Then he seemed to remember something. 'I going to bother you again, Ma Kuskus,' he said wearily.

'What's it?' And now the old woman turned her face towards the bed.

'I have a house in town . . .'

'You *did* have a house.'

'What you mean?' he asked, but there was little concern in his voice.

'Dem burn it down same night de boy dead.'

He took the news quietly, then said, 'I did have some money there, too.'

Ma puffed a little cloud. 'Yes. Five hundred poun' bury in a tin under de floor board.'

'How you know that?'

'You talk 'bout it all de time.'

'When I was off me head?'

'When you was *mad*.' She would not spare him.

He thought a while, then asked: 'What happen to it, you know?'

'It not dere!'

The news of his loss did not seem to surprise him.

'Any more question?' she said sarcastically, but he did not take offence.

'No thank you, that's all.' And he carefully turned on his side with his face to the corner.

Ma Kuskus sat staring at the back of the man, still puffing tiny clouds out of her mouth with the gentle 'phut' of her lips as she released them. The birds outside chirped in the trees and the slight breeze rustled the leaves of the pimento, and swayed the long pointed leaves of the banana tree.

Ma Kuskus broke the silence. 'What you have in you mind, why you ask 'bout you house an' money?' She knew he was awake and waited for his reply; her cold pipe still in her mouth.

'Just curious,' he answered without turning round.

'I is curious too!'

'You don't need to.'

'Why?'

'Because you know everything.' He turned towards her again, resting on his elbow. His one eye gleamed in the half light as if he was once more on the verge of madness. 'Yes, Ma Kuskus, you know everything. You can do everything as well! You can put a curse on a man, you can make him run mad, you can make him dead, and if you like to play with him, you can bring him back to life again.' His voice rose higher as he spoke the bitter words. But if his taunts roused her in any way, she did not

107

show it. She only looked at the hard ground which formed the hut floor. A slight gleam passed from her eyes down to the place where they were focused before her, but he could not see it from where he was.

'Awright. I tell you my mind what I think of you. Now kill me.'

Ma Kuskus got up from her seat and the Constable fell back exhausted. She stood looking at him without speaking, her pipe still in her mouth. Then she walked into the sunlight.

CHAPTER TWENTY

Dimlight stood on the fringe of the crowd at the dock gates. He was hardly noticed. Every man was tense, hoping to get a ticket which would mean work for a few hours or perhaps a whole day; but whether four shillings or eight, it would provide bread for themselves and their families.

The boss came out and stood on the bank by the gate, flanked by subordinates, while two men stood lower down, leaning on club-like sticks. Names were read out while the wharfinger stood in his spotless white suit, his cigar pointing to the sky.

'Here!' 'Here!' Those who were summoned shouted eagerly. When about thirty had been called there were still a dozen tickets left. All the men still waiting anticipated the next move and drew closer to the remaining tickets which were tossed into the air. The scramble started. Forgetful of dignity, they fought to get hold of the little card which would mean a few shillings' work. Hands were crushed and heads bruised, but though they strove for possession, it was not done in anger and no one attempted to take a ticket another had picked from the ground.

One ticket was blown at Dimlight's feet and as he was standing alone, he retrieved it unopposed, bemused by his good fortune.

Two months had gone by since he had spoken at Sonna's grave. He looked different now. He was dressed in a khaki shirt and blue trousers, with cheap canvas shoes and no socks on his feet. His hair was high on his head, making it seem larger than it really was. He had been everywhere seeking work; to the canefields, the banana plantations, even to far-away Kingston. He had found nothing but he had learned much. He had seen the degradation of his people and had shared the little he had with the most unfortunate. He had sold his black serge uniform and his cornet for a few shillings. In the past two days he had only eaten a few rotten bananas and a bruised orange. When he had arrived at the dock he had been teased by some and called turncoat or Captain, but when they had seen that he took it without a frown or a murmur they had ceased and had let him be.

With his ticket in his hand, he now moved forward with the rest of the men and showed it to the gateman.

They were to unload a tramp ship containing flour. Each bag held one hundred and ninety-six pounds. Dimlight was given a barrow and he began to haul two bags at a time to the warehouse. Hungry and unused to such work, he staggered with his load across railway lines to and from the ship, while others, more used to running a handcart, moved with startling speed. After an hour, Dimlight's hands were badly blistered. He struggled to cross the raised lines and recross before reaching the storehouse. Sweat ran down his face and his shirt clung to him, though the sun was still low in the sky.

After three hours, the dock was merely a sunlit blur to Dimlight. Hunger and exertion were making him dizzy and weak. He began to pull the next load, not seeing the boss, cigar in hand, coming towards him. As he tried to negotiate the railway line, the two men collided, sending the handcart over and spilling the flour. Vaguely, Dimlight realized he had been the cause of an accident and he began to apologize, but the boss angrily raised his voice, 'Gateman! Send two men here to throw this man out!'

Stunned, Dimlight tried to reason with him while the other workers looked on from a distance.

'Get out before my men carry you out between them!' was the shouted reply.

Dimlight forgot his discomfort. 'I said I am sorry, it was an unfortunate accident and both of us were at fault. I have a ticket which entitles me to work and I wish to continue.' As he spoke, the onlookers were impressed by his calmness and dignity.

Aware of this the boss demanded loudly, 'Where the hell are the men I asked for?'

Two men approached from the gate with sticks in their hands. As they stood beside their employer, Dimlight began to speak to them; though outwardly cool he was raging inside.

'I have done no harm,' he said. 'What happened was an accident. Why do you treat me like this? We are all workers fighting to earn the bread we need to live. Must I be set upon unfairly by you just because it is your master's wish? Must I be chased like a dog through the gates without my pay though I came in honourably, just because your master orders it? Must you face me with great clubs as if I am a wild animal that cannot understand reason?'

The two men looked at each other and then at their boss. They, it seemed, were on the verge of rebellion, and their master knew it. He said, 'I am going aboard the ship. If, by the time I reach the gangway, this man has not been set to his heels by the use of your sticks, you will cease to work for me.'

He walked away without looking back.

The two men stood perplexed and embarrassed. 'Look,' said one, 'we have no quarrel with you, but we can't make we wife and picni starve because of you. But tell you what you can do. The wharfinger not looking. You run and we will run after you and pretend we licking you till you pass through the gates.'

'And that would please your master?'

The word 'master' upset the two men. Dimlight's scorn made them angry as well as ashamed.

'We trying to help you,' said one.

'You are trying to help me?'

'Yes!'

'Very well. You will have to help me out!' Dimlight suddenly grabbed the stick of the one nearest to him and flung it over the heads of the spectators into the sea. Taken totally by surprise, the two men did nothing for a moment. Then, the one who had lost his stick charged and swung his right fist wildly at the same time. Dimlight ducked out of the way. The crowd laughed. He made a second, bull-like attack but Dimlight dealt him a heavy blow. Then the second man joined the fray with his stick . . .

When Dimlight recovered his senses he was in a narrow lane near the wall of the wharf. A man was bending over him, giving him a drink from an enamel mug. Still in a daze, Dimlight allowed himself to be led away from the docks towards the poorer quarter of the city, until they reached a yard which he did not recognize until he sat down. It belonged to Ironman. At once, Dimlight experienced a deep sense of humiliation. His presence was explained by his companion and Ironman came, forcing spirits down his throat and making him swallow hot soup. While they fussed over him, Dimlight wondered how to tell them he could not pay them. But he was too hungry to refuse the food that was put before him.

As he ate and began to recover his strength, he became aware of his surroundings and of the people, men, women and children who came through the gates for their midday meal. Ironman was sometimes their waiter, sometimes cook, sometimes cashier. A table-cloth served as an apron tied round his chest. Everything was clean. Dimlight was surprised to see that dish-covers had been put on all the items not in use and those who helped with the dishes dipped them in steaming water before passing them on to be washed, frequently changing the water and cloth.

When the place was almost empty, Ironman brought two large mugs to Dimlight's table. He sipped one, expecting water and found it was lemonade with ice.

'Hear you have a brush with the dockman this morning,' said Ironman, sitting beside him and taking a sip from the second mug.

Dimlight looked up quickly, thinking he was being mocked, but there was only concern in Ironman's face. Dimlight decided that he had not been recognized and said, with a wry smile, 'I got a beating. It seems I would be better blowing trumpets and beating drums in the Salvation Army. I am certain I can beat a drum, but I'm sure of nothing more. They were right when they nicknamed me Captain Dimlight.'

Ironman merely said, 'A man must do what him conscience tell him is right, Cap'n. Even if you lose, and you mostly lose, you have the satisfaction of knowing you didn't do the easiest thing. And everything what you conscience tell you to do is always the hardest!'

Dimlight was surprised into silence by his response.

'Sorry I can't talk to you more now, Cap'n – I going still call you Cap'n, I hope you won't mind. I going give a hand with the serving. Come every day for you dinner.' As he lifted the mugs from the table he bent forward and said in a low voice, 'Don't mind 'bout the money. You will get a job, and if you find youself hard up for a bob or two, don't be 'fraid to signal me. We start serve evening food six o'clock, but come when you can.'

Before Dimlight could answer, Ironman was behind the counter again, dishing up meals for latecomers.

As he walked through the door, the Captain said to himself, 'Dimlight, you are truly dim. We search for miracles when we have them about us every day, never recognizing them as such.'

CHAPTER TWENTY-ONE

The man seemed afraid to take his first step. He put one foot solidly on the ground while he stood only on the toes of the other. From the way he bit his lip it was plain that even this caused him some pain. He had grown so thin that he looked much taller than he really was. His famous belly had disappeared. One eye was open but the other was permanently closed. His face, once clean-shaven, was bearded making it seem long and melancholy, no longer round and puffy. But his lameness, above all, had changed him; he was almost unrecognizable.

Nearby, at the door of the hut, Ma Kuskus sat smoking her pipe while her birdlike eyes watched his effort to walk barefoot with a semi-useless ankle. Before he had taken half a dozen steps, sweat appeared on his forehead and he faltered. He glanced towards Ma Kuskus. Her expression spurred him on. This time he did not stop until he was through the door and out of her sight. Then he dropped to the ground, burying his face in his hands.

When, at last, he rose and began to make his way back to the hut, his steps were more regular though still unsteady. Ma Kuskus was still at the door; she had not moved in the hour that he had been gone. Her pipe remained in her mouth but no tiny streaks of smoke issued from it now. As he came within a few feet of her, he smiled and it was the first smile she had ever seen on his face. Yet it was sad and there was mockery in the one eye.

'You know what, Ma Kuskus? I have a new name for meself.'

As he had expected she did not answer. He turned his face so that his good eye caught the sunlight and the hardness of his expression was laid bare. 'My name not going to be Robinson Crusoe like what them use to call me at school. And it not going to be Bangbelly . . . it going to be either One-Eye . . . or Tip-Toe.'

He fell silent as if considering which it was most likely to be. He then looked back to Ma Kuskus and said, as if she asked his preference, 'I would rather them call me Tip-Toe – and Tip would be better still.' He pushed his hands into the pockets of the trousers which hung loosely on him.

Ma Kuskus took the pipe from her mouth. 'Betta come an' get de foot rub . . . Tip.'

There was a pause and then he followed her uncertainly, shaking his head a little as he went.

As the days passed, he discovered one more change in himself. He now had a slight stammer that prevented him from speaking in his usual assertive and abrupt manner. He had been aware that he was speaking much more slowly but he had expected this to pass as his strength grew. Now it seemed that the change was permanent; there was no sign that his old way would return. It was as if he had suffered a stroke and could only pronounce his words in a slow drawl. At first, the loss of his normal voice had distressed him greatly, but he was becoming accustomed to it now. In any case, he seldom had the chance of conversation for Ma Kuskus kept communication to a minimum. It seemed that his whole life had moved into a slower sphere; there were long hours of isolation and enforced idleness and his slow speech seemed to reflect this new pace.

Ma Kuskus had been bathing his feet daily in boiled herbs and salt to harden the soles. Now, after much practice he was able to bear the feel of the sharp, hard stones that covered the area around the hut. Twice he had gone into the hills after Ma Kuskus, hoping that she would find him something to do, but she had dug everything herself, even the large tuber-like roots which were bought from her as a base for tonic mixture. She would not give up the sharp cutlass and as there were no other tools, he could not assist her. She would not even let him carry the bundle she collected, preferring to tie it in hessian and haul it down the hill behind her. When she was away he sometimes gathered firewood or filled barrels with spring water from the hill. Though she never openly acknowledged what he had done, he once thought he could detect the absence of the usual hardness in her eyes as she looked upon him. Later he was sure he had imagined it.

As he sat thinking of all this, her call reached him: 'Dinna . . . Tip.' Hearing her address him by this new name, though not for the first time, made him want to show that he appreciated it. But when he reached the door of her little room and looked at her face, he saw the same cold, remote expression and the words he had been planning to say died inside him.

He sat before the meal without making any attempt to start. He disliked being beholden to Ma Kuskus, who so obviously considered him worthless, and he knew that she had little money to spare for his upkeep. He looked around the room that he had come to know as well as his own. The wattled walls were pasted with magazines or newspapers in lieu of wallpaper and a rush mat was spread across the floor. There was a large table covered with ancient bits of patterned plates, cups and saucers and heavy tumblers which must have been the first the

113

glassmaker had attempted to blow. In the centre stood a large oil lamp with a patterned globe. In the far corner there was a wooden bed, neatly made and covered with a patchwork blanket; its many colours brightened the room. Beside this, there was an old trunk that might once have held ships' treasure and pirates' doubloons.

'What wrong wid de dinna?'

Tip did not see how she could tell that his meal was untouched; she had been standing with her back to him since he had entered the room. 'I don't feel hungry,' he answered.

'Well you can get up an' leave it, nobody forcin' you.' Now she turned to face him, resting her back lightly against the papered wall.

'Is not that the food is not good, Ma Kuskus, is just that I don't feel good eating what you provide all this time, and me not doing anything to help.'

'I don't complain.'

'All the same, I feel bad about it Ma. Besides, why should you be feeding me and treating me good? You is not me relation. If I 'member right, me and you is enemy.'

He waited for a response but there was none. She was looking at the sunlight that had come through the little window to shine on the table of china, making it glitter and sparkle.

'All the same, I thank you for what you do, enemy or not,' said Tip.

'I tell you befo', don't t'ank me yet.'

'Yes I know you say that Ma Kuskus, but I still thank you.'

'Why?'

The question was unexpected and Tip considered it before he replied. 'Because these months give me time to think and see everything different from how I see them before.'

'So you t'ink it wort' it?'

'Yes Ma, I think so.'

'Even ef you suffer later?'

'I can't suffer worse than what I gone through a'ready, Ma Kuskus.'

'Don't be too sure.'

'If that is true Ma Kuskus, then you is a cruel woman to save me!' He forgot his resolve to avoid taunts or bitterness; his mind could only dwell on the horror he had passed through and the hint that worse might follow. His angry speech brought new hardness to Ma Kuskus' face. She came to within arm's length of him and said:

'You 'member a man you swear on de Bible dat you see him tryin' to broke de bank one Sunday night? You know it was not true. You was tellin' lie!' She spoke with a hatred he had only seen once before – on the day she had cursed him, and all the fear he thought had been exhausted now returned.

The old woman stared into his face. 'You don't answer,' she taunted. 'Four years de man get, four long years! Yet you know dat him was shelterin' from de rain when you see him dat Sunday night, but jus' because you know him got in trouble one time befo', you challenge him, search him an' when you fine de stick of dynamite in him bag, you wouldn' believe him when him explain dat him was goin' to dynamite fish. You could have arrest him for havin' de dynamite, tell de truth an' him would get prison, but not four years. But no, you mus' tell lies. You mus' say you see him tryin' to broke into de bank.' Her voice came low and sinister with the next words: 'You didn' care 'bout de man wife an' young picni, eh Mista? Two years him serve out of de four, den him wife hear de news . . . him dead in prison. You know how him dead Mista what-you-name? Him dead because him complain him have pain in him side, but de bosun wouldn' believe him. Dem march him out to de quarry an' beat him when him tell dem him sick, an' all de time him was sufferin'! Dem fine him dead nex' mornin'! You know you guilty of dis as well as all dem innocent what you send to prison . . . an' death. An' now you have de cheek to tell me 'bout sufferin' an' call me cruel because I didn' leave you to dead when I fine you dat mornin'!'

Her voice penetrated like a knife, making little cuts with every word. She stood with her arms folded, watching his bowed head and his trembling body. Perhaps his demeanour prevented her from lashing him further with his past, for she said nothing more, but quietly turned away. He, in turn, softly and painfully made his way out of the hut and into the sunlight. When he was a short distance away, he stumbled and sat down on a stone which stood half buried in the earth and remained motionless.

At last he got up and knowing he could no longer stay, he returned to the hut. Looking round, he realized there was nothing he could make up into a bundle. The trousers and shirt he had on were the only clothing he possessed. Ma Kuskus had bought them with the money she had found in his pocket. He fingered the fifteen shillings change she had returned to him, refusing to accept it towards his keep. Just as he was leaving, he saw a small box at the side of his bed, tied up in a large bandanna handkerchief. He untied the knot and found his District Constable's badge and his handcuffs, rusty now with stains he took for blood – his blood. The marks of the handcuffs were still on his wrists.

Bearing these relics in the handkerchief he walked slowly from the hut. When he was some distance from it, he tied the items up, and flung his hand back with the intention of tossing them far into the bushes beneath him. But he could not let go of them and instead he made the knot which contained them more secure and forced the bundle into the back pocket of his trousers.

'You didn' t'row dem 'way? Why?'

He jumped, almost losing his balance. The sun had dipped behind the mountain and now there were shadows all around.

'Why you change you mind?' Ma Kuskus asked again.

'You in charge of me life Ma Kuskus, maybe you could tell me.'

'Ef I could take charge of life as you say . . . one little life I woulda like to take charge of wid all me heart. Want to hear de name Mista?'

'*No!* Ole woman, why you won't stop this torment?'

She did not answer.

'I going away,' he said.

'When?'

'Now. I was coming to say goodbye and thanks for everything.' It was hard to tell from his tone whether he was mocking her or not. She ignored his thanks this time.

'You still weak . . . Tip,' she said.

And he said to himself: she say that almost like she thought I was a human being like anybody else. Aloud he said, 'I will manage.'

'Dat foot you have still weak.'

'All the same, I going Ma Kuskus.'

'You need money . . . Tip?'

'I got money in me pocket . . . Ma.'

'Fifteen shillin'?'

'It will do.' His tone conveyed that he did not wish to be questioned further. His head was bowed but he could smell the home-cured tobacco now, and a scratch and a blaze of light told him she was lighting her pipe. Then came the phut, phut of her lips and the smoke from her tobacco which he liked to smell . . . just a little.

'I could len' you some money . . . 'bout a hundred poun'.'

Tip stood dumbfounded for a moment. 'I can see you don't done with me yet, Ma Kuskus,' he said at last. 'Where you would get a hundred pound? When or how, even if you did got it, you would get it back?'

'I am a ole woman.'

'Don't give me that. Ole people want money more than young people.'

Silence.

'Ma Kuskus?'

'What?'

'It don't make sense. Why should you of all people want to lend me money, if you got it in truth and really mean what you say? You hate me like hell, yet you offering to lend me enough to take me far from this place, instead of seeing to it that I can't leave Santa Lucia! Why?'

'T'ink out de answer youself, Tip.'

'Only one answer I can see, Ma Kuskus.'

'Well?' The mildness of her tone made him feel ashamed of hitting out, but he could not help himself. Besides, she must have guessed his thoughts.

'Maybe . . . maybe that hundred you offer would just make the last of you prophecy come true, Ma Kuskus!' He steeled himself for the lashing he feared would come.

'De answer is a good one. So, you mean to go back to Santa Lucia?' He was dumb for a moment, hardly believing she was letting him off so lightly.

'Yes, Ma. Santa Lucia,' he said.

'You gwine into danger!' He wanted to be rude, but instead he said, 'I kinda guess that, Ma Kuskus.'

'So you don't want de money?'

'No. I don't want the money, Ma Kuskus. Thanks all the same.'

He began walking down the hill in the dark, without another word and without looking back. But a couple of chains along the dim path, he relented, and shouted, 'Goodbye, Ma Kuskus!'

There was no answer. He stopped and peered back in the half darkness, but either she was not there, or his one eye was not strong enough to see. He turned his head once more towards the road – towards the city.

Tip thanked the charcoal cartman who had given him the lift to town. It had been a slow journey with the mules plodding along, the driver hunched over his seat and Tip perched on top of the hessian bags. It was fortunate that he had been offered the lift, for after only three of the ten miles his bare, lame foot had made further walking impossible. He was glad that the cartman had asked no questions. Now dawn was approaching.

Tip was even more afraid than he had anticipated now that he was back in the heart of the town. He knew that his illness and unkempt appearance had wrought a disguise that would be difficult to penetrate but his memories of Ma Kuskus and her prophecies made him acutely conscious of the dangers around him.

He went to a barber and had a haircut and a trim rather than a shave,

117

in one of the privately owned areas known as grass yards, which were like private market places. Although the barber teased him about the length of his beard and the height of his hair, he gave no signs of recognition. When he went for a cheap meal at one of the cookshops he was stared at, but he knew this was because of his beard and the abundant hair he still had on his head – seldom seen among West Indians then – and the patch he wore over his eye.

Later, as the day became brighter he took courage and went to the place where handcarts were usually for sale. He remembered how, only a few months before, he had felt way above those who went barefoot and how he had scorned the pushers of handcarts. He wondered if Ma Kuskus had anything to do with this change in him and then began to realize that it was only the awakening of his own conscience.

CHAPTER TWENTY-TWO

She was a mighty woman. Everything about her was big, from her red blouse and cretonne skirt, to the great bib-like apron which reached nearly down to her ankles. Her white canvas shoes spread themselves out as if the pressure of the feet inside was getting fiercer with each stride. The big round face under the plaid headkerchief boasted a pair of cheeks which danced with each movement of her feet, accompanied by the jingling of earrings and two pairs of silver bangles, which must have been made for the large wrists they adorned. Tip watched her coming down the lane of handcart men, but only out of curiosity, for he knew that being at the end of the line of eager men, he had no chance of being the one to be called. To his surprise they were not behaving as usual. They were not calling out to the woman, telling her of their readiness to take her load, whatever it was, for the fewest possible coppers. He decided that they knew her, and that she probably had a special man whom she was seeking, and they did not wish to rob this cartman of his regular patron. For he had learnt in a short time that they had their own code of practice.

She continued to walk, rocking on her big feet like a sailor on the deck of a ship, peering into the face of each man without halting until she had reached the end of the line, and stood before him.

'Come!' she said, looking at him with a pair of eyes too small for her great face. With that single word, she turned and started back up the lane. Tip followed hastily with the handcart. As he passed the men they said something but he was in too much of a hurry to catch it; besides they were probably just annoyed at being passed over.

The woman glanced back once or twice to see if he was still following. Once more he heard the men and managed to make out the word 'mule', but once again he put it down to resentment. When they were out of sight of the other cartmen, the woman slowed down and allowed him to walk beside her. He could hear her breathing and noted with his one eye that she was sizing him up – noticing his lameness perhaps. He got scared in case she was thinking that his foot was going to make him unworthy of his hire.

'Is awright lady, it don't make any difference. I still strong.'

The woman grunted, 'You new here, never see you befo'?'

'Yes lady, not round here long.'

'I got my regelar man, take me load every week, but him mus' be sick, or perhaps gone to prison, I can't fine him, dat's why I take you.'

'Thank you lady.'

'Him was a good worker . . . an' we never quarrel. I take him every week an' pay him one shilling to take me t'ings. De trouble is, sometimes I can't fine him, jus' like today.'

'Yes mam.'

'I like a regelar man. Ef you do dis work well, I take you every week, an' I will pay you de same as what him always charge, one shilling. You agree?'

'Thank you, lady.'

'Awright, I will pay you de shilling now.' She hastily pushed a shilling at Tip.

'How far we going, mam?'

'Not far, not far at all.'

At last they came to the street where a number of trucks were parked, filled with baskets and bags of vegetables. The woman stopped beside one of these. She called out in a masculine voice:

'Sideman!'

A big man detached himself from a group, and came towards her.

'Get me load, dis is me han'cart man.'

'Where de other han'cart?' the man asked, first looking round, then looking incredulously at the woman. 'Him one can't carry all dat load!'

'Mine you own goddam business an' take off de load off de truck,' the woman shouted in rage. 'You got too much goddam mouth, I gwine to complain to you driver, make him fire you from him truck. See Gawd! I gwine tell him I won't put me foot in him truck aggen till him fire you!' Frightened, the sideman tried to calm her.

'I didn't mean anyt'ing, Miss Hilda, didn't mean anyt'ing at all! Was only a joke I was makin'.'

'Take me load off den, an' long as you see me, don't interfere in my business.'

'Awright Miss Hilda,' said the man, and he climbed on the back of the truck and started unloading under watchful eyes.

Tip accepted bag after bag, until he saw that the handcart was full. He wondered whether he would be able to raise the shaft when he wanted to start. Mistaking the rest that the sideman had taken for the completion of the loading, he was about to lift the shaft to test its balance when the woman said roughly, 'Why you don't hurry up an' give de man de res' of me load, Mister Sideman?'

'But lady, the handcart full to the brim! It can't take any more!' said Tip.

The woman turned on him, her big bosom moving up and down. 'What de hell you mean? T'ink I gwine pay you what I pay you jus' fe dis? You like all de res', want money, an' don't want to work fe it. I work fe every penny I get an' nobody gwine to get anyt'ing from me and don't work fe it!'

'But I don't have nowhere else to put anything more, lady, and them bags full of coconut make the load too heavy a'ready!'

'What you t'ink rope fe? Why you don't get out you rope an' tie de bag down when de han'cart full? Dat's what all dem other han'cart men do. Where is you rope?' she asked, her big earrings shaking with the vibration of her face.

'I don't have any rope,' said Tip, bewildered and half defiant.

'You don't have any rope an' you call youself han'cart man?' she said. 'What you people expeck, eh?'

The sideman was perched on the edge of the truck, waiting patiently with his mouth shut for the battle to subside. His expression showed that he had witnessed such disputes before, and could predict the outcome. As he anticipated, the woman addressed him now.

'You ever hear anyt'ing so in you life? Han'cart man an' him don't even have a rope to tie up anyt'ing when him get a job.'

But the sideman, still smarting under the lash of her tongue, would not be drawn. He folded his arms and looked up at the sky as if he were seeing it for the very first time.

'Awright,' said Tip wearily, 'I going to cross the road and buy piece of rope.'

As he went she called after him. 'Dat's betta! An' you betta be quick, I wastin' time a'ready.'

When Tip returned he saw that the sympathetic sideman had used his experience of packing to arrange the bags until he had made use of every little space in the handcart. Then he climbed back, avoiding Tip's eyes and began the unloading once more.

When the sideman signalled the finish, Tip looked at the handcart in despair. It resembled a mountain and the bags were perched so high that it seemed they would slide off at any minute. Tip tried to secure them with the ropes. After watching for a few moments the sideman took them gently from his hand and made an expert job of tying the load down. When the task was completed he stood up and pressed Tip's hand. Tip recognized that with this gesture he was saying, 'Good luck, my friend,' and he thanked him but the sideman said nothing as he climbed back into the truck.

The woman, who had been watching silently all this while, moved from the wall where she had been leaning and took up two bundles which were lying at her feet.

'Follow me,' she said abruptly.

Tip raised the rough shafts of the handcart and its weight lifted him off his feet and almost threw him over. He bore down with all his might so that his full weight was on the shafts he held, like an acrobat doing a handrise on a crossbar. With a desperate effort he eventually managed to get his feet back on the ground. The woman stood at a distance looking, but she did not turn back to help. The great load was evenly balanced, thanks to the sideman and Tip slowly pushed off, walking as smoothly as possible and trying not to hold the shafts too low or too high. The wheels of the cart were only wooden ones from some old T-Ford and had lost their tyres. Tip hoped that he would not have to go far or face any hills.

As he drew level with the woman, she began to walk ahead again. He nearly ran into the back of a car as he could not see over his load. The driver swore at him. It seemed to occur to the woman that if he ran into anything she might not be recompensed, for she suddenly came from the sidewalk to guide him along. As they walked, Tip found it hard to keep the resolutions he had made on the bed in Ma Kuskus' hut.

After thirty minutes, they had left the busy streets and reached the country lanes, which presented equal difficulties, for they were rough and untarred. The cart was so heavy that Tip had to bend, bracing each foot at every step. The pain seared through his heel, his chest burned with each breath and sweat ran into his one eye, yet he could not release his hold on the cart to wipe it away. The woman was also sweating, not because of the light bundles she carried, one on her head, the other under her arm, but through the intense heat of the sun and her own great bulk. A sudden rage took over Tip and he brought the cart to a halt and eased the shafts to the ground. Painfully he tried to straighten himself. The woman stopped too, lifting up the side of her large apron to wipe the perspiration from her face.

'How much further we have to go?' Tip's voice was cold and assertive, quite unlike the one she had heard before. She began to wish she had been a little less aggressive when they had been loading up.

'Not far now, not far!' she said, trying to sound pleasant but it didn't alter Tip's expression.

'You said the same thing long time ago.'

'But it is not far. It only look so to you because you not use to it. Yes I can see you not use to it. In fack I was sayin' to meself all dis time dat you is a decent man, not like dem han'cart man, dat's why I take you.'

'You lie!'

This sudden attack from the previously weak man rendered the woman speechless for once.

'You take me because you know the others wouldn't take you damn job. You know is more than a handcart load. And you do this to you own colour, you own people!'

Tip suddenly remembered why he was now a handcart man. This was his first experience of the lives of those he had once hounded and his rage went and shame took its place. He said, without looking at the woman, 'I sorry I said so, lady. Is only because I tired.'

This abrupt return to meekness surprised the woman even more than his outburst.

'Is awright,' she said, keeping her peace but only because she wanted to get the load to its destination. 'Res' a little more ef you like.' But Tip took up the load again. It felt even heavier than before. He braced his sound foot behind him and pushed, and at last the cart moved forward. They went on for some ten minutes more. Then the woman said, 'We turn off dis way.'

Tip knew the road, it was Mango Walk, barely wide enough for two handcarts to pass each other. It looked more like the bed of a small, dry river than a lane. It had many ruts and rose steeply and there was a

122

sharp, downhill slope if they went far enough. He could not trust himself to speak. Inside, he struggled with Bangbelly who wanted to rage and argue, fight and curse.

As he prepared to push up the steep incline, the woman said: 'You will have to zigzag, else it won't go. I will give you a han' when you want help.'

'When I want help!' Tip said to himself bitterly. As he went, his feet slithered on the gravel and sand. On two sides of the lane, great cacti grew forming high, impassable fences. He stopped to get his breath and to summon more strength for the third time since he had started to negotiate the slope. He was still only half-way. It was afternoon now, so the sun was less fierce but he hardly noticed. His clothes clung to him. He started to move again. Every time he slithered or was forced to stop, the woman would stretch out her free hand to assist him. As soon as he started on his zigzag course again, she would draw her hand away. He knew without looking that the skin had burst in several places on his hands. He decided not to look up again to see how far he was from the ridge, lest he should lose courage. He kept his head down, pushing and slithering and he ceased to think.

He heard a voice say, 'You over now, you over,' and as if to confirm it, he was aware that he no longer needed to brace himself. Slowly he rested the shafts on the earth. Then he sat down in the middle of them and cried, only the eyewater could not be seen for it fell inside, and his one eye kept it secret.

Fifteen minutes later, Tip was poised for the descent with the cart behind him instead of in front. He was aware of the risk that he might lose control and be trapped between the shafts but he said nothing. He noticed that this time the woman had placed her two bundles on the great pile and he concluded that she had realized he could not control the cart alone.

'I will stay at de back,' she said and he nodded.

The cart began to roll down the hill, gathering momentum as it went. Tip struggled to control it.

'Hold it back, hold it back,' he shouted to the woman behind him. He could feel her pressing the back of the load causing him to lose his balance.

'Hold it back!' he shouted again. 'Don't press down on the cart I tell you!' It was rolling with such speed that Tip knew he could not hold it for long. 'Oh God,' he whispered, 'and I don't get to do a thing I promise to do.' He was running now, barely able to grip the shafts as they propelled him forward. The noise of the wooden wheels came behind him, threatening to catch him up. Just in front, he could see a large rut and he remembered the woman. If the load were to fall and she was behind it, she could be killed. He swerved and there was a jerk which almost pulled him apart. He was thrown over in a kind of arc and the cart behind him came to a standstill. Stunned for a moment, he just lay there and then he remembered the woman. She was coming down the hill, still some distance away. He sighed with relief and as he looked at the cart he could see why it had stopped. Some of the load was hanging precariously to one side and the axle was broken. One wheel lay at the edge of the road.

The woman was charging towards him. 'You see what you do?' she wailed. 'You mash up me load, you broke up all me t'ings!' She was trembling with her efforts to run.

As if to make her cry come true, Tip saw a bag slip. A coconut broke loose and cracked on the hard road, spilling water and gathering speed as it rolled to the foot of the hill. He tried to save the load, knowing that the rope was not so taut as before, but he was too late. Before he could hold the burst bag, more coconuts came banging down. Tip barely managed to jump out of the way of some five-gallon kerosene tins of molasses-type sugar, before half the contents of the cart followed.

Momentarily, the woman could not find her voice. Then she gave a piercing yell. Tip looked at the wide-open mouth and the stream of tears that came from her protruding eyes and rolled down her balloon-like cheeks, and could not help himself; he burst out laughing.

'You laugh? Eh, you laugh?' she screamed. 'After you broke up all me t'ings, you good fe nutt'n man? An' is jus' because I was sorry fe you! I pass all de strong , healthy han'cart man, an' take you wid you lame foot an' one eye an' I pay you, even befo' I give you de load, an' dis is what I get! All me load 'pon de ground, mash up to nutt'n!' She was out of breath and her breasts heaved like blacksmith's bellows.

Tip's temper rose, and for a moment he was the Constable again.

'You goddam lie, woman! You take me because nobody else would come if you ask them, that why, them all know you! Only me didn't know!'

His rage frightened her, and she turned to self-pity. 'Jus' because I is a poor woman an' don't have nobody to take up fe me, dat's why you want to take advantage of me. An' me a poor widow woman don't have a soul to take up fe me, not a soul but God. What I gwine to do now? What I gwine to do?' She lifted the end of the great apron and wiped the streams of tears, her mouth twisting terribly. 'How I gwine to get me load home now, eh? How I gwine to manage? You have to help me! You have to get it home, for is you fault an' I pay you a'ready!' Her voice was half whining, half accusing. Tip remembered his time in Ma Kuskus's hut. He felt ashamed.

'Awright, I will get up the load, and see if I can go back to town and get something else to carry you things.'

The woman's eyes gleamed and her tears stopped almost at once. 'An' don't t'ink I got any money to pay, cause I pay you a'ready! An' what 'bout de t'ings you mash up? Who gwine to pay fe dem?'

Tip was about to lift a bag of nuts to the side of the road. He stopped and opened his mouth, then seemed to think better of it and resumed his task of moving the items. Eventually he found that, apart from half a dozen broken coconuts, and a couple of badly bruised yams, nothing more had been lost.

'You stay with the load, I going to town to find a cart.' Without waiting for an answer, he made off up the hill as fast as his lame leg would allow.

'You 'member dat you mus' pay dem youself, cause I pay you a'ready!' the woman bawled after him, but he climbed the hill without answering or looking back. When he reached the busy part of the city he saw three men waiting by their handcarts for customers. They recognized him.

'You de man what pass we wid a mountain of load 'pon you han'cart?' asked one, and before Tip could reply, another said:

'Man, you make de woman treat you like a mule. Dat load I see you have 'pon dat cart could fill two more, an' lef' somet'ing behine. An' dat woman, you shoulda know she is de mos' dishones' woman in de Island; when she not sellin' wid bad scale an' bad measure, she buyin' wid dem, or gettin' people what don't know her to take her load an' pay dem little an' nutt'n. What happen wid you an' her?'

Tip realized how difficult it would be to get help from these men. Long before he had finished his explanation he knew that they would only assist if he would pay their price.

'Dat load need two han'cart, maybe all three, an' we know where dat woman goin' is more dan a mile from de place where you cart broke down. De job will cos' you five shillin'.'

'But I don't have that!' said Tip. 'The woman only pay me one shilling.'

'What? Only pay you *one* shillin' from Market Square to her shop?'

They stared incredulously, then roared with laughter. They slapped their thighs and held their sides. At last they managed to control themselves and wiped the water from their eyes. They looked at each other, then someone said, 'One shillin',' and they all started laughing again.

Tip stood like a little boy, too ashamed of his folly to move away.

'Five shillin' we will do it fe,' the men repeated.

'I don't have five shilling, or I would pay you to take it just to get me out of the trouble.'

'Well, you shouldn' be so foolish,' scolded one.

'When man foolish, him mus' pay fe it,' said another.

'But him didn't know,' said the third. 'De man is a stranger. Don't you know de ole sayin', "Stranger don't know deep water"? But even dat, man. Good God, him common sense shoulda tell him dat was double time han'cart load, an' was worth more dan shillin' to carry even a chain distance.'

Seeing the distressed look on Tip's face, one of them asked:

'How much you can afford?'

Tip pushed his hand in his pocket expecting to find about four shillings, including the shilling the woman had paid him in advance. But all he found was two and nine; the woman had made him buy rope for his cart.

They looked into his hand, and at each other.

'Awright, we will do it fe two an' nine, but only because we sorry fe you, you understan'?'

'Yes. I thank you, I understand,' said Tip with gratitude.

Without another word they followed Tip, who knew that they were doing it out of kindness. When he had paid them he would have neither money for food, nor the sixpence necessary for a night in the Salvation Army hostel. But he could not ask them to take less. At last they reached the spot of the accident.

It was now dark, and the men took their storm lanterns from under the carts, drew matches and lit them so as to be able to see to load the goods – as well as to keep on the side of the law.

The minute the woman saw them she came up to Tip and warned: 'I hope you pay dem. I hope you make dem know dat I don't business wid de pay!'

But one of the men, remembering what she had paid Tip said with a drawl:

'Lady, you pay de man one, single shillin' an' between me an' you an' de doorpost, ef it was not fe him, you an' you blasted load could stay by de road an' rotten, an' ef you blow hard between now an' we move off, me an' me frien' gwine to take off de two han'cart of load, cut de bag, an'

126

make dem roll to hell. Ef you don't want dat, shut you blasted big mouth!'

The woman was silenced.

At last they were ready and Tip saw with anger that the load filled the two carts and there was some left for the third. He handed over the two and nine. The men hesitated, their lantern held high. 'You sure you is awright, cause we don't want to leave you dry, you know?' asked one kindly.

'Yes, my friend, I is awright, I going stay here with my cart for a while,' replied Tip.

'Goodbye,' they shouted to him. 'We won't come dis way when we comin' back, is too bad!'

Tip managed to get the damaged cart to a part of the roadside where there was a rainwater culvert, and so left the road free for any vehicle that might need to pass. He wondered what he would do. He did not have a penny in his pocket, his cart was broken and he was far from the city. He realized that he had no lamp for his cart, which was against the law. He remembered that he had prosecuted many for just this offence. His body ached. He had a pain in his side and hunger was making his stomach feel hollow. But tiredness was his greatest trouble. He sat back deep in his cart with his feet hanging out. It was awkward; the missing wheel and the broken axle made the cart tilt, but he was too tired to make it more comfortable.

He was awakened by a heavy blow to his legs. He opened his eyes and a light shone in his face, dazzling him. At first he did not know where he was, or the meaning of the light and he sprang up fearfully. His gesture was taken as a sign of attack and a second blow was dealt to his head.

'Get up you son of a bitch. Get up and tell me what the hell you doing here this time of night.'

Tip could see the heavy boots and black trousers worn by members of the regular police force. He stumbled to his feet but could barely discern the outline of the officer behind the torch.

The policeman played the light up and down his body and then commanded roughly, 'Turn out you pockets.'

Tip felt panic as he remembered that his handcuffs and badge were in his back pocket, wrapped in a handkerchief. He turned out his two side pockets and then, to his relief, the policeman said, 'Now tell me what you doing here this time of night.'

Tip remembered how he had once questioned suspects with much greater force and bore the man no grudge. He began to whine just as his victims had done when he had threatened them. 'Please Officer, me cart broke down, and I was just sitting resting, and didn't know when I drop off to sleep.'

'What's you name?'

'My name is . . . Tip . . . Tip, Sir; see, I got it write down on me cart.'

The policeman turned his torch, saw the white painted letters and seemed satisfied. Footsteps could be heard coming from the road and he decided to end the matter quickly; perhaps he realized he had been more aggressive than was strictly necessary.

As he moved off, Tip thought he heard footsteps drawing closer, and then all sound suddenly ceased and he slid to the side of the road losing consciousness.

As he came to, he heard a young voice saying: 'You feel better Sir?'

He mumbled, 'Yes, thank you,' and realized that there were several children round him. Somebody lit a match, but before he could see their faces, the light went out. He felt himself helped up to his feet, and one of the voices said, 'Come with we Sir, don't make the policeman come back and find you.'

He allowed himself to be assisted along the short distance to their home. He barely listened to their subdued chatter but it still made him uneasy. And then, as he was about to enter their room, someone said: 'Mobel, I going to put some water to boil for him cut head.'

'Oh God, it can't be,' he said in his heart, but the children noticed nothing as they sat him down and went to get a light. He could hear them in the kitchen as they got a fire going:

'No Sista! . . . when Pazart draw de match . . . maybe was because of him eye . . . poor man . . . look sick . . . you think him hungry, Sista? Make some cornmeal porridge . . . Don't give anybody Sonna cot to sleep, Pazart, you hear? I will give him mine . . .'

Tip jerked himself up from his low seat with a sound that brought the children to him. He staggered forward to push past them but in his haste he stumbled. Pazart grabbed him, breaking his fall and they gathered round him asking if he were badly hurt and preventing his flight.

'Come and lie down Sir. Sista, open that cot. Make I and Pazart get him to lie down on it.'

'But Mobel, 'member what you say outside?'

'Bout what?'

'Bout the cot, Sonn . . .'

'Do what I say and shut you mouth, Sista.'

'Awright, no need to bawl after me.'

Tip released the children's hold on both his arms as they tried to guide him to the clumsy, home-made cot. 'No, no please,' he said.

'Sir, the cot is clean and a good one,' said Sista, but they did not press further. He rested on a stool and they brought him mint tea and dressed his wound. He could not eat the biscuits they offered him. They saw that he was adamant about the cot and made him a bed on the floor. Then the girls returned to their room, leaving him alone with Pazart. He dreaded the boy's questions but none came. Pazart merely asked if he were comfortable and then discreetly let him be.

He had accepted their help and hospitality and had drunk tea from their meagre store. He felt the urge to shout: 'I am the man who swear him would lay hands on you in spite of God. I am the man who kill you friend,' but Tip did not follow his impulse. He lay with his eye wide open thinking of his past. He could tell by Pazart's even breathing that he was asleep. Carefully and quietly he got up, rolled his bedding into a bundle and placed it by the door. He went outside. The night was warm and there were many bright stars. He found the gate and made his way back to his broken cart. The cruel irony of the policeman's attack and the comfort the children had offered seemed like a punishment from God. He could not bear the realization of what he really was. He had been a fool to think he could escape it just by changing his name. He would let the sea take charge of him.

He passed through the town. Twice, lights flashed on his face. Once, the dark figure behind the torch ordered him to take off the eye-patch, but he was not recognized. At last he entered the long lane leading to the fishermen's beach.

Dawn was starting to break as he reached the first line of boats on rollers, high on the sand. As he rested beside them he heard the whining of a puppy. He peered under the rollers and saw two eyes glaring through the darkness. The whine turned to a snarl. The puppy's bravado made Tip laugh out loud. He bent low and put his hand out. The snarl became a fierce bark. Tip laughed again, his pain subsiding for a moment. He admired the courage of the puppy which seemed so much greater than his own. It began to understand that Tip was a friend and no longer struggled but started to whimper again.

'Don't mind, little dog, don't mind,' said Tip soothingly. He sat for a while, cradling the animal, whispering kind words. He saw the similarity between them; both were hungry, alone and afraid. He drew some comfort from the knowledge. 'Me and you will go hungry together,' he said. 'We will have a good fight, you and me.' The puppy licked him and its trusting gentleness touched Tip. He turned his wet face away from the sea and strode along the beach, making plans – impossible plans – and all because of the skinny pup with the big head that was lying contentedly in his arms.

CHAPTER TWENTY-THREE

Tip was sitting on the beach watching the waves that glittered in the sun. Despite the golden colour of the sand, there was nothing clean about it. Seaweed, refuse from ships, and sewage from open drains had been deposited on its surface. John Crows circled and perched boldly on idle canoes, searching with beady eyes and ugly noises for crabs, fish entrails and any other morsels that might have been left by the fishermen at the end of a night's work.

And yet there was beauty too. For several miles, the long strip of sand was dotted with bent, storm-tossed coconut trees, while a little further back where the ground was swampy, there were lines of mangroves. Great wild grape trees grew where the sand stood firm and beneath it all broad leaf creepers thrived away from the salty sea. There were also private beaches, sometimes half a mile or more, separated from the rest by fences.

It was nearly four weeks since Tip had fled from the house of the Sparrows. He had built himself a small lean-to with coconut boughs which he had hauled a long distance across the beach. He did not think it had been seen; it was too small and low and far up the beach to have been spotted and he had deliberately erected it where the worst of the waste from the ships could be found.

Tip, his shirt and trousers worn, his beard knotted and his hair high, looked at himself in a broken pocket mirror. The image he saw revived a memory. He recalled that when his parents had died, he had gone to live with an uncle, his wife and son and had worn his cousin's old clothes. His schoolmates had laughed at him and had christened him Robinson Crusoe; they had been reading about him in their school books. When it had all become unbearable, he had run away. Now he was the image of the castaway, only as far as he knew, Robinson Crusoe had been neither lame nor blind in one eye.

The puppy that had rekindled his instinct to survive, was lying beside him, no longer weak in the legs and growing less frail. Tip had not yet found a name for him. All those that came easily to mind were too closely associated with his past and he feared using them. He could not afford to hold on to any part of the life he had had as Bangbelly, and he wanted to forget all about his former existence. But apart from the puppy, his memories of the past were all he had.

As he thought, the puppy, always alert for intruders, bounded up, and caused Tip to look along the abandoned beach. Some distance away, there was a small figure. The puppy seemed satisfied that the visitor was a friend, for he lay down quietly, with his head and ears up, still watching intently. The child continued to come slowly towards them. She could not have been more than four. Her small plaits stood like spikes on top of her well-proportioned head. Her frock of brightly coloured stripes fitted her closely and he was reminded of the costumes he had seen skaters wearing in films. Her face was jet black and her firm little knees almost rubbed together as she walked. She trod warily, feeling with bare feet for the small mounds of sand which might trip her up. She was carrying something carefully but every now and then her eyes left it and she surveyed the scene before her.

As he watched the progress of the child, Tip wondered at her being left to carry whatever it was in her hands, on a beach full of seaweed and crab holes that might make her fall. He was aware of his concern for her and it surprised him. He had not noticed small children before, except as nuisances that had to be dealt with. He would have gone over to help her but he remembered his appearance and that his trousers were full of holes in the worst places. The child could not have seen him properly or surely she would have run away?

Now she was so near that he could see a tiny pair of earrings that caught the light of the sun whenever she moved her head. He knew that she could see him now and yet she was still not running, she was smiling. The puppy raced up to her as if they were old friends. Bewildered, Tip continued to stare as the child approached timidly but with a smile on her face.

'My mammy send this for you dawg, Sir, she said she hope you won't be vex but she like puppy . . . and me like them too.' Tip was sure the last line was all hers. His smile must have banished any lingering uncertainty in the child for she smiled back again brightly. Before he could think of anything to say she was speeding back, running and jumping and splashing in the water with all the abandon of one who had completed a mission successfully. Tip watched her go, noting that she disappeared amongst a great cluster of wild grape trees on the wider section of the beachland. He remembered having seen a hut nearby and guessed that the child and her mother must live there. He also remembered that the puppy often disappeared mysteriously whenever he approached that place and sometimes Tip had had to whistle for a considerable time before he returned.

He looked down at the warm bowl in his lap. There were bits of shrimp, boiled green bananas and a sprinkling of rice. There was also a spoon. Tip wondered what excuse they would have found for giving him food without the puppy. He smiled as he tasted the meal, and felt warmth and gratitude. He remembered that he had not had time to send a message of thanks to the child's mother. He could not see her in his tattered clothes and he had to return the bowl and spoon. *The spoon.* That made him laugh and he showed it to the puppy saying, 'This was for you to eat you soup with. The lady said the dinner was for you but she put a spoon in it.'

Tip finished his share of the meal and gave the rest to the puppy. He lay down on his back for although few people came to the beach at that time of day, he was afraid to get up, knowing that the woman and her child could easily be somewhere nearby seeking firewood. He was ashamed to be seen as he was. He began to worry that if he could not find a way of returning the bowl and spoon, the mother herself might call to recover them. He could no longer rest. He decided to go to the hut. He thought that if he let his shirt hang out over his ragged trousers, he could hide some of the most embarrassing holes. And he could also roll up the tattered trouser legs like the fishermen sometimes did.

He waded into the sea and washed the bowl and spoon and again he surprised himself. It was a simple politeness but it would never had occurred to his old self. Sometimes the division between Tip and Bangbelly frightened him. He could not explain or understand it.

The puppy jumped to his side and they walked towards the spot where the child had disappeared. The pup ran ahead and brought Tip to a hut. A woman saw him approaching and came to greet him, remarking on the friendship between her child and the dog as a way of opening the conversation.

Tip listened to her. Her voice was as pretty as the child's. He was grateful to her for trying to put him at his ease.

'Please come in Sir,' she said. Tip thought that a blind man on hearing

132

her might suppose she was entertaining royalty. Her courtesy somehow made him feel even more ashamed of his appearance.

'You must excuse me for the place and because I can only offer you a box to sit down on,' she continued. 'I hope you don't think I take too much liberty with the puppy. By the way, every day him always come to say good morning to me and my Thelma – that's my little girl name – and talking 'bout name, we always want to know what you call the puppy.'

'Sonna,' answered Tip. The name had been in his mind for so long that it had slipped out before he could stop himself saying it.

'I like the name very much,' was all she said, but her tone convinced Tip that she had heard about the Sparrows.

More anxious than ever now, he only wanted to get away. 'I come to thank you for you kindness, lady, really I didn't mean to come and take up you time.'

A silence followed that discomforted them both. Tip looked at her and saw that she was tall and slim and not more than twenty-five. There was a serene beauty in the fine face with its slightly flat nose and the upper lip that turned up just a little. She was watching him too, and as he caught her eye he felt conscious of his own strange appearance and how repellent he must be to her.

The little girl burst in, dispelling the awkwardness, 'Oh mammy, I love the puppy, I love the puppy,' she cried, throwing herself into her mother's lap. The pup pulled at her frock.

'Don't be naughty . . . puppy, don't pull you friend' frock . . .' said Tip haltingly, afraid that the dog would tear it.

The woman just laughed. 'You shoulda seen him and Thelma this morning, Mr . . . I don't even know you name.'

'They call me Tip-Toe because of the way I walk,' he said, 'but I don't mind . . . in fact I paint the name 'pon a cart which I had at one time. But I like when them just call me Tip . . . is the best name I ever have.' He said the last words as if he were talking to himself.

'It's a nice, friendly name but I sorry it come from you lameness, Mr Tip.'

The little girl turned to him impulsively and rested a tubby hand on his knee. 'I like you name Mr Tip and I not fright'n now at all, at all. You is nice gentleman, even if you only have one eye.'

'Thelma, come here this minute! I going to give you a spanking.' Realizing that she was in disgrace, Thelma went back and hid her face in her mother's lap.

'Mrs . . . Don't scold the child. You want I tell you something?' he paused and then said, 'Is the nicest thing a child – or anybody – ever say to me.'

'I don't believe you, Mr Tip. I don't mean you is telling a lie, at all, but I mean you only say what you say to pull shame out of my eyes.'

But he shook his head. 'No lady, is true, and I will always want to 'member what the little one said to me today.'

She stared at him and saw that he was sincere. She wondered how any man could have lived in a world where no one had ever said anything nice and she pitied him, though she hid this quickly, sensing that he would not like it. 'Thelma, go and tell the gentleman you is sorry for what you said,' she ordered sternly.

'No lady, don't force her to do that, I tell you . . .' But the mother silenced Tip with a look and the child came shamefacedly, head down to apologize. Tip forgot his own shyness and pulled her down to him. Feeling the soft hands of a child for the first time since his own childhood, he passed his palm over the little plaits on her head and she responded by nestling closer.

'Alright now, you and puppy go outside and play,' and Thelma went with the dog immediately, as her mother had requested.

The mother sighed. 'It's such a hard thing to bring up a child without a father,' she said quietly.

'I didn't know she don't have a father,' said Tip, genuinely sorry for the woman.

'Her father dead when she was two.' He felt the sadness in her voice.

'I am very sorry to hear, Mrs . . .'

'Oh I am sorry, I forget, I didn't tell you my name. It is Salome. Don't bother 'bout the rest of the name, just call me Salome,' she said hastily, remembering, perhaps, that he had only told her his nickname.

'Salome! Is a nice name,' said Tip.

She reminded him that the woman in the Bible was bad, but her eyes conveyed that his way of saying it made it sound nice.

Tip said, 'Is not the name what matter, Mistress Salome,' he did not want to sound familiar, 'is the person what make the name important. Sometimes a person worry 'bout the name they may call him or her, and it can make him mind as twisted as a barbed wire, but that's cause him make the name take hold of him, instead of him taking hold of the name. And that is a bad thing when a man make him name take charge of him. But mostly that happen when somebody give you a name what you don't want, and make you feel that them is calling you so to make you feel bad. But if you show them you don't mind even if you do, after a time them

134

either don't call you that name anymore, or them make the name sound good. But mostly we never know all that till too late.'

His voice trailed off as he wondered why he was able to talk so freely to the woman whom he had never met before. Usually the few sentences he spoke to anyone came out of his mouth like the words of a man who, knowing that he might stammer, tried to get it all out before the impediment came on. Now he found that he was speaking without effort on a subject he had never even considered before.

Salome's response was reassuring. 'It's true, Marse Tip, I feel so,' she said and her expression warmed him because it acknowledged and respected his experience of life.

Tip suddenly felt that he wanted to tell her all about himself . . . everything, and the need blotted out caution and reason. It became irresistible – that impulse to tell her of his life; his lonely childhood and his isolation. He tried to find an opening but it was harder than he had anticipated, not because he doubted that she would understand but because he could not find the words.

Tip thought of the puppy and the idea came to him to begin with the morning when he found it on the beach. Then he could go from there back to his past. But before he could begin, Salome, trying to put him at his ease, said, 'It make Thelma so happy. The puppy come to her like a little brother.'

Tip closed his mouth again, and then asked sympathetically, 'She have no brother nor sister?'

'No, Marse Tip, she is the first and only one.'

'I sorry to hear, lady. It is hard when is an only child, for the parents, too.' He remembered again the loneliness he had experienced in his own childhood.

'We . . . me and my husband, did want a lot of children,' said Salome sadly. 'We promise weself that as soon as we get fifty pounds we was going back to the mountains where we was born. We was going to build two more rooms on the one we build already, and we have five whole acres of good fruitland, with coconut trees, breadfruit trees and orange. We would buy a young cow, and plant corn, and raise fowls. Fifty pounds would do all that, 'cause in the country people is even kinder than town people. Them people in the districk would come one Saturday – every single man, woman and child – and them would dig you plot of land, and plant all the things you want to plant, and not a soul would take a penny for them time, all them would take is the food and the little drink you provide for them, and even that them help you to get.'

She paused, looking beyond the beach, her mind away in the mountains which evidently held her heart, and Tip, knowing the country himself, and the way people helped each other there, nodded in agreement. A whole village would join in erecting a house for a new family, for the customs of ancient Africa still lived in the country parts.

Salome was speaking again. 'My husband and me work hard to get the money to go home 'cause we didn't like the town, but as we know it was only till we could do the things we want, we didn't mind. I use' to work in one of the big people house – cooking and washing, and cleaning five apartments for eight shilling a week. Only one Sunday a month, seven days a week. You know what it is like, Marse Tip. Start work six in the morning, finish nine at night. My husband work at a bakery, fifteen shilling a week, no holiday, every day. One day I take sick at my workplace, but I still try to work, but the lady wouldn't believe me . . . she say I was lazy and discharge me without even a week wages, even though it was Wednesday already. When I come home, my husband take six shilling out of what we save and take me to the doctor. Doctor said I was going to have a baby and I must rest. Well, Marse Tip, we didn't save much a'ready, 'cause we have to pay taxes for the land in the country, pay rent in the town and everything. Doctor say I must get tonic. I have to pay fifteen shilling in advance to have my baby at the hospital when it born, then I have to buy baby things. By the time Thelma born, the fifteen shilling my husband was earning couldn't keep we and pay the taxes.'

Tip watched her intently, his feeling for her driving away his own trouble. He saw that she hesitated before going on and, for no reason that he knew, he felt apprehensive.

'One day my husband did a bad thing. Him know we didn't have any money, 'cause my grandmother write from home to say gover'ment going to take away we land 'cause we didn't pay the taxes. So him take a pan of bread from the bakery where him work, and try to hide it in old newspapers. Them catch him. Him get thirty days. You know what it is like, Marse Tip, the disgrace, him handcuff and go to jail for thiefing.'

She did not see the effect her words were having on Tip. He looked away from her and moved his lips silently.

She stared outside. 'When him come out of prison, nobody want him, even though him was a good baker. Him started going out fishing with another man. It didn't pay. We nearly starve and couldn't pay rent. Some of the men use to dynamite fish. It was against the law, it was wrong, and it was dangerous, but him agree to go with them, for him could swim and dive good.'

136

Tip moved backwards and forwards in his seat as a mother does when she rocks her child to sleep. He could not stop Salome. He could not even raise himself and so break the spell or escape the pain he saw before him. Her voice sounded distant as if she were speaking through a narrow tube.

'One Sunday night, when him was going, him look nervous, and I say to him better don't go tonight, Joseph . . . Rain was pouring and thunder and lightning, like we was going to have hurricane, but him said that the gover'ment say them didn't expeck any hurricane, and if, when him go to the beach and him find the weather still bad and the other fishermen not going out, him would sleep down here in this hut, what him and him friends make to keep them things dry and take a nap sometimes. I didn't know till the next day what happened. A Districk Constable see him sheltering from the rain under a bank piazza. The man tell lies!'

Her voice rose from its low, dead murmur to such an angry pitch that the child playing outside, stopped digging the hole in the sand, and looked towards the house. But when the words came again only as a murmur, she resumed her digging.

Tip sat rigid, his fists tightly closed on his knees, like a man expecting to be struck.

'Them didn't believe Joseph, though him told the truth 'bout the dynamite in him bag. Them believe the man who tell the lie. Joseph got four years! I stand at the roadside when him walk to the train with the handcuff on him hand. Him try to wave to me and Thelma. It was like him know we wouldn't see him again.'

As she finished speaking, Thelma ran back into the room. 'Mammy the gentleman, him sick!' she cried.

Salome turned in alarm to her visitor. His face was grey and his lips were covered in some white substance.

'Give me a cup with water, Thelma,' said Salome, raising Tip's head. She managed to get him to take a couple of mouthfuls.

'I awright.' He gently loosened her hold.

'But you not Marse Tip. Is my fault, talking and talking, telling you all my troubles when you feeling sick.'

Tip knew he had to get out into the open air. He stood up, holding on to the cornerpost of the house for support.

'Marse Tip, stay even a little longer, till you feel better.' She feared he was ill through her neglect.

He shook his head. 'Thank you just the same Mistress and for everything . . .'

Tip was still walking when the sun disappeared and the sudden darkness spread over land and sea. Only the twinkling lights from the ships far out in the harbour or those from the distant piers stood out; the sea roared and splashed as it hurled itself against the rocks, but he neither saw nor heard these things as he threw himself, face down, in the wet sand.

The dog crept close and licked the salty substance from his cheek.

When dawn came, Tip was able to identify the part of the seashore where he had slept. It was the worst area of beach, so full of waste that the stench kept most people away from this part of the shore.

Up ahead, Tip glimpsed the puppy chasing large, white crabs which scuttled back to the swamps at its approach, their claws held defensively as the dog tried to find out about these hairless creatures with so many feet but no tails.

Tip wanted to bathe and wash his clothes but he had to walk some distance before he found a brackish pool where the water was almost clean. As he took off his shirt, he recalled his childhood nickname once again and called to the puppy, 'How would you like to change you name to Friday?' The dog, delighted to hear Tip's voice after such a long silence, bounded up and down. 'Awright then, you will name Friday from now on, and between you and me, you can call me Robinson Crusoe.' As he said it, he realized he no longer resented the name.

He washed his clothes clumsily, hanging them afterwards on the branch of a wild grape tree until they were dry enough to be worn. Once he was dressed he called Friday to him and with a resigned sigh he started along the path to the city.

CHAPTER TWENTY-FOUR

Tip and the dog had been in the city for more than a week. He had found no work, and was looking for food in the rubbish bins around the shops and cookhouses. Suddenly Friday bolted through a gate and Tip pursued him anxiously. He collided with a man who caught hold of him to prevent him falling. Tip looked into his face and saw that it was Ironman.

'So this is how it will end,' he thought for no reason that he knew. The presence of his old adversary filled him with apprehension. Ironman had somehow been part of all his recent sorrows and forebodings. He shrank from him, fearing his voice. Yet Ironman gave no sign of recognition and merely said:

'I hope I didn't hurt you man? If the pup is yours, him gone behind the kitchen.' He steadied Tip with a reassuring grasp. 'You just take it easy man, them going to serve you, you soon be awright and don't worry 'bout the money.'

He steered Tip forward and left him with Noname who went to fetch a bowl of soup.

Tip wanted to leave but his need for food was too great. He ate the meal that was put before him. Even Friday was fed, he licked his plate clean and then went to rest under the table.

As Tip finished his meal, the three children walked in. Mobel was the first to see the pup and she dashed forward with a shout. 'Look, is my Bulla come back! Is Bulla, Sista, same black dog with white 'pon him paw and over him eye. And same stump of tail.' She held the dog to her face.

Ironman looked on, knowing that the dog was the only thing to arouse their interest since Sonna's death. Tip was staring at them. Suddenly they became aware of him. 'We never see you from that night Sir,' said Pazart, coming over to him with the others. 'We look everywhere to find you for we fix up you handcart good, with new wheels and axle, but we couldn't find you. The cart is in we yard right now.'

Tip received the news with mixed feelings. He would be able to find work now but he was more deeply beholden than ever to the people he had harmed. The burden of guilt was becoming an ever greater part of his punishment.

Ironman told the children that the puppy belonged to Tip who saw how attached Mobel was to the dog and said that he really didn't know how to dispose of him. He could tell that Ironman approved of the indirect offer from the way he hastily promised to feed and care for it when the children were busy.

Later Tip went with Mobel, Sista and Pazart to retrieve the cart. It looked almost new, with a pair of good wheels in place of the old ones and a strong axle instead of the one that had been broken. They had even painted the body, leaving the name intact. He promised to repay them as soon as he could but they said there was no need as they had not bought anything. Thinking that they were only saying this because of the pup, he spoke again of payment. Mobel, trying to reassure him that it had cost them nothing said:

'Them wheels come off the cart what we did make to carry we friend to the cemetery.'

Tip suddenly felt cold and in his mind, the faces round him turned accusing and hard.

Then the dog broke the moment of tension by barking at a neighbour's chicken that had crowed audaciously from a tree-stump opposite. The children laughed but Tip could feel nothing but misery and foreboding.

Tip had left the children and was half-way down the narrow one-way street when he saw her sitting before a heap of herbs and roots. He could not turn back; he was drawn towards her despite himself. They were close to the market and a crowd was gathering. Perhaps she would expose him now and take her revenge. Yet still he moved forward, wanting to get it over with. He was cold, but sweat stood on his brow. He remembered that once or twice he had managed to think of her as a friend. He had even called her Ma before he'd left her. He knew that she despised him, and would hurt him if she could, but he could not walk away from her. The shafts of his cart slid in his moist hands. He had almost reached her now. He stared at her half hypnotised, and she looked back but she did not seem to see him.

'Sorose? Good fe bellyache, penny a bundle! Kuskus roots? Smell sweet! Keep moth from you clothes.'

Tip realized he had passed her. She had not denounced him, she had not even seemed to know him. He did not understand.

CHAPTER TWENTY-FIVE

Tip had always planned to see Salome again to thank her for her kindness and after a few weeks of working with his cart he had been in a position to do so, though he suspected that Ironman had helped by asking the market people to hire him as often as they could.

It had shamed him to tell Salome the kind of work he was doing; handcart men were usually despised. But she had said that there was no shame in honest work. He had brought her gifts of vegetables and groceries, knowing how little she had in her house. He had been able to tell from the way she received them how much she needed them and in consequence he had returned almost every day, making all kinds of excuses and always with something in his hands. After a while, she asked him to have supper with them and he agreed, knowing that otherwise she would feel unable to accept his gifts of food.

Tip had also managed to present the Sparrows with small gifts boasting about the smartness of his cart and reminding them that but for their help he might have been in prison.

He often thought of Salome's dream house. His cart would seem to say, 'Fifty pounds, fifty pounds, fifty pounds', as the wheels revolved. The train wheels would pass and say it and the chop-chop hooves of the horses that drew the carriages for tourists changed their tune to, 'fifty pounds', whenever they passed him. He wanted to present her with the money but it was impossible. His earnings would never allow him to save that sum in years, even if he had not pledged to use all he had to help those he had wronged.

One day an idea came to him which made him stop suddenly in the middle of the road with his cart. 'Ma Kuskus!' he whispered. Then he realized how extremely unlikely it was that the old woman would lend him the money she had offered that day as he was leaving. Perhaps – more than likely – she had only said it then to see how he would react. He could not fool himself; he still feared her. What could he tell her? Lies? Perhaps she would know the truth, and the reason why he was asking for the money. In any case she had probably just been playing a cat and mouse game when she'd offered it. His head began to ache. He felt it was hopeless. How could she have money, selling a dozen bundles of herbs and roots at a penny a time or maybe telling fortunes at three pence a time? But all Tip could hear was Salome's voice:

'Fifty pounds, Marse Tip, that was all we need! With the land what we have a'ready, and the kind people in we districk to give a hand to build we little house and cultivate we land . . . fifty pounds could make we never want for anything again!'

Even if he could get the money from Ma Kuskus, he would still have a job persuading Salome to accept it. For he knew that she would not take it, and to owe it would only be a burden to her. But he would find a way of getting round her scruples. Perhaps he could pretend he had won the money on the Chinese lottery.

He decided to see Ma Kuskus. If he took a bus, it would drop him only a couple of miles from her isolated home. He would have to negotiate rugged paths and tiny tracks but he knew that he could find it for, by then, the moon would be up.

Tip discerned the outline of the one-room house in the moonlight.

He saw that the old woman was standing in the clearing before the lean-to hut with her back to him, gathering bundles of herbs and tying them together. He moved closer to her, then stopped and thought:

'She still have her back towards me. I can go back down the hill without she knowing! I shouldn't come! What a foolish idea! Yes, if I walk softly I can go back . . .'

'Well?'

With just one word, the old woman froze Tip. She had her back to him, yet she knew that he was there. Perhaps she had known he was on the verge of running when she had spoken. He licked his lips but said nothing.

'What you want?' She turned to face him now, her eyes probing him.

'One . . . one time . . . Ma Kuskus, you offer to lend me a hundred pound.'

'What 'bout it?'

'You still mean it?'

'Why?'

''Cause if you did mean it . . . I . . . I would like to borrow it now!'

'I always mean what I say.'

'But Ma, why should you want to lend me the money?'

'Who de hell say I want to? You come all de way to ask me dat?'

'No, Ma Kuskus, I really want the money! You right, I shouldn't ask you question since I want the money.'

'When?'

'Soon as possible, Ma Kuskus.'

'Come to me tomorrow at de market gate. Ask fe a bundle of dry sorose. Pay me a penny an' take it an' go. You will fine de money inside.'

'But . . . but Ma?'

'What?'

'It's not what you think . . . 'bout the money . . . I mean I not going to use it for what you think!'

'How de hell you know what I t'ink?'

'And . . . and I don't have any security, and you may never get it back!'

'You see any worry in me face?'

'No Ma . . . Well, since I can't get to say thanks when I come to you at the market gate tomorrow, I want to say it now!'

'Betta go befor' you fall 'pon me neck an' kiss me!'

'Awright Ma. But I wish I could make you out!'

'A little parcel wrap up, on de stone side a you, take it!'

'Thank you . . . thank you Ma. See you tomorrow!'

There was no answer. The old woman was busy with her herbs again.

As Tip returned to the city he opened her parcel and his bewilderment intensified when it yielded a lovely, warm, fried fish and a large cassava bread known as 'Bammy'. This made him more certain than ever that she had been expecting him. She had even known that he had not eaten for nearly eight hours.

For the rest of the journey he contemplated how he could present Salome with ninety of the promised one hundred pounds. By the time he arrived in the town he had it all worked out. But he had new fears now. Suppose Ma Kuskus was fooling him? Suppose she reconsidered the whole thing and changed her mind? Suppose she did not turn up at the market gate as promised? Suppose she was planning a trap for him, right at the place that he had always feared . . . the market?

'Will I ever live without being 'fraid of something?' he said to himself.

He reached the Salvation Army's men's hostel which was his home. But he did not want rest; just a bath, a cup of coffee, then he would go to Salome with his plans, and after that it was only a question of waiting to see if Ma Kuskus would keep her promise . . .

Salome was glad to see him. He could tell that by the way she smiled, and by the way she took her hand out of the soapy tub and hastily wiped it on her apron so that she could meet him partway and shake his hand. She had always been like this but he felt that there was a little more in her greetings that morning. It was as if he had gone away for a week or more and had just returned.

'So sorry I couldn't come yesterday as usual, Miss Salome, but I just couldn't make it.'

'That's awright, Marse Tip. I was only worry cause I think something might happen to you . . . you know, you might not be feeling well.'

'Oh I am fit as a fiddle as them say, Miss Salome!'

'I so glad, Marse Tip,' she said with a sincerity that Tip could feel. Thelma came to greet him and they went to sit down.

'Miss Salome, you ever buy Chinese lottery?'

'Joseph . . . my husband use to buy it now and again when him could afford the sixpence or the shilling, Marse Tip, and two time since him dead, I take a chance, but we never win anything. We always hear that somebody win forty-five pound for sixpence and ninety pound for one shilling, but we never know if it's true for we never know anybody what win it. And it so dangerous! If police ketch you with it, five pound or prison!'

'That's true, Miss Salome. But I going to try my luck today! Last night I dream I mark eight numbers on the paper and when I go to see the result, it win, Miss Salome, the 'ole eight, and I get ninety pound for my shilling! When I wake up and find it was not true I was so sorry! All the same, I 'member the place where I mark it on the paper and I going to take a chance. I have sixpence what I was going to give Thelma for her birthday tomorrow, but I just feel lucky, Miss Salome, so I going to put one shilling on the mark for myself, and I want you to see if you can find sixpence to put with the one I have and was going to give to Thelma so I can put a shilling on it for you and her as well.' He saw her looking a little embarrassed and guessed that if she had a sixpence it was either for some special purpose or it was all they had left for food but she moved without a word towards the house. She returned in a little while, counting out some money with fingers which seemed over clumsy as she walked slowly towards him.

'I couldn't find any sixpence change 'cept this, Marse Tip. Please excuse me for it is all in farthing and ha'penny.' She kept her head low, and he guessed that it was because she was ashamed at having to tell a lie. He thought of the hundreds of lies he had told to win his cases, some with fatal results like . . . God! Now he could see why people hated him so much, but he took the money from her, knowing that if his plan went well he would be able to present her with hundreds of sixpences.

Tip was still waiting for Ma Kuskus at the market gate. There was no sign of her. He paced up and down unevenly on his lame foot.

'What a fool I was to believe her when she said she would meet me with the money. What a damn fool I is! Two time I go there and she not there. Look at the time now – half past ten. What a fool I make of meself! She must be sitting down at her room doorway laughing her head off. She guess what I want the money for and she just playing with me. And me like a fool dream 'bout what I going to do with that hundred pound. No use going back again to that market gate. She not coming . . . Maybe Salome won't even have oil for them lamp when night come, and me have to go back six o'clock to tell another lie to say I buy the mark and it didn't play like I dream it! One more time to the market gate. I know she won't come now but I will just go one more time . . .'

'God! She come! Wonder if she bring the money? Wonder if it is a trap? Suppose when I reach to her, she bawl out who I is? Maybe is what she mean to do to me! God, I must go all the same . . . I must go! She don't see me coming yet. God, I feel frighten'. I right before her and she still don't see me yet! What she say I should do? Take out a penny and ask her, yes I 'member what she say I must do. God, but I feel frighten'!'

'Nice bush fe you cold? Penny a bundle. Kuskus roots? Lovely smell. Keep moth out you clothes. Penny a bundle. Sorose Massa? Good fe belly ache . . . '

'I want a bundle of dry sorose, mother.'

'Yes Massa. Here you are. One penny. T'ank you Massa. Kuskus roots? Lovely smell . . .'

Tip walked quickly with the bundle of herbs in his hand, feeling certain that a hoax had been played. The old herb-seller had not looked up until after he had paid for the herbs and it looked exactly like any of the dozens of bundles of sorose she had had piled before her. He pushed his empty cart until he reached a public convenience. It seemed a waste of time even to open the bundle; it was so small that his fingers closed completely around the middle when he squeezed it. But he did open it and stood astonished when he found that it contained one hundred pounds exactly, in notes.

The rest of the day was endless but at last the sun went down and he was able to go to Salome . . .

'Marse Tip, please forgive me, but I couldn't help meself. I had to cry. To think . . . I can tell you me secret now, Marse Tip, when I give you that sixpence this morning it come out of Thelma saving box . . . only one farthing left in it and there was not another farthing in the house; not a crust of bread . . . not even a spoon of sugar! And through you, Marse Tip, look what we got on the table tonight! Me heart so full . . . oh Marse Tip . . . Thelma don't cry chile. Mammy is crying because she is happy. See Thelma those things on the table is money. Paper money. You will live in a nice place. Marse Tip, you will never be able to understand what this money mean to we. But not the whole ninety

145

pound Marse Tip! I know you win the same amount as you say, but half of this ninety pound will do all we want to do. Besides, half of it is really you own for though you say the sixpence was for Thelma, now that we have more than we need, you should take back what you sixpence win!'

'I wouldn't hear of it, Miss Salome. I got more than enough! You get ninety pound for your shilling and I get ninety pound for mine. Why should I take back half of yours as well?'

'But before we go home if you change you mind, Marse Tip, I will gladly give you the half, for if it was not for you, we would have only a farthing in the house tonight!'

Salome stood by the side of the bus, glancing at the man beside her. She thought of the many things she had never had the chance to ask him. She wanted to know how he had lost one of his eyes, how he had become lame, and other personal things; if he was married, and where he had lived before he had come to the city, for she felt that if he had been there all the time she would have seen him. She knew he was lonely; perhaps this was the reason why she felt so close to him. And now she was going away, perhaps never to see him again.

Three days had passed since Tip had brought the money to Salome's house. On his advice she had made sure of not losing the windfall, by sending most of it away to the government savings bank in her district. She had bought the necessary things for herself and Thelma, and a few little gifts for relations and old friends. He had gone with them on the shopping spree. It had felt good to have him beside her. Now Thelma was inside the bus making friends with a girl her own age, and in half an hour they would be on their way.

'Marse Tip, I don't know how to begin to thank you.'

'That's nothing, Miss Salome, you must thank you luck!'

'Marse Tip . . . just walk up the lane with me . . . I must talk to you in private. Thelma, Mammy not going far, just up the lane with Marse Tip for a minute.'

They stood at the top of the lane. They could still see the red bus.

'Marse Tip, Thelma . . . she love you very much.'

'She is a lovely child Miss Salome.'

'She is always talking 'bout you.'

'I get to love her as if she was me own, Miss Salome.'

'It seems you so fond of children . . . The little girl what you tell me

146

you give the puppy to . . . it show you have a good, kind heart, Marse Tip.'

Her words pained him; she did not know what he was. But he merely said: 'I did feel bad afterwards 'bout not offering the pup to Thelma first, Miss Salome, but the little girl need it . . .'

'Marse Tip, you do the right thing, I tell you so over and over. I would vex if you didn't give it to Mobel. I know she and her two friends well. Marse Tip, I never ask you, you have any children of you own?"

'No Miss Salome not a chick nor child.'

'Marse Tip, we don't have much time to talk. Is 'bout where I going; it is a nice place, right up the mountain. My place is right at the top. Me alone will be up there. Not a soul anywhere near. The land is fruitful and good. You don't see a soul 'cept you really want to see them.'

Tip looked at her, believing that he understood what she was asking him, yet at the same time, unable to believe it. He felt so close to her. He pushed the feeling aside, it made him afraid.

'You should see the place when it light with the moon! And the smell of night jesmin, orange blossom, and all the plenty sweet-smelling things make the place smell like nothing you know . . . for nothing else smell like it.'

With all her feeling in her eyes she looked directly in his face.

'Come with me, Marse Tip! Come with me now! Later if you like you can come back for you things! But don't mind 'bout it now, just come as you is! I feel shame because a woman don't have no right to say such a thing to a man first, but I can't help. We will be happy, Marse Tip. I will be a good woman to you. I know you will make Thelma and me happy.'

'I didn't think I could care for anybody after Joseph dead . . . Funny, him use to say if him ever dead and I ever want to judge a good man, I must go by Thelma. Him say if Thelma like the man, I would know that him is alright, for picnies always know good people. Thelma love you Marse Tip! That's why I feel so sure!'

She stopped as if she had said more than she intended, and as the wonder of it all pressed itself upon him, Tip realized that this woman, who would be his only love, must be told that he could not accept the home and the love that she offered. He searched for words and Salome misread his hesitation, thinking he would be going with her. Then she remembered that he had told her that he too had won a similar amount to hers, and she grabbed his arm without knowing it.

'Marse Tip, I didn't 'member you win some money youself! Oh, Marse Tip, you must think it was 'cause of you money why I ask you to come with me! If I did 'member I wouldn't open my mouth, Marse Tip, don't mind how I feel!' She took her hand away from his arm and now she was almost in tears.

'Salome. Look at me! You think I would believe such a thing?'

She looked up at him slowly and she smiled, seeing in his face that her love was not one-sided. 'So you will come, Marse Tip! You will never regret it.'

'Miss Salome, what . . . what you say to me just now make me head grow big . . . and make me heart full to the brim. It make me proud. It is a great honour to me . . . with my one eye, lame foot and ugly face.'

'You musn't say such a thing 'bout youself, Marse Tip! I won't hear it.'

'Awright, Miss Salome, I won't say it again. All I can say is I would be happy to come with you . . . but I can't! Don't ask me why, Miss Salome, it will only make I feel worse. All I can tell you is it would mean a thousand time more to me, than it could to you. I beg you, don't feel vex', and don't ask me why I can't come!'

Salome saw pain in Tip's face.

'Awright, Marse Tip. I won't ask you why, and I not vex'. Let we go back. Them nearly ready.'

As they walked back to the bus, Tip whispered to himself: 'And the night jesmin – and the other things – smell like nothing you know . . . for nothing else smell like it.'

Salome felt the shame lifted from her face as she heard Tip repeating her words, for she knew then he had not turned her down because he did not care for her, or what she had offered.

'Marse Tip?'

'Yes Miss Salome?'

'This little piece of paper . . . it have my address, and it tell you how to get to where I going after you come out of one of these bus. It would be hard to find it without the paper Marse Tip, for it is a long way from where the bus pass, so keep the paper carefully. If any time you change you mind . . . just come. No need to write.'

'Thank you very much Miss Salome, I will keep it.'

Thelma looked at them both as they approached and called out, 'Mammy, why you don't kiss Marse Tip like me?'

'Thelma! Now you see? You make everybody laughing at me!'

And then finally the bus moved away. Long after it had gone Tip limped across the road. He bent down wearily and lifted the shafts of his clumsy handcart.

CHAPTER TWENTY-SIX

Night had come. Tip had spent the evening alone, just as he had always done in the days before he had known Thelma and Salome. He had thought of the hut on the beach and imagined it empty and bare, as bare as he felt inside.

He walked along the sand where he had first seen the mother and her child and felt that in Salome he had recognized beauty for the very first time. Through her he had begun to see the world around him with less hardness, and the emptiness that he had felt for as long as he could remember had subsided until he had scarcely been able to feel it at all. Now it had returned with all its force. He would almost have preferred to have remained Bangbelly, who had known only loneliness, than to be Tip who had been given a glimpse of something he could never have.

He walked on, brooding over his loss, with his hands deep in the pockets of the trousers he had bought with part of the ten pounds he had kept back from the hundred that Ma Kuskus had lent him. He wondered if he would ever hear from Salome and then remembered that she could not write because he had not given her the address of the hostel. Perhaps he had been a fool not to jump at her offer. How was it that he now thought about whether things were right or wrong before he acted? It was his dream – fresh mountain air, food dug from his own patch, eggs from his own chickens . . . a woman who also loved the earth and would have been the kind of wife he had not even dared to dream about. He thought of Ma Kuskus and wondered how much of this she knew. He would not have believed that his greatest pain could come, not from bitterness or hatred, but from love.

And suddenly, Ma Kuskus was there by his side. He was not frightened to find her there. He did not even ask how she had found him on the loneliest part of the beach when it was not his custom to be there at that time of night. She walked with him, looking smaller than ever, engulfed in her bundle of clothes.

'I suppose you come to ask me 'bout the money – I mean what I done with it Ma Kuskus.'

'Why should I?'

'Well in the first place, it is you money!' he said, turning his face from the sea to the old woman. Then he added, 'You . . . you don't mean you know what I do with the money a'ready, Ma Kuskus?' But all she said was: 'Why you didn' go?'

Her question was so abrupt that he answered at once.

'I don't know. Maybe, maybe because I think it won't work. But how you know, Ma Kuskus?'

She ignored his question. 'You still have time – Tip.'

'To go you mean, Ma? Or to choose?'

'Take it how you like it.'

'What a hell of a answer!' he said in disgust.

'To a hellava question!' replied Ma Kuskus.

Tip was surprised at her mildness and at the bold way he was speaking to her. It was as if he had lost his fear of the woman – as if they were friends.

'Dat money . . .' she said, and Tip thought: so she really going to ask me 'bout it!

'It was not my money,' she said.

'You mean you take somebody money what don't belong to you and lend me, Ma Kuskus?' he asked in a voice full of anger and panic. 'You have no right to lend me anybody money. Well, you can't get it back now. You know everything, you should know that as well!' As he spoke he was aware that his words still tumbled over one another from time to time and he realized that he could reveal himself in a burst of temper.

'I don't want de money back,' said the herb-seller quietly. 'De money was you own money.'

'What . . . what you mean? I don't have no money. You tell me them find the money I did have hide under my house.'

'I tell you de money wasn't dere. Dat was true. But I didn' tell you, dat after you keep talkin' in you madness 'bout it an' where it is, I go an' fine it, jus' like you wrap it an' de gun as well.'

She fumbled with the buttons on the front of her thick cotton blouse, and brought out a package, which she handed to him. He took it from her without knowing what he did.

'It was five hundred an' eight poun' fifteen shillin', all 'cept de hundred what you get befo', an' de gun, is inside de package.'

He looked towards the sea, the package unopened in his hand, then he began to speak quietly.

'You didn't have to give me back a penny Ma, and I wouldn't know. You must take some of it – half – take half Ma, take . . . ' He looked around. She had gone as silently as she had come and but for the package he would have thought he had been speaking with a ghost.

CHAPTER TWENTY-SEVEN

The day after Ma Kuskus had given the money back to Tip, he went to see Ironman who had become his close friend.

'Ironman I want you to help me.'

'Anything I can do Tip, man you just ask.'

'Well it's like this. I get back some money what I never know I would see again. I want to use it to help people – mostly the picnies like the Sparrows. I want to know how I can do it.'

'How much you got to spend?'

'Four hundred.'

'Four *what*?'

'Four hundred pound.'

'Jesus, and I think you was a poor man!'

'I is a poor man, Ironman.'

'And you want to use it to help people? How much?'

'Every penny of it, Ironman, every penny.'

'Jesus, you is a man after me own heart! Come. Me and you going to put we head together man! . . .'

They found a place which was turned into a shop within a week. It was in a side-street, surrounded by lock-up shops, with a big backyard with double gates and another entrance in a narrow lane. They had almost quarrelled over Tip's insistence that the business should be set up in Ironman's name but agreement was finally reached on condition that the people were told of its true ownership.

Soon after they had started their venture, Tip discovered that the government had bought corn for a newly-built cornmeal factory. When it seemed that the spare parts necessary for the running of the machinery would not arrive from England before weevils had spoilt the grain, they panicked and offered it to wholesalers at half-price. Noname swore that the missing parts had arrived and been misplaced somewhere and urged Tip to buy the corn at the prices offered and Ironman had agreed, saying you could always depend on the government to back the wrong horse. The day after Tip had paid cash for the corn, the missing parts were found. Anxious to hide their blunder, the government tried unsuccessfully to get the sale cancelled. At last, to avoid a scandal, they repurchased the corn through a 'private' buyer, giving Tip a profit of two hundred pounds.

However, despite this good fortune, there was still much to be done. Just before Christmas Ironman and Dimlight went to the Syrian stores. When they explained that they were trying to assist the poor, for once the storekeepers let them have remnants at very low prices. Ironman said that Captain Dimlight had converted them. They asked the Salvation Army to help make up the fabric and this was done even though Dimlight was no longer one of them. The market women also asked their customers to help with the making and a week before Christmas piles of clothing were ready for distribution.

Tip supplied the children, at cost price, with most of the items they liked to sell on the streets. He rented a stall in the market for Mobel, Pazart and Sista, giving them goods to supply to their friends on consignment. Onions, garlic and grains were sold to the market people at the wholesale rate.

Tip continued to remain in the background and he lived in a room at the back of the shop. He only ever slept for about four hours a night and he was glad that no one lived nearby. The silence around gave him time to think and he preferred to remember the past in isolation.

CHAPTER TWENTY-EIGHT

Captain Dimlight, who had joined in the venture at Ironman's insistence, reopened his evening classes as part of his contribution to the well-being of the children. Although it pleased him to see the improvements that were being made in the lives of the people around him, Dimlight saw something in Tip that made him uneasy. He could not put it into words, but he often felt that Tip was not quite what he seemed. The way he had suddenly appeared among them and his reluctance to answer any direct questions, however trivial or well-meant, made Dimlight suspect he had something to hide. He reasoned to himself that this was true of many of the people in Santa Lucia, and in itself no sin; perhaps like Ironman he had been in prison. But Dimlight could not dispel the feeling that Tip, unlike Ironman, was not honest about his plans and had some motives for his actions that no one could begin to guess at. Although he was polite to Tip, even friendly sometimes, he was careful to keep a distance between them. He tried hard to like Tip, yet something held him back.

Although Dimlight often helped in the business, he continued to find work wherever he could. One day he returned to the dock. The same manager was there with his assistant wharfinger and his two body-guards. They had called the names of the regulars and were about to throw the remaining twenty-five tickets in the air to the eighty or so men who were still assembled, when Dimlight said, 'Wait a minute!' from the back of the crowd.

'Well, what is it?' asked the assistant.

'We would like to change the way you dispose of the rest of the tickets.'

'And who the hell do you think you are?' roared the manager.

'Just what I am – sir – a labourer waiting for work.'

'I know you now, you were that blasted troublemaker. Well, haven't you learned your lesson?'

'No – sir – I don't think so.'

'Then by God, you will learn it well this time!'

Someone in the crowd said, 'Beg pardon, sir, but we would like to know what the man was suggesting . . . I mean 'bout the ticket!'

Dimlight replied promptly. 'After the names have been called for the regulars, I am suggesting that the rest of the tickets should be distributed through a ballot.'

A hum of voices followed. The manager shouted, 'What the hell! Do you think I would waste my time arranging ballots when I can have a hundred men waiting for a single ticket for an hour's work?'

'I am not suggesting you waste your time doing this; we could take care of that part of it.'

'Well, let me tell you, Mr Troublemaker, all these years I have handled my wharf and my labourers as I see fit. No goddam man has ever asked me to change my system, they know better! Now you get to hell out of here and let us get on with the job, or by God you will be sorry. You two men, see that by the time I count to five that man is on his way.'

The men, the pair who had fought with Dimlight before, moved forward hesitantly. They came within a few feet of Dimlight, then stopped.

'Get on with it, men. I order you to see that the man is helped on his way; what's holding your hands? Frightened? He is one man, not a dozen – do you want to look for another job?'

They wavered, then heard a strong voice say:

'Don't lift you hand my friends, if you do you will be sorry.'

Everyone turned. They recognized Ironman who was wearing his usual shiny peaked black cap – a favourite item worn by ship's firemen.

The two men retreated like soldiers commanded by an officer. The assistant wharfinger whispered to the manager, then without warning he threw the handful of tickets in the air.

'Don't touch them, men!' called out Dimlight quickly. The stampede which had always followed, did not happen. The tickets remained on the ground.

'Come on you men, all you whose names have been called, this will mean more hours' work for you if these fools don't want it. And, as for you two, you can consider yourselves fired from this minute, you hear me? You are *fired*!'

He turned to his assistant. 'Take the men who have tickets through the gate, I shall telephone the police to clear the rest of them away.'

'Come on, you men who heard your names,' said the assistant, but not a single man moved. The manager stared in disbelief. Ironman stood behind Dimlight, his arms folded and a strange smile on his face. Dimlight's face registered nothing.

'Are you coming you men, or do you want to be barred from this wharf forever?'

Still nobody moved. The manager whispered to the assistant who in turn whispered to the junior standing close by. Then the manager walked away.

'Alright, you men, you can pick up the tickets and have them balloted between you,' said the assistant and he began to leave.

'Beg pardon, sir,' said Ironman, 'it would be more polite to give them to we in we hand, then we could ballot for them.'

The assistant glared at Ironman, and Ironman glared in return. Without a word, the assistant and his junior retrieved the tickets at the men's feet. They tried to give them to the first man available, but each indicated that Captain Dimlight should receive them.

It was the beginning of a change.

CHAPTER TWENTY-NINE

Two men – one a Syrian, the other an almost white Jamaican – stopped talking as soon as Tip reached the counter to buy his usual five bags of onions.

The Syrian said: 'Ask this gentleman.' The other, who had been sizing

Tip up, looked doubtful but then decided to try. He explained that he had a lovely consignment of onions on offer but the shopkeeper already had his full quota and could not afford to buy. The price was very low and was Tip interested in making a very big profit in a very small space of time?

He was a good salesman and Tip soon followed him to his car. They drove to a large office building with glass-panelled doors and rich interiors, for the deal to be closed and signed. One thousand bags of onions. Two hundred and fifty pounds down, balance in thirty days. Tip signed, was rushed in the car to collect the money for the down payment and at the end of the transaction all he really knew was that he had a thousand one hundred pound bags of red onions at the warehouse for which he had agreed to pay ten shillings a bag, and that this was a bargain for he had been paying twenty shillings a bag to the Syrian.

He had thirty days to find the other two hundred and fifty pounds and he was broke. The onions would rot within a week once they were taken from the ship's hold but he was sure he would sell his five hundred pounds' worth within days. The salesman had assured him of it. He had also assured him that if he were in any kind of trouble he only had to call at the office and ask for him – Mr Karl – by name.

Tip planned to give the people of Santa Lucia a great surprise. He would sell them the onions at twelve and six per hundred pound bag, seven and six less than they had been paying the Syrians. He would sell them quarter-pound and half-pound bags too and supply the children of the streets at cost, through the Sparrows, leaving them with all the profit.

As soon as he got back to the shop, he told Ironman what he had done and was told:

'But Tip, Santa Lucia and Kingston is full of onion.'

It seemed that through dock strikes at other West Indian islands, perishable goods were being diverted to Jamaica and five shiploads of onions had arrived on the same day. Four of these were in Santa Lucia harbour.

Still hopeful that the news was not as bad as it seemed, Tip and Ironman went to the market, but there they discovered that people had been buying extra supplies at seven and six a bag – half a crown cheaper than Tip's.

They tried to solve the problem. Ironman offered his fifty pounds' savings but obviously this was not nearly enough. Unless Tip could move the onions within two days, he would also incur additional warehouse charges. Then Tip thought of something. He would borrow

Ironman's money and use it to rent space in the town's two cold storage depots. However, the manager of the first could only take two hundred bags and demanded payment in advance at a high rate. The second manager was able to take the rest, but on seeing Tip's shabby appearance demanded high rates and cash in advance. He and Ironman barely managed to meet the cost.

For the next few days Tip became depressed. He had to turn away most of the people who came to him for help and he had vowed never to do this. He knew that people had sometimes taken advantage of what they considered to be his good nature, but in his anxiety to make amends he had been prepared to make mistakes and suffer losses. It seemed that he now had nothing left to give.

He decided that he would return to the salesman for advice. He arrived at the company's reception desk feeling extremely uncomfortable in the opulence of the great office around him. He was assisted by a beautiful girl and was immediately conscious of his poor clothes, his one eye and his hair, which had not been combed since early morning. He explained that he had bought some onions and had been invited to return in case of difficulty.

'You bought the onions last week?'

'Yes lady, one thousand bags.'

'Good lord! Wait a minute, did the salesman say his name was Mr Karl?'

'That's the name, lady.'

The girl picked up the phone. 'Mr Karl, a gentleman says he would like to have a word with you about the purchase he made through you last week. He says you had told him to call on you . . . Mr Karl, I cannot give such a message! I am bringing the gentleman up. Come with me, Mr . . .'

'My name is Tip, lady.'

'Follow me, Mr Tip,' she said and led him to a glass-panelled door, knocked, and without waiting for a response, pushed it wide open.

'Mr Karl, here is Mr Tip. Perhaps you would like to give him your message in person?' She closed the door behind her. Her sarcasm had clearly embarrassed the salesman.

To hide his confusion, he said, 'The lady referred to you as Mr Tip . . . that, of course, accounts for your difficulty in seeing me . . . for I could not place the name. You see, on the documents you signed you had a different name. Here they are: J. Power! Now, how can you account for this?'

Tip had no idea he had signed his original name on the documents. 'Well sir, most people know me as Tip – and that is mostly how I sign my name – but Power is the name I was born with.'

Although the salesman believed him, he decided to get rid of his visitor as soon as possible by being on the offensive.

'Well, I suppose I must take your word for it, but I do wish you would make up your mind about the name you want to use. As it is, I can get myself in trouble with the firm over this. I am sorry about the onions, Mr Tip, I had no idea the market was like this when I sold you the consignment!'

'You lie! You know I couldn't get rid of them onion just like how you couldn't get rid of the blasted thing till you find a damfool like me. You sell me at ten shillings a bag when everybody else was buying at seven and six a bag! You say I must come and see you, give me all kinda sweetmouth talk, then soon as you get me to sign the paper and take my two hundred and fifty pounds out of my hand you don't want to know! If it was not for that nice little lady out at the office I wouldn't see you at all! Now, I did come to see what you could do for me like you say, but now I don't feel I could trust you even if you promise to help me. You is a real twister, I telling you this to you face! Good thing we have people coming up like that nice little young lady outside. As long as we have people like them we will have a better Island . . . Now that I talk my mind I will go,' he said, and left, leaving Mr Karl wondering how one meek man could have changed so much. It was like seeing two different people . . .

As Tip walked to the front office, he cursed himself for losing his temper. But when he remembered the difference between seven and six and ten shillings, and thought of the one thousand two and sixpences, not counting the other loss he was still angry, especially as Noname had told him that the insurance companies had ordered the onions to be brought from the strike-stricken islands to be sold for what they could fetch before they all rotted.

The lady was there at the counter to greet him with a smile which made him feel a little better.

'I have a confession to make, Mr Tip, I eavesdropped – I mean I listened at the keyhole – I am proud of the way you spoke to that man!' she said, in almost a whisper. 'He is the only one like that in this office, Mr Tip, we all detest him and he knows it!'

Tip saw the friendly glances of the rest of the black, brown and nearly white staff; all young people, and he felt pride and hope.

'Cheer up, Mr Tip, you may yet find a way!'

He stepped out into the sunlit street, feeling that he had only just begun to know his own Island.

CHAPTER THIRTY

Less than a week before the money was due, Tip saw that bags of onions no longer leaned invitingly in shop doorways, and back at the shop Noname and the Sparrows were waiting to tell him that they, too, had discovered that onions were scarce. He called Ironman, Captain Dimlight, the Sparrows and Noname to a conference. They would check that there was a demand and, if so, start hauling the onions the following day with all the handcarts they could find. After a tiring tour, it was confirmed that onions were not available anywhere in quantity.

Early the next day Tip, who had still been taking odd jobs with his handcart, returned to open his shop and found market people blocking his door and crowding the street.

'Them find out who I is!' was his first thought, though he could not run.

'Plenty people want onion,' shouted the Sparrows from the shop and he realized his mistake. But those few minutes kept coming back and convincing him that he would never be able to acquit himself bravely if he were threatened by another mob.

A while later a car nosed its way through the crowd of market people, and a chauffeur-driven Packard, out of place in such a back-street, drew up in front of the shop.

In the back of the car, smoking a fat cigar, was a huge gentleman. Though it was still morning, his face was red and perspiring. Sitting beside the driver was Mr Karl.

'Ah, Mr Tip! You remember me surely?' he said. 'Of course you do! Glad to meet you again!'

Mr Karl kept on talking as he jumped out of the car and shook Tip's hand vigorously. 'I have brought you *business*, Mr Tip . . . big business! I did promise I would help you out, remember? Well, I am a man who keeps my word. This gentleman is Mr Bonetti of Bonetti Hotels, you must have heard of him. Everybody knows the name.' The speaker paused, bowing towards the great man, who in turn let go of his torpedo-like cigar to wave a royal acknowledgement in Tip's direction. The salesman continued: 'Mr Bonetti is a valued customer of the firm, Mr Tip. We have a supply of onions . . . on the way . . . which should arrive within a couple of days, but in the meanwhile, I have persuaded the gentleman to purchase some to tide him over. So there you are. The gentleman does not deal with things in a niggardly manner. He has generously offered to take five hundred bags of your onions at fifteen shillings per bag of a hundred pounds, and the remainder at twelve and six per bag, right away!' The big man managed to lean forward and lift a bulging briefcase from beside him which he tapped with the back of his ring-laden fingers.

'I pay you now, and not wid da cheque! I pay cash!' and he settled back to enjoy his cigar. A policeman, seeing the crowd waiting for the onions around the car, stopped to investigate just as Tip asserted that he had no intention of selling his onions in this manner.

'Alright, I am a busy man!' declared Mr Bonetti with a flourish of his cigar. 'I will take da lot at fifteen shilling per bag!'

'There you are, Mr Tip,' said the salesman grandly, 'think of it! A clear two hundred and fifty on your five hundred, Mr Tip, and nothing to do but to sign a bill of sale of the cash!'

'But I tell you I not selling my onions that way!' said Tip quietly, and some of the people who were beginning to move away, stopped as they heard what he said.

Mr Bonetti forgot his cigar now. 'How much do you want for da onions? One pound? OK It is da robbery but I give one pound. One thousand bag, one thousand pound cash! You will be rich! Maybe you will buy da Roll'Royce, eh?' His stomach moved up and down as he enjoyed his own joke.

They listened with open mouths as Tip replied:

'You can't buy them onion like that Mister, them belong to me, and I will do what I like with them. In fack I sending for them now!'

Mr Bonetti became angry. 'It is blackmail! You know I already take da onion from da cold storage. Da cold storage you put da eight hundred bags in belong to me. Yestaday I tell my men: Take da onion out. I will see da man! I will pay him! Now I get da blackmail and you da policeman speak nothing!'

The policeman was surprised to find that he was being accused, and his dark face suppressed the anger he felt. He said to Tip:

'Have you given this gentleman permission to take you' onions from the cold storage?'

'No officer!'

'And as far as you are concerned the onions are still in the cold storage?'

'That's right, officer!'

'And what are you' plans for these onions?'

'I plan to sell most of it to the market people, Constable!'

There was a murmur of appreciation from the waiting crowd.

The policeman turned to the embarrassed Mr Bonetti and the fast-talking Mr Karl, who was now looking alarmed.

'So that is the situation, Mr Bonetti, and I don't see how the charge of blackmail fits in. I think you will be in a very awkward position if Mr Tip insists on his rights.'

The Constable's words made Mr Bonetti look towards the sky, by way of the car's upholstered roof, for the help that was not forthcoming on earth. But no assistance came. 'OK! OK! You win!' he cried, like someone in pain. 'I pay thirty shilling per bag for da onion I already take from my cold storage, and I offer two pound per bag for what you have left! Done!'

This time when Tip shook his head, even the policeman felt he was crazy.

'I is collecting one pound apiece from these people,' Tip said to the astonished crowd. 'That mean I will owe them all one bag of onion apiece. When them get the paper I give them for the money, them can go for them onion at you cold storage. It will be up to them if them want to colleck the onion . . . or you want to pay them what them ask for it! The balance of the onion is for them street picnies to sell and make a good little break for once. Not my business how much you want to pay them for the onion what you say you take away behind my back. That up to you and them. All I want is one pound apiece from them, and as far as we is concern' the onion is still at you cold storage. Now if me was you Mr Bonetti, me would drive like hell before all these people pay me them pound apiece, and come to colleck them onion!'

Tip finished by walking back through the jubilant crowd to his shop where he directed Noname to begin collecting a pound from each person.

Mr Bonetti vented his anger on the salesman, but Tip had won. He was loved and respected by the market people more than ever before.

CHAPTER THIRTY-ONE

Just after the success with the onions, when Tip was trying to find another investment for the profits, an idea came to him. He remembered that as a boy he had worked with some of the small dealers in agricultural produce, lifting heavy bags of grain, bales of hides and bundles of roots, all of which had been exported. He remembered now that most small dealers had been dishonest and had graded the coffee, pimento and ginger brought to them by the poor people from the country, at the lowest possible rate – regardless of quality – and cheating them further by altering the scales. His boss had taught him to prepare the sellers for the worst by pretending that the produce was not worth buying, and in this way these dealers had made massive profits.

Tip hastily called a meeting and it was decided that the business would branch out into the buying of country produce for export but would offer the fairest prices. Word was sent out, but the sellers were advised to sell half their goods to the usual buyers and bring half to Tip so that they could see the difference for themselves.

This simple test impressed the country people who found that Tip paid twice the usual amount for half the goods. The news spread. Handcart men, feeling that Tip was still one of them, showed their loyalty in their recommendations. Remembering how much they owed Tip for the onion deal, the market people extolled his merits to everyone who came to town with produce to sell, and Dimlight, though he still had reservations about Tip, took on the business side; setting prices, finding storage and dealing with exporters. After only a month the results had exceeded all expectations; Tip's name had spread all over the Island, the business seemed set to thrive and the country people were at last getting a fair return for their labours.

Now that the business seemed well-established, Tip felt he could afford a holiday. At first, he planned it with the idea of getting away from his memories; every part of Santa Lucia contained some reminder of his former self. But as the idea grew, he decided instead to take the Sparrows with him to Kingston.

To Pazart, Sista and Mobel it was the most wonderful thing that had ever happened to them. Their boarding-house stood in a dingy street and was in no way luxurious but they felt like millionaires: eating in restaurants, being waited on and visiting the funfair booths which were

161

always there near Christmas time. They returned to Santa Lucia loaded with the gifts that Tip had bought them and before they did anything else, they went to visit Sonna's grave, feeling a little guilty because they had forgotten him for a while and wanting to share their excitement with him. It was then that they discovered that the grave was not there. A new tomb stood in its place with a headstone and iron railings with a little gate.

Panic-stricken, they ran back and forth, searching desperately for the simple pot with the wild flowers in it they had left, unable to believe that in the short time they had been away it could have been taken from them.

Then Sista caught sight of the inscription on the headstone and made Mobel and Pazart look too. The name *SONNA* had been etched into the stone.

When the Sparrows arrived at the gate of their shacks, a second change awaited them. In place of their huts, they found two neat cottages with blue-painted verandahs, galvanized roofs, and sashed windows, while the outside had been painted over and dashed with golden-coloured sand. There was a neat kitchen just across the yard and further still, there was a small latrine.

Ironman, who was there to greet them, explained that Tip had provided all the money for the cottages and when the Sparrows were calm enough to take in the smaller details, they found that furniture and everything else that they could ever want had been provided. Their tin oil lamps had even been replaced with lamps with flowered glass globes. They could not believe what was happening to them. They were overwhelmed with gratitude and happiness. From that time onwards they called Tip, 'Godfather'.

CHAPTER THIRTY-TWO

Tip had grown to love all three children, but he loved Pazart best. The boy seemed to need the companionship of a man – perhaps to replace his father who had died when he was very young – and little by little, Tip had filled the vacant spot. Pazart had always seemed the most helpless

162

of the three. Mobel could think fast and was dependable in a crisis. Sista, though sentimental, was highly intelligent, and unlike her companions, she had received the guidance of adults for the first few years of her life. But Pazart was so open and simple. It was always possible to read what was going on in his mind from the changes in his face. He was clumsy too, but he was also the first to recognize his own shortcomings. Tip had taken to the boy and the love was returned. Sometimes they would go fishing together from a borrowed boat or from a rock along the beach. They did not need to talk in order to communicate. Any fish they caught were merely a bonus; the real pleasure was in the sharing.

In the light of this unexpected happiness, Tip was able to push the predictions of Ma Kuskus into the background. Sometimes, when the children held his hand or the adults shouted, 'Watch you Marse Tip,' with genuine affection he was even able to doubt her words. After all, almost two years had passed since his return as Tip and his happy hours with Pazart, his talks with Ironman and the thoughts of his love somewhere in the hills, all combined to make the nightmare vague. He could not entirely forget his past but often he thought of Bangbelly as someone he had never met. Sometimes he wondered at the loneliness of his former life and remembered the flashes of envy he had experienced when he had seen others enjoying the companionship he had craved; Ironman, Noname, Dimlight – even the Sparrows had all seemed to possess something that had eluded him. Now he had it too, but sometimes the happiness this brought gave him anxious thoughts and sleepless nights because he knew that if he were discovered now, he would have so much more to lose. The days were passing too quickly; he wanted to do so many things.

He wondered if she would come as he waited on the beach near the mouth of the river. He had been so anxious these past few days that he had dared to pass Ma Kuskus with his cart and say: 'Tonight near River-Mouth. Must see you!' She had not looked at him; her head had remained low over her bundle of herbs. He did not know what he would do if she did not come . . .

'What is it now?'

As usual her arrival startled him. She had seemed to raise herself out of the earth and was now standing by his side, barely visible in the darkness.

'You t'ink I have all night?' she asked, and he realized he had kept her waiting for a long time saying nothing. He felt nervous.

'Ma, I have to see you! I couldn't bear it any longer. I must know!' His breathing grew loud.

'I waitin'! said Ma Kuskus softly.

This made him angry. 'Doing like you don't know what in me mind! You well know, Ma Kuskus! You damn well know!'

But the old woman kept silent and Tip was forced to speak again.

'You think it fair – something bad might happen to me, you know all 'bout it and keep it to youself? Me must sleep and wake night and day and don't know what going to happen, how it going to happen, or when it going to happen? You won't even tell me if is *you* put the curse on me or not.'

He suddenly stopped, feeling he had gone too far.

'So, Mista Tip feel to himself dat him can put on Mista Districk Cons'able Bangbelly clothes aggen, eh? Him can bawl at people! Bully dem! Make a poor ole woman tremble when him talk!' Her scorn bit deep. He was glad the darkness hid her eyes.

'Mista Tip who is Mista Bangbelly don't feel grateful him did get a warnin' dat somet'ing to happen! No! De gentleman feel him shoulda know every little t'ing 'bout it, how, when an' where! An' ef what de poor ole woman tell him gwine to happen is not what him like, all him need to do is to say: I don't want dat at all, at all, ole woman! I want so an' so, or else . . .'

'Stop, Ma Kuskus! For God sake stop! I sorry for what I say! Can't you see you killing me? Don't you have any pity? Better I end it now with the gun you give back to me or is that what you did have in you mind?'

Tip covered his face with his hand and there was silence. When he took his hand away, he expected to find himself alone, but she was still there by his side – a short, vague shadow whose face merged with the night.

'What you want to know?'

He was surprised not only by the question but also by the quietness of her voice.

'I think I know the answer to most of the question I was going to ask, Ma, according to what you say.' His voice sounded sad and humble now. 'As you say, I should be glad that I did get a warning.'

She said nothing; only the waves could be heard.

'An' de balance of de question?' she asked.

And he said to himself: 'She know everything!' Then aloud: 'When

. . . when whatever going to happen, happen . . . anybody going to know who I is?' He held his breath as if breathing would mean drowning.

'Yes . . . Tip.'

He exhaled and inhaled and knew he was drowning and tried to lay hold of a straw.

'Anybody . . . close . . . to . . . me?'

'Yes . . .Tip.'

The straw went down with him. They stood silently on the sand looking at nothing.

'Ma?'

'What?'

'I know now you don't have anything to do with . . . with what going to happen, but why you won't tell me exactly what and how? Don't get vex' again, Ma, is a idea what come in me head why I ask you this time.'

'What is de idea?'

'I just think: Suppose you don't want to tell me because it is a bad end and you don't want to hurt me no more . . . 'cause you . . . like me?'

'What dif'rence dat would make to you . . . even ef I did feel so?'

He spun round eagerly to face the little figure beside him. 'The 'ole world of difference, Ma!' he said excitedly.

'How come?' asked Ma Kuskus softly.

'You see Ma, you would be the only one who know me . . . what I was before . . . and still like me! It would make I feel good Ma Kuskus! Real good!'

He peered vainly to see her face, after he had spoken.

'Ef you t'ink dat will help . . . Tip, den t'ink so.'

He stood trying to digest the meaning of the herb-seller's words, trying to bring himself to feel that he was right; and before he could ask her for a clearer confirmation, she seemed to disappear.

And then he began to chuckle to himself. 'You do well to go so quick, you ole fire-eater, for if you did stay a minute more you would have a fit! For I would kiss you right on one of them wrinkle cheeks, so-help-me-God!'

He walked home brooding over what he learned, yet feeling for the first time since he was a little child that he was not alone in the world. 'It make such a difference,' he kept saying to himself, as he reached the lighted city.

CHAPTER THIRTY-THREE

'Tip?'

'Yes Ironman?'

'Them tax and water rate due. Make I take the papers and pay it today.'

'I don't have them down here. Them is at my room at Mango Walk, in the ole trunk.'

'Is awright. Cap'n ask me to give Pazart a book him want him to read. Give me the key for you door and I will colleck them on the way.'

'Thank you, it will save me a journey. The key is hanging up behind me, please take it.

'Awright. See you later, Tip.'

'Right Ironman. Thank you . . .'

'Oh God! I send Ironman to get the papers for the tax in the ole trunk and *it* is in the same trunk. What I must do? Oh God! He will see it and look what tie up inside – then he will know. Oh God! Oh God! I must lock the place and go and see if I can ketch him before he go into the room. Maybe . . . maybe he will go to see Pazart first. Maybe he will sit down and have a talk with him. Yes, he gone 'bout twenty minute now but I got a chance . . . I must get rid of them things. I was foolish to keep them so long. I going to get rid of them soon as I get there – if he only don't find them. He mustn't find them! Oh God, why I didn't throw them away long time ago? I must hurry, get a bus to take me part way. If I didn't have that bad foot I could go quicker. Oh God, don't make him find it, please God . . .'

'Marse Tip, where you goin'? My goodness look how you sweatin'! You mus' take it easy, Marse Tip! You can overdo it, you know?'

'I is OK Shepherd. I just going on a little business.'

'The Lord go wid you my brother. But you shouldn' hurry like dat! Not good fe you at all, at all!'

'Thank you Shepherd . . .'

He was almost running now. He saw a bus coming and rushed across the road towards it, colliding with a bicycle. He lay there, dazed, blood oozing from a cut over his good eye.

'You hurt bad, Marse Tip?' asked someone.

'Don't try to get up Marse Tip! Give him something to drink, him don't come to himself good yet.'

'I is awright. Please make I get up now, I didn't get a bad blow. It was my fault but I feel awright now.'

He tried to stand but the crowd would not let him go. They helped him into a nearby house. 'Is no use no more,' he thought. 'The people won't let I go because of the cut. Anyway, is too late. The same people what helping me now will tear me to pieces when them hear who I is. Oh God! And the Sparrows, them will know. So this is how it going to end . . . Oh Jesus! I won't be able to stand it when them taunt me.'

He could not lay still. People saw his agitation and thought he was in pain. Then suddenly Ironman was there, sorry to see him injured, trying to help him. He had not gone to Tip's house; he had put the key down while searching for the book and forgotten to pick it up . . .

Late that night, Tip dug a hole behind his room at Mango Walk and buried the contents of the handkerchief – the relics of his past.

CHAPTER THIRTY-FOUR

As Salome alighted from the loaded truck near the great Santa Lucia market, she saw an unattended handcart parked near the kerb with the name Tip painted on the side.

She stood still and looked for its owner, hoping to see the gaunt, one-eyed man, yet frightened now that she seemed to be so close to him.

She had told her friends and relations that she was making the journey because she had a lot of produce to sell and had heard there was a business in Santa Lucia that paid good prices, though she knew nothing more about it. However, her biggest reason for coming to the town was her need to find Tip.

After more than a year of good fortune, she was very comfortable. Shortly after her arrival, the people of the district had come up to the hill and, as was the custom, with the guidance of the village carpenters and masons, they had taken the materials she had bought and built a two-roomed cottage with a cedar door and floors of hard broadleaf boards, that were stained until they were slippery and shining. It had taken four

Saturdays for the able-bodied people in the village to raise the house and they had accepted nothing more than the food and rum bought for such an occasion; and then to the improvised tunes of digging songs they had dug and planted her lot in a single day. To try and show her thanks, Salome had made dresses for the women and children.

She had invested in a few more acres of land, rich with fruit trees. Her pigs had littered and thrived; one of her two cows had calved; her hens were laying, the fruit trees were laden and her vegetables promised a second crop even better than the first. She had prospered but although Tip had brought her luck, there was no contentment. Every young bachelor in the surrounding villages had paid their respects but she had never shown them any interest. From the day Salome had waved Tip goodbye, she had known that she loved him. At first she had not realized the depth of her feelings; she had told herself that she would soon forget and think of him only as a friend. But she came to recognize that she was deceiving herself. Had it not been for her child, she would have come to him within a week with the shame in her eyes asking him to live with her even if he did not wish to marry her or to return to the mountains with her. But she had known that she had to build a future free of hunger for her daughter so she had worked and planned, spending her money with great care. As the days had turned into months, her feelings for Tip had only deepened. Thelma too had thought of him; whenever she heard the roar of the bus as it climbed the hill she would say: 'Mammy, suppose we just see Marse Tip coming now, wouldn't we feel glad? Maybe him is on this bus Mammy. Maybe him climbing up the hill right now,' and Salome would agree that it would be good to see Marse Tip, and like the child, she too hoped he would arrive as every bus came by.

Then finally she had decided that she would go to town to search for him. All through the journey she had hoped to find him alone, poor and in need of her, only in order to be able to show him that she wanted him, not his money.

And now she was standing looking at the handcart with his name painted on the side. Then someone came and took the handles of the cart but it was not Tip. Salome felt as if she had been robbed. The man brought his cart alongside the truck and asked her if he could take her load and she gave him her four bags of coffee, two bags of ginger and one of pimento, saying that she wanted to go to the shop where they paid good prices. He knew exactly where she meant and as she walked beside him, he promised that she would get a very fair price.

Salome wanted to ask him about the cart and its former owner, but fearful of disappointment she could not bring herself to do so at first.

168

Supposing Tip was ill or had gone away? Eventually she said, 'Somebody . . . somebody else did have a cart with that name . . . you know him?'

'Oh maybe you mean Marse Tip, lady?'

'Yes! Yes, where him is?'

The handcart man smiled tolerantly at her. 'Marse Tip down at de shop lady.'

'Which shop?'

'De shop what buy produce, de one we going now lady. Marse Tip him own de shop,' he said patiently.

In a hushed voice Salome asked: 'You mean all the business belong to the gentleman name Tip?'

'Yes lady.'

They were soon there. As they approached, the handcart man called out, 'Noname, dis lady bring produce to sell. She ask after Marse Tip.'

And as Salome went inside and looked around she saw that Tip had a thriving business. Noname praised him saying what a good friend he was; her produce was weighed and priced and Salome suddenly felt she could not stay. Tip had prospered. No doubt he was happy in his new surroundings. He had probably forgotten all about her by now, anyway. She no longer felt she had the right to disturb him, it was not fair of her just to arrive like this. He had given no explanation for not wanting to be with her but no doubt he had had a good reason. She did indeed obtain a fair price – one that surprised her until she remembered how generous Tip had always been and how willing to help those in need. She could not try to take him from people who now relied on him. When the transaction was finished, Noname asked if she wanted to wait for Tip.

'No, I won't wait this time,' she said. 'Please only say for me that Salome called.' She turned her face away. 'Please tell him that everything is just the same . . . and it will never change.'

Before Noname could answer she was hurrying from the shop towards the truck that had brought her to the city.

'Tip?'

'Yes, Noname?'

'A nice young lady call to see you and left a message!'

'Oh? What her name?'

'Salome.'

'Where she is? Which way she go? How long ago she gone?'

''Bout six hours ago, Tip. Maybe she home now . . .'

Ironman and Tip were enjoying an evening together. Sometimes they would talk but they were just as happy to be silent. They were sitting on the back steps of the shop on two empty soap boxes. The moon was coming up, but it had only reached the tall tops of the few coconut trees scattered round the city.

'I can't get the little fella out of me mind,' said Ironman suddenly.

Tip's face twitched but he said nothing.

From the way Ironman had spoken of Sonna on the few occasions he had mentioned him, Tip knew how deeply he had loved the boy.

The glow from Ironman's cigarette brightened as he took a couple of pulls from it.

'I never tell anybody before, Tip, and only 'cause you is me best friend why I going to tell you now.'

The cigarette burned, intensified and faded.

'I did lost a boy what would be the same age as Sonna if him live, and I sorta feel Sonna was me own son what come back. When I look 'pon him hard, it even look like me and him resemble.'

Tip still did not speak.

'That night, when the nurse call me in . . . when I see how bright the little fella was, I feel cheer' up. I say to meself, him will be back from the hospital by nex' week the longest.'

There was no red glow from the cigarette now.

Tip asked himself: Would I have come back if I'd known I would feel like this? Then he remembered Pazart . . . Mobel . . . Sista. He remembered the woman somewhere in the mountain district where the smell and beauty of the night was beyond description . . . He remembered the man who was speaking to him, and for whom he would do anything . . . The hundreds who greeted him with love and affection. Yes, perhaps later he might regret returning . . . but not yet, in spite of the pain . . .

'Him make me promise not to kill that son of a bitch. Him never stop till him make me promise!'

Tip shuffled his feet on the earth and mumbled something. He wondered if Ironman had noticed the strain in his voice. But Ironman was too deeply involved in the past to have noticed anything and now Tip remembered how he had nearly killed him, then had flung him away from his grasp with a cry that even Bangbelly – so much less aware than Tip – had recognized as the most intense sorrow.

The moon was higher now and he could see the blurred face of his friend, but he dared not look long, lest his own face betray his guilt. Now he began to feel like a relative of the dead boy coming after the funeral and being told how it all had happened. I getting mad, he said to himself.

'When them call me in the nex' time, I look at Sonna and say to meself: Him just feeling bad . . . maybe a bit of a fever. Him soon be awright. But it was nothing like that. Him was dying and when I see it, I couldn't do one thing 'cept take him in me hand. Him . . . him try to put him hand round me neck . . . and then him was gone, Tip . . . gone forever!'

Ironman ended as if he was glad the telling was over. Then he got up and said good-night to Tip who sat where he was, the weight of his own suffering leaving him unable to move or speak.

CHAPTER THIRTY-FIVE

Tip was in the produce-buying department of his shop. He sat on a box thinking about Ma Kuskus and her strange ways and when he lifted his eye from the ground, he was looking right into the face of the old woman of his thoughts as if he had somehow summoned her. She had a bundle tied up in a great piece of coarse material, balanced so well on her head that both hands were free, though one held the staff she carried when in the city. Taken by surprise, Tip almost asked why she had come, a question that might have aroused the curiosity of the others in the shop. But the old herb-seller saved him from making the blunder and said, 'I jus' come to fine out ef you buy root like sasiperilla?'

'Yes . . . yes, Ma . . . mother, we buy it,' said Tip though he looked frightened as she moved closer to him. Confused, he wondered if she was ready now to denounce him.

Ma Kuskus took the bundle from her head before he could help her. He took it out of her hands and fumbled with unsteady fingers at the knots. Gently the old woman assisted him and the coarse cloth was spread open to reveal the clean little roots of the sarsaparilla. The sight of them seemed to help Tip to think more clearly and it occurred to him that perhaps she had come like any other seller – because she was short of money and he gave the best price. As he weighed the bundle of roots he was shamed by the thought that this woman, who had returned his money to him when she could easily have retained it for herself, should now be in want. He felt in his pocket again, unaware of his customers, but once more she anticipated him. 'Ef you tell de man how much money I mus' get fe de sasiperilla, I will get some onion from him fe it,' she said, and Tip knew she was telling him that she did not want money and that, in any case, to offer her anything in public was dangerous. So she would not expose him . . . at least not at that moment, he thought.

He shouted the total due to the old woman to Noname and the herb-seller walked forward, like a daily visitor who knew the arrangements by heart.

As Noname gave the woman the onions, Tip guessed that Ma Kuskus wanted to see him. He wondered how she would manage a message when it was so easy for them to be overheard. But the old woman came back and collected the cloth which had carried the roots without once looking in Tip's face. When she had gone, Tip found a broad leaf, newly plucked, on the box where she had rested her bundle. It was a leaf of the wild grape tree, to be found only on the sandy beach. He guessed that she wanted to see him there and, after long consideration, realized she would not expect him to be there until nightfall.

Tip went to the part of the beach where the river emptied itself into the sea, for this was where they had last met. He never doubted she would find him.

This time there was no mystery about her coming. She came out of the darkness like any other human being just when Tip was beginning to think he had read the message wrongly. She seemed to have shrunk in height since he had last seen her.

'Ma Kuskus?'

'What?'

'I don't know what you want to see me for, but first of all I bring some money for you.'

'I don't want you money.'

'Just because it is *my* money, Ma?'

'No.'

Tip waited, trying not to show how anxious he was about the reason she had summoned him to this meeting.

'Tip, why you don't go?'

The voice was not hers. Not the voice he knew. The suggestion from her meant so much. She sounded so human. And eagerly he turned to face the blurred figure beside him.

'You think it would work, Ma? You think so?'

'I didn' say so.'

172

'No Ma, you didn't say so, but you think it have a chance?'

'I don't know.'

'You mean it, Ma . . . when you say you don't know?'

'Yes . . . I mean it.'

'God A'mighty! I could give up everything . . . leave it for them and go tomorrow! She wouldn't mind at all, not Salome! I got her address and how to get there in my pocket, Ma! From the time she give me, I never open it, never look at it . . . but night and day it in my pocket!' The man grabbed the old woman by the arm without knowing he had dared to touch her.

'Ma, I could leave everything this very minute . . . everything, I tell you! Ironman and Cap'n would see that the Sparrows would be awright from what I would leave! Most of the business arrange a'ready just in case anything happen to me. Yes Ma Kuskus, I could leave the 'ole business and the money what I have for them. God, it would feel so good to go up in that mountain place to her and to Thelma – just like I was her own fath . . . ' The man stopped in the middle of the word. Finding himself with his hand on the arm of the person he used to be more afraid of than anyone else in the whole world, the dreamer seemed to awaken. He snatched his hand away as if he were afraid that he would lose it if he touched the herb-seller for another second and turned away, so that now she was almost behind him. He stood, squeezing one fist in the palm of the other hand with a grinding movement.

Behind him came the scratch of a match, followed by a sudden flare which lit up the area briefly, then began to go bright then dim alternately as the old woman put it against the tobacco in her pipe. Just before the light went down for good, the ex-Constable swung round and grabbed the withered hand savagely as it held the half-burnt match and the light fell to the sand with one last glow. Tip then grabbed the other hand of the unresisting herb-seller, and by feeling for its shape he found the little box containing the rest of the matches. Breathing loudly, he took the box away, struck one of the sticks and, as the flame came to life, he put it against something he had fished from his pocket. For less than half a minute the drawn face of the man and the creased face of the old woman showed plainly against the glow. Then darkness took over again.

'What you burn, Tip?' The voice was still unlike Ma Kuskus's.

'Don't you know, Ma?' asked Tip, and without waiting for a reply, went on: 'You can't temp' me again, Ma Kuskus! And I can't temp' meself again, either . . . for now I don't know the address, or how to find her now!'

173

It was hard to tell if his voice contained laughter or tears as he ended the sentence.

'Is that all you did want to see me for, Ma Kuskus?'

'Yes, dat is all.'

'Well I going now. Good-night Ma Kuskus.'

'Tip!'

'Yes Ma?'

'Maybe de road not so lonely after all!'

'Lonely like hell, Ma.'

'Even when you believe what you did ask me?'

'I must ask you a million things by now, Ma Kuskus!'

'But one of dem was diff'rent, Tip, an' when you fine out what it was . . . de answer to dat one shoulda been . . . yes.'

He was the first to say good-night, but he was standing peering in the dark after the little old woman who had left him, suddenly, as if she had been swallowed by the night.

Lying sleeplessly in his bed he thought over all the questions he had asked her since she had brought him back to life two years before – and then he remembered one which made him sit upright. He dismissed the answer as fantastic, but the thought kept returning to him. He did not want to think of any other answer to the riddle.

CHAPTER THIRTY-SIX

Ex-Captain Dimlight, still puzzled about Tip, had been asking questions in the surrounding neighbourhood, trying to discover where the man had come from and why. He found no answers and that in itself had puzzled him. There was something in his gaunt, weary face that was familiar and Dimlight felt compelled to know what it was, not from idle curiosity but from his instinct that the secret – whatever it was – concerned them all and somehow was set to do them harm.

Dimlight was surprised at the depth of his own feelings in the matter. Sometimes he even wondered if he was spurred by envy; when he had been Captain he had inspired the kind of love and admiration that Tip was receiving now and Tip's business had done more for people in need than he had ever done. But he soon dismissed this from his thoughts. He wanted to protect Ironman and Pazart and Sista and Mobel, nothing else.

And then suddenly a thought had come to him, a thought so preposterous that he wondered if he was in his right mind. He could see the face of the ex-Constable and then the face of Tip and the two looked different yet somehow strangely similar . . .

Dimlight was working on a campaign designed to raise wages in the various industries of Santa Lucia and the possibility of strike action was to be discussed. He decided to catch Ironman before the meeting to discuss with him his suspicions about Tip. With this purpose in mind Dimlight waited for him to come along the beach. He soon saw the large frame of his friend moving towards him.

'That you Ironman?' he called and was greeted warmly. The two men sat down on some tree stumps. Dimlight began warily, not quite sure of his ground. He wanted to put his suspicions to Ironman before he confronted Tip. Perhaps he was imagining the similarities – it would not do to jump to conclusions. After all, Tip had given much to the people and he had many friends, not least Ironman and the Sparrows.

The Sparrows! That settled it for Dimlight. Sonna's face appeared before him and he knew that he had to voice his uneasiness for the sake of the children. If he was right, they had been lied to, taken in, made fools of . . .

'Something on you mind Cap'n?' said Ironman.

Dimlight spoke slowly, 'I . . . I think I may have found out something . . . something bad about Tip.'

'Tip?' Ironman's voice was no longer friendly. 'You better don't say it. You see the work the man do, yet in spite of all this you want to drag up him past?'

'I think he is a bad man.'

'We is all bad! 'Member how them call me thief and make I stay in prison?'

'That was different. He may be a liar, even a murderer . . .'

Ironman jumped up and grabbed hold of Dimlight, shaking him violently. 'You take the man money, you see what him do for the poor and now you say him liar and murderer!'

'Listen . . .' said Dimlight.

'You shut you goddam mouth!'

'You must listen to me. I think he . . .'

Ironman dealt Dimlight a blow that sent him reeling. The idea that a man who had refused all but the most basic comforts and had given everything else that he had for the benefit of others, could be so accused – whether rightly or not – incensed Ironman so that he did not care where his fists landed. He only knew that he had to defend Tip and that he would always believe in him because of the man he was and because of their friendship.

But Dimlight was fighting back now and he crashed his fist into Ironman's face just as Tip and Noname and Shepherd Peter arrived for the meeting. They rushed in between them and held Ironman back.

'Lemme go,' he roared and tossed two of them aside. Only Tip remained and Ironman, blinded by fury, tried to give Dimlight still more blows. Tip was caught between them and received a punch on his jaw and fell. Ironman came to his senses and helped him to his feet.

'Now you owe me something, Ironman,' he said.

'I know it Tip.'

Tip turned to Dimlight, 'And you Cap'n you owe me something.' For a moment, Dimlight was silent. He was staring at Tip, trying to match his features with those of the District Constable and he found he was less sure than ever. 'Yes, I owe you something Tip,' he said with emphasis, feeling now that his envy had caused him to imagine the impossible. He was glad that Ironman had not allowed him to speak.

'Shepherd Peter and Noname, witness a debt going to be paid.'

Tip grabbed the hands of Ironman and Dimlight and brought them together swiftly before they could protest. 'Now shake and I will feel that you both pay me what you owe me for my broke' jaw.'

They shook hands but neither spoke to the other. Tip wisely called off the meeting.

CHAPTER THIRTY-SEVEN

Tip heard someone coming through the back gate, then across the large yard, and wondered who it was. He was not expecting any visitors that night except the three children, and that would not be until after the serial at the cinema. He could hear his visitor stumbling in the dark.

'Who that?' he called, just a little afraid.

'Is me, Marse Tip,' came a high-pitched, sing-song voice.

'Is that you, Shepherd?'

'Yes, Marse Tip, is me! I want to have a word wid you!'

For the first time, Tip associated this voice with the nightmare experiences of two years before. Apprehensively he got up from his seat by the table where he had been replacing the strings on his eye-patch. He hesitated, for he had never allowed anyone to see him without it, though the blind eye was always closed. But there was no time to fix it so he opened the door as he was. Shepherd Peter entered rubbing his bony hands.

'Fancy you knowin' me jus' by me voice, Marse Tip! You got a good mem'ry! Now me, I can't tell one voice from de odder, don't matter how I try, *but when it come to a face* . . . Marse Tip, it might take me a long time, but I never does rest till I place it, once I feel I see it befo'!'

Tip's good eye suddenly got itself blurred, so that he had to feel for the chair by the table, though the big oil lamp was burning brightly. Shepherd helped himself to a seat opposite Tip, with the light between them.

The ex-Constable had always tried to imagine how he would act in the face of exposure but there was only numbness. Perhaps he could buy his way out? He felt that the man sitting before him would wish to make him pay. Perhaps he would hope for a new church? He was just that kind of fanatic. He would consider it justice to make his victim pay for a House of God. Shepherd was talking but Tip was too busy imagining what disclosure would mean to hear much of what he was saying.

' . . . So I say to meself: Marse Tip is de only one who would help me. So here I am, Marse Tip. I want you to len' me some money.'

'How much?' asked Tip, feeling that his guess was right and that he would not be denounced until he was bled dry. Fleetingly he thought of putting Shepherd off his guard, getting his gun from the room at Mango Walk . . . but he pushed the thought of murder from his mind.

'How much you can help me wid now, Marse Tip? Say fifty?'

'I don't have fifty here, Shepherd. Perhaps twenty, but not fifty.'

'Twenty will do fe now, Marse Tip!' and the ex-Constable noted the 'fe now' in the sentence as he wearily pushed his hand in his pocket.

'As I was sayin' a while ago, Marse Tip, I don't like how it look wid we two friend at all, at all! I know somet'ing bad gwine to happen! One of dem gwine to kill de odder, mark my word!'

'Who you talking 'bout, Shepherd?' asked Tip, still with his mind on his own danger.

'Gosh! You mean all de time I was tellin' you, Marse Tip, you wasn' listenin'?'

'You don't mean Ironman and Cap'n, Shepherd?'

'Yes, Marse Tip. I was tellin' you jus' now, somebody tell me on de quiet, him hear Ironman swear him gwine to kill Cap'n! You know dat trouble dis evening . . . I know Ironman would never make Cap'n get away wid de blow what him give him when we part dem. De Bible say: Man' heart is desperately wicked, above all t'ings! An' Marse Tip, ef Ironman should kill Cap'n as him say, dem would hang him, an' it would depen' on me an' you alone to take over de union movement what Cap'n organizin'! Not a soul would be left to do it but me an' you! Me bein' so experience' wid organizin' would make it easy fe me to run de 'ole business – don't feget God ordain me a Shepherd – an' you could help same as you doin' wid money, Marse Tip!'

'But Shepherd, Ironman would never do a thing like that! You talk 'bout it like you believe it will happen! You wrong, Shepherd. I know you wrong!'

Tip's fear for himself returned at Shepherd's next words.

'Make I help you count de money, Marse Tip. You know, you look diff'rent widout de piece of leadder over you eye? It make you face look so diff'rent . . . like you is anodder person, Marse Tip!'

With that comment, Shepherd stretched his hand across the table and took the roll of notes from Tip's hand, then scraped three heaps of silver which were on the table. He got up and, without counting the money, pushed all in his pockets, silver in one, notes in the other. Tip sat motionless.

'Don't worry, Marse Tip, ef what I t'ink gwine to happen really happen, me an' you can manage de 'ole business! Good-night. God bless you.'

'Good-night Shepherd.'

Tip saw his visitor out and then walked back without knowing he had done so. The small hope that he had not been recognized had gone when Shepherd had commented on his appearance without his eye-patch. Could he still escape? As long as Shepherd thought he had money he was safe but after that, he would either strike him down himself or leave him to the market people. He now connected the preacher with his capture and disposal. He had had an instinctive fear of the man since his return. Suppose he went away? Suppose he found where Salome lived? It might be possible. Ma Kuskus had suggested it only two nights before.

Perhaps he could disappear to Salome's place, leaving everything in the hands of his helpers. He had been to a solicitor and willed most of his belongings. He could draw all he had from the bank, give it to Ironman, and he had no doubt his wishes would be carried out to the letter. Perhaps the children need not know. But what would Shepherd do when he found he had disappeared? Would he tell the secret? And if so, would they believe him? Perhaps he would think it best to keep his mouth shut rather than be blamed for Tip's – Bangbelly's – escape.

Then without warning as so often happened, Tip remembered the wrong he had done Salome when he had been Constable and it dovetailed with his thoughts of escape, just as it had done on the beach when he had burnt the address. No, he could not go to Salome and her child. The secret would always be there between them. Tip rested his aching head on his arm over the table. At least he would be safe for as long as he had the money. But he vowed that the money he had set aside for the children would not reach Shepherd's hands. Perhaps that would be the cause of Ma Kuskus's prediction coming true. He wondered if Ma Kuskus was still certain how it would end. She herself had suggested he should go away and had admitted she did not know what would happen if he did. Was she right in saying that those he cared about would also know who he really was? Perhaps he could have altered everything by killing the skin and bone Shepherd, squeezing his little neck when he had bent forward to take the money . . . Yet he knew that while Bangbelly might have done such a thing, Tip could not.

He could hear the Sparrows coming through the gate. He tried to pull himself together as he listened to them crossing the yard. Then he remembered that he had not finished mending the strings for his patch over his eye, but there was no time. No, even without the patch he was safe – except for Shepherd. He stood with his back to the door and tried to compose himself.

They knocked. 'Come in,' he said, carefully making his tone cheerful. He heard them enter.

'Well, Pazart, tell me what happen to the girl what them did tie on the train-line last week,' asked Tip in an over-happy voice.

'Bangbelly!'

The name reached him with the force of a blow. He turned round slowly. Standing before him was Mobel, the Mobel he had known in the old days with a torn red frock under a man's faded jacket, her hair disarranged, legs sprawled, chest heaving.

Standing by Mobel's side was Pazart, in the man's trousers cut short at the knee and an old moth-eaten pullover, without shirt or vest underneath. Only Sista was absent. Tip saw all these things and then realized that Pazart was pointing something at him. It was the automatic revolver he had had in his room at Mango Walk.

'Is him, Pazart! See how him look now? I tell you it was him!'

'Yes, Mobel! Him is Bangbelly! See how him look when him see we? We going to kill you, Bangbelly! We going to kill you like you kill Sonna! Tell him, Mobel! Tell him!' Pazart pointed the gun at Tip's chest.

'For God sake listen to me. Them will ketch you and you will hang for murder! Put down the revolver. I won't run,' pleaded Tip, not for his sake, but for theirs.

'Hear how him beg now, Pazart? Hear how the man what kill poor Sonna, beg?'

'Yes, Mobel, I hear him beg!'

'Listen to me, I don't care 'bout my life. It is you I worrying 'bout! Police will know what you do and them will hang you, or since you is young, you will go to prison for life!'

'Think we care 'bout that, Bangbelly? Think me and Pazart care? We find out who you is because of this, Bangbelly!' spat Mobel as she threw something she had been holding behind her on the table. It made a jingling clatter as it fell by his hand. He turned his head slowly like a clockwork toy and his eye looked down at his old rusted handcuffs and his District Constable's badge.

'Is the dog find it, Bangbelly! The dog what you give me, find it!' said Mobel.

'We didn't believe, me and Mobel!' cried Pazart excitedly. 'Even when we see J. Power write beside the badge, we didn't believe, but when me and Mobel go in you room and see J. Power on the onion paper what you get when you buy the plenty onion, Mobel and me know it was you, Bangbelly, and then we search you trunk and find the gun, and now we going to kill you!'

'Yes Pazart, we going kill him!' Mobel was heaving as she spoke.

Tip said, 'My God! My God!' as the depth of their hatred reached him. He could not shield himself from them. He knew he would be remembered now with even greater bitterness than two years ago. He looked at Pazart and saw that his eyes were dilated. Sweat was on his forehead, and he stood unsteadily. His lips parted slightly and he said, almost inaudibly, 'Don't make them throw water on me!'

'Pazart, what wrong with you?' cried Mobel, still standing behind Tip, opposite her companion.

Tip recognized the symptoms as the beginning of a fit but he could do nothing. Mobel took the gun from Pazart with one hand and tried to steady him with the other, but then the convulsions took hold of the boy. Tip saw that he must reach him, and at the same time, get the gun from Mobel who seemed to anticipate this for she said with fear in her voice,

'Stay there! Don't move, or by Jesus I going to shoot! I don't care, now! I going shoot, I tell you!'

Tip moved forward fast and reached them as Mobel pulled the trigger and Pazart crashed to the floor. Tip intercepted his fall, saw Mobel's hand with the gun somewhere in the confused heap, and took it. She did not resist but sat dazed on the floor, barely knowing what had happened. She could not tell if she had shot but not killed him, or if she had missed. She did not remember hearing the loud blast of the gun, nor did she know whether this strange weapon was one of those which they had read about in the Sexton Blake Crime Club story where the men used silencers. She saw Tip bending over Pazart, trying to cushion his head, trying to prevent him from biting his tongue. He had not been shot. She began to sob. 'Why you didn't dead?' she cried. 'Why you do what you done . . . ? You kill Sonna, and, and you come back . . . and you make we believe you is a good man? You fool we . . . you made we . . . we . . . Oh God, what we going to do now? Why the gun didn't kill you? It woulda been the best thing . . . Oh God!'

Tip looked up from the helpless Pazart to Mobel's bowed head. He heard her rocking cries of anguish. He thought of the gun now in his pocket and knew that nothing had happened because the two children, when they had come to kill him, had forgotten the safety-catch.

He thought: This is the end of everything. He wondered if he should make it easy for them. He could take the gun from his pocket and turn it on himself. He felt that Ma Kuskus had been right when she'd said that he alone would choose his fate. He knew now that the man Shepherd had been connected with the attempt on his life that day after he had tried to hang himself. But for the fit which had overcome Pazart he could have been killed, but none of these attempts had been successful because it was not to be. He would be able to choose the end. He looked at Mobel, weeping silently now with her face hidden, he thought of Sista somewhere, unsuspecting, even at this moment, because the two, he was sure, had wished to protect her. Even if he could live without their love, they would not be at peace while he remained. There was no place for him now. The time had come to choose his end. They all heard footsteps coming through the gate and guessed it was Sista. Mobel raised her tear-stained face and Tip, glancing at her, thought: When Sista come through that door the last link will be severed . . . And then Sista came in, breathless with excitement.

'Marse Tip, you know what? I go to Captain Dimlight house and knock . . . ' she broke off, looking from Tip to Mobel, who, in her long discarded old jacket and frock, slowly stood up and leaned dejectedly against the wall of the room, with both hands in her jacket pockets. Sista's bewilderment grew into alarm as she looked over the table and saw Pazart lying on the floor.

'What . . . what happen?' she asked turning from one to the other. Tip prepared himself for what was to come by slowly sitting down at the table.

'*Him* is Bangbelly, Sista!' Mobel said hopelessly. The dreaded name caused Sista to jump and she glanced fearfully around the room as if expecting a ghost. Bewildered, she turned again to Mobel, while Tip sat with bowed head.

'I don't understand what you mean, Mobel. Bangbelly dead two year now. And you don't tell me what wrong with Pazart?'

Mobel took one hand out of the pocket of her tattered jacket and pointed to the table where the handcuffs and badge still lay: 'Them belong to *him*! I tell you *him* is Bangbelly!' she cried, getting excited again. But despite the evidence Sista could not believe it.

'Mobel! You mad! Calling Marse Tip, Bangbelly?'

Mobel stopped leaning against the wall and stood straight, her face filled with anger.

'*I* getting mad? Awright Sista, ask *him* what call himself Tip, who *him* is! Go on, ask him!'

Sista looked at Mobel's face then, with a frown, moved to the far side of the table so that she could see Tip's face properly. She still didn't believe Mobel but she wanted to look at him so that he could, by some sign or other, confirm what she feared about her girl-friend's reason.

'Marse Tip, you hear what Mobel saying? She . . . she say I must ask you . . .'

Tip felt it was better to end it quickly. He slowly lifted his greying head and looked at Sista, giving the answer he could not speak. His one eye stared at her and the weight of the misery that showed through, forced the girl to see the other eye. There was silence as she gazed at him in the strong light without his patch. Mobel stood with her hands in the pockets of her old jacket watching them both. Then Sista touched her lower lip. 'No!' she whispered and took one step backwards. 'No!' she said again, and then, 'Oh God! It him!'

She backed away until the wall prevented her from going further, her hand still up to her mouth, her fingers still touching her lower lip. Mobel spoke:

'Him can't get away, Sista! I not worrying now! You know why? 'Cause when everybody hear, them going to hunt him down like a dog! Marse Ironman alone will tear him up!'

Mobel's eyes gleamed as if the thing she had in mind gave her great pleasure.

'Yes, Sista, I not worrying even if him want to go out of this room now! And you know why, Sista? Because . . . because him only have one eye, and him foot lame as well! Him can't hide, Sista! Him can't hide!' She subsided triumphantly.

Tip seemed immune from further hurt. He sat with his chin touching his chest, his hands hanging at his sides as if he were asleep. Sista, still leaning back on the wall, spoke at last.

'And we use to love you . . . love you so much that we call you Godfather behind you back all the time!'

Tip found that there was still a place left in him which was not crushed into numbness, for each word spoken now by Sista made him flinch.

'Yes Sista! We . . . we love him! And we even call him Godfather! And all the time *it was him what kill Sonna*! Yes Sista, him fool we!' It was as if Sista's words, after the long silence, had woken up Mobel's anger once more and given her new strength, for she rose and walked to the table where Tip sat.

'Fancy me, you and Pazart calling the man what kill Sonna Godfather, eh Sista? And we did eat with him and share with him, and all the time him saying to himself: "I smart! I fool them! Them can't know is me!" ' The girl stopped speaking as Pazart, still sleeping on the floor, moved his head uneasily, and Sista, also looking at the boy lying there, remembered what she had been saying when she had come in a while before. She moved from the wall and went towards Mobel.

'As I see Pazart on the floor,' she said, 'I 'member what I did come to tell . . . *him*. You know you say I must go to Captain for some homework? Well, I call and knock but I didn't get any answer, and when I peep through the keyhole, I see like him laying down 'cross the bed, but the lamp was low, and I couldn't see good . . .'

Dazedly Tip took up the thread of what Sista was saying. Something told him that it had to do with what Shepherd had hinted at earlier. Now he paid full attention to her words.

' . . . I did want to go in the room to see what wrong with Captain,' continued Sista, 'but I hear like somebody moving behind the house, and I get 'fraid, for the place is so lonely, so I run and come to tell you, and when I see you and Pazart wasn't home, I come back here.'

Suddenly it was clear to Tip that something terrible had happened to the ex-Captain, and he was sure that Shepherd was responsible. It gave him something else to think of and his brain began to work once more, yet all the time he was aware that once he left the house he would probably never see the children again. He groped for the leather patch with its broken strings, and turned to go.

They stood silently watching him, with Pazart still asleep on the floor. As he stretched out his hand to open the door, he stopped and turned to face the two girls.

'I just want you to know, before I go, I is not the same man you use to hate. I didn't mean to kill Sonna.' He paused and the children stood close to each other staring at the man who now looked so old.

'I know you not going to believe me when I say I is changed, and I don't blame you, but if you could only believe that I come back because I was sorry for what I do, and that since I come back I get to love you all, even the dead Sonna, more than I love my own life, I wouldn't feel so bad when I go, not even when everybody hear who I is.'

He smiled sadly before he spoke again. 'What you say is true, Mobel, it wouldn't be any use if I try to run away. One thing I glad 'bout, you didn't get to kill me youself. Goodbye, and tell Pazart goodbye, and God bless you.'

He walked through the gate and along a deserted back-street, which he selected deliberately, as the route he would take to Dimlight's little room. The Captain lived in isolation at the end of a muddy lane. All the way to his destination one hope was in Tip's heart. He hoped that all that had happened was another of the many nightmares he had had throughout his life. He hoped that he would open his eyes to find that it was time for him to dress and go out to the market. It was only when he slowly pushed open the door and saw the ex-Captain lying battered and motionless that he knew there would be no waking from this nightmare. He saw a torch, and the old police instinct told him to look for clues which Shepherd might have planted if he was behind the murder.

He searched round the outside of the house unsuccessfully and was just about to enter the room again, when his torch picked out a black object between the low wooden steps. He bent down and picked it up and muttered: 'My God!' For the thing he held in his hand was the shiny peaked cap which everyone knew belonged to Ironman. He went back into the room and searched for further clues, but as far as he could see there were no more. For a while he stood in contemplation and then he pushed his hands in his pockets, took out the patch he had worn at all times before this night, and placed the small piece of leather with the broken strings on the bed, almost under the dead man's body. Then he pushed the cap he found inside his shirt and with a whispered,

'Goodbye, Cap'n,' walked out of the room and closed the door softly behind him.

Half an hour afterwards Tip weighted the cap he had found with a stone and flung it far out to sea. Then he walked back to his room behind the shop. The children had gone. He took paper and pen and began to write. It was nearly dawn when he finished all he had to do. Then he stepped out again after locking the door. Twenty minutes later he walked up to a policeman and said: 'Please take me to the station, I commit a murder.'

Just as he reached the door of the police station with the policeman behind him, he glimpsed a small figure in a bundle of clothes in the early light. He walked inside the station feeling that he was not quite alone.

CHAPTER THIRTY-EIGHT

Shepherd Peter thought of the man who now called himself Tip. When no one had been able to tell where this stranger – who was so good to the poor – had come from, or how he had got his lame foot and had lost an eye, he had guessed like Dimlight, that the man had wanted to hide his identity. It had taken a long time to put two and two together. But, this time, there would be no escape. Bangbelly would be drained of every penny which would go to build a church to glorify the same God his very life had mocked, the same God who said: 'For I am The Lord thy God, and a very jealous God!' Then Shepherd would turn him over to the wrath of the people. He could not escape with that lame foot and one eye.

He thought of the ex-Salvation Army Captain he had left dead in the room. He did not regret what he had done. The man was a turncoat, 'putting his hand to the plough and then taking it away again'. God must hate a man like that. It was no sin to destroy him. Nor was it a sin to put the blame on Ironman who deserved whatever he had coming to him. He and the Captain had been encouraging people to think of earthly things – asking for more pay, having a union – and the foolish people had listened to their Godless talk until now, even his own members had deserted him. No longer did people offer him gifts of food. And when he had told them they should fast, they had told him that

185

Dimlight – the turncoat – had said when people started a fast, they should have something on which to break it when it was over! Now with those two out of the way – the ex-Army man dead, and Ironman arrested for the murder, he would take over the affairs of this union, until it was crushed and the people were won back to the fold. All the factory workers, dockers and the other labourers who were joining up secretly, would soon discover that they were without their leaders, and that only himself and Bangbelly remained to look after their affairs. There would be no strike in two weeks' time as planned. Perhaps the authorities would thank him on the quiet. It would not be the first time he had tried to help them; he had burnt down the little chapel of his rival, Brother Paul, an imposter. God could never have called him, Shepherd was sure of this. He had hoped to kill two birds with one stone by burning down this chapel and getting the people to blame Dimlight, but somehow nothing had come of it. Well it did not matter now. He had the man, Tip, in the palm of his hand. All those who had forgotten to pray to God for food just because the fool Ironman was ready to give them a meal for nothing, would have to go back to praying tomorrow.

He had planned things well, he said to himself. He had told everyone he intended to go out fishing for the night and would not be back until the next morning. There was nothing to connect him with the night's happenings. He passed his hand along his pocket and felt the roll of notes lying there. He felt good. It was useful to know that he could get lots of money whenever he wanted it. This man Tip was a gold . . .

'Shephad Peter?'

The suddenness of the voice close to his ear, when he had thought himself alone, made him draw a sharp breath. He saw three shadowy figures around him, one on each side and another breathing on the back of his neck.

'Who you?' he asked shakily.

'Is awright, Shephad, we is all brothers in de Lord! Is me, Brother Paul, wid two of my church brothers.' The voice had a note of mockery, and it made Shepherd uneasy.

'Oh, is you, Brother Paul. I didn' know it was you. I is sorry to hear dem devil burn down you chapel!' said Shepherd in his preaching voice.

'T'ank you kinely fe you sympat'y, Shephad. No, no need to stop for we all gwine de same way!'

Shepherd tried to speak lightly:

'Look like we all gwine fishin' tonight, Brother Paul, but dis time de soul what we gwine to fishin' fe is fish sole! One spell S, O, U, L, an' de odder is S, O, L, E! Dat's a good one, don't you t'ink so, brothers?' He threw back his head and laughed but no one joined in his mirth, or made any comment. They walked along the lane leading to the beach.

'You feelin' worried, Shephad Peter?'

'I don't have no cause to feel worried, Brother Paul.'

'Same t'ing I say to meself, Shephad. I say to meself: Shephad can't be worried jus' because we walk wid him to de beach. Even ef him was goin' to lose him life, him wouldn' be worried, fe I say to meself, such good Christian like Shephad an' meself, who is always tellin' people what a wonderful place heaven is, an' how dere will be no more hungry an' want, an' everyone gwine to have golden slippers an' golden harp, an' crown of gold, an' how every day will be Sunday, an' we will wear lily-white robe an' such like, same as de Bible tell we, well, I say to meself, it would look bad ef we tell people 'bout all dem nice t'ings an' get dem to come to Jesus t'rough it, an' when we time come to go an' enjoy all dem niceness, *we don't want to go*! It would be a bad t'ing, Shephad, fe *it would look like we was tellin' a lie!*'

Shepherd swallowed and tried to find something to say, but could find nothing for the first time in his life. Suddenly one of the men who had not spoken before, hissed in his ear:

'How much, Shephad?'

'How much what? I . . . I . . . don't know what you talkin' 'bout!'

'Fe de church what you burn, Shephad Peter,' the other said, through clenched teeth.

Shepherd instinctively brought his hand to his hip pocket and someone immediately flashed a light to see the meaning of his gesture, while the man from behind grabbed his neck in the crook of his arm, with a knee pressed in the small of his back.

'Search him,' said a voice, and because of the hold around his neck he could not protest. They gave a satisfied grunt as they came across the wad of notes and the silver in his other pocket.

'Jesus, look like him bank him money in de sea!'

He tried to say something but they put a cloth in his mouth and bandaged it in and tied his hands. He saw that they were going in one boat and were arranging to tow his own boat behind. There was no need for Brother Paul to quote from the scriptures by saying, 'Thou fool, tonight thy soul is required of thee.' But they found it hard to persuade the Shepherd to be happy in the thought that the longed-for heaven, with all its attractions, would soon be his.

The boat was found the next day, floating upside down, far out to sea.

CHAPTER THIRTY-NINE

'. . . I tell you, Mobel, me foot walk on it and when I take it up and feel it, it was a cap, and the peak feel smooth and it kinda glisten, but the light from the lane was too far for me to see good. All I know is it was black and look like Marse Ironman cap. But when I hear like somebody was moving behind the house, I get 'fraid and drop the cap on the step and run.'

'And now we see Marse Ironman two time and him don't have him cap! Suppose we go and say we was with *him* the night, and we did see the thing what him wear over him eye on the table, them might say it was Marse Ironman what kill Cap'n! We couldn't tell them 'bout the cap, only what you see in the room and the noise you hear back of the house.'

'Mister Pazart, who the hell say we was going to police to tell them anything? Since when we and police is friend?'

'But . . . but, Mobel, we have to tell the truth!'

'Truth 'bout what, Mister Pazart? *Him* tell police him kill Cap'n, you want we to say is not him? You 'member how him kill Sonna? You just wait till I tell all them people in the market who him is! Just wait!'

'All the same, I feel we shoulda tell we was at him room the night.'

'See how you fool! Don't him coulda kill Cap'n before we go to see him? Don't him coulda have another piece of leather for him eye, and it might be it him have on the table when we see him? Maybe him was going to make it look like it was Marse Ironman what kill Cap'n and . . . and when him see that we find out who him is, him talk truth and say is him.'

'But . . . Marse . . . him wouldn't do such a thing, Mobel!'

'No, Miss Sista? How him kill Sonna and, and pretend him was so good? Give we so much things, make Sonna tomb. God! Wish we could give back the tomb and this house as well as all the other thing what we give away since we find out! . . .'

'Corporal.'

'Yes, Sir?'

'What do those children want?'

'Don't know, Sir.'

'Find out. They have been sitting there a long time.'

'Yes Sir. Come here, you children. Who you want to see?'

'Nobody special, Sir.'

'Come to report something, then?'

'Yes, Sir – I mean no Sir.'

'Make up you mind, boy. What's you name?'

'Pazart, Sir.'

'Pazart what?'

'Pazart Wilson, Sir.'

'And you and these two girls are together?'

'Yes Sir.'

'Well now, tell me what you come here about.'

'The murder, Sir.'

'What murder?'

'The one what a man name . . . name . . . Mar . . . Tip, Sir.'

'You mean the one-eye' man?'

'Yes Sir.'

'Well, what can you tell me about it at this time?'

'Is . . . is not me Sir, is this girl, Sista . . .'

'You sister?'

'No Sir, only friend . . .'

'And the other girl as well?'

'No Sir, she don't have any evidence to give.'

'I am asking you if the other girl is also just you friend or a relation? Whether or not you are related to the other girl?'

'Yes Sir!'

'Yes Sir what?'

'What you say Sir . . .'

'Pazart, don't you see him just trying to make you look foolish? I said you shouldn't come to this place.'

'What the . . . Who are you, Miss?'

'Name Mobel . . . Sir.'

'What was it you was saying?'

'I say you just trying to make him look foolish and you know is true.'

'I . . . think I have seen you somewhere! Come to think of it, all three of you!'

'We never go to jail yet, none of we!'

'Shush, Mobel. Don't say anymore.'

'Don't tell me shush, Sista. If Sonna was here him wouldn't say shush. We don't do anything bad, all we come to do is tell them something. Don't look like them want to hear we.'

'Alright, Miss what's-you-name, enough of you cheek. You are in a police station and speaking to a police officer. Now, what are you here for? You friend here said something about this man Tip who is here on a charge of murder. What about him?'

They looked at each other, for now that it was time to tell what they had planned to say they found that in their embarrassment they had forgotten just how they had planned to say it.

'Is 'bout the night when Cap'n dead . . . Sir. We did see 'pon the table . . .' began Pazart.

'Now, wait a minute, let me get this straight. You are here to make a statement. Is that so?'

Pazart answered, 'A statement, Sir?'

'Yes, boy, a statement.'

'He mean to give evidence, Pazart,' put in Mobel.

'Oh, not me, Sir, is Sista want to give evidence 'bout what she hear, and what she see on the table.'

'Now, listen to me, three of you, I have had enough of this. I don't know what you are trying to tell me, but whatever it is, I'm sure it will not matter, for the man has already pleaded guilty to the charge. By the way, you know something about this case, you say, and you kept it to you self all this while? You know, of course, that it is wrong to withhold evidence? Answer!'

But the three stood silent.

'So, you have all suddenly lost you tongues? Right, wait here.'

'You can't frighten we, you know, sir. We come here weself, and we don't do anything bad,' said Mobel.

'What is it, Corporal?'

'I thought I knew their faces, Sir.'

'Yes, the man Tip used to look after them. A kind of fairy godfather, I hear. Isn't that so?' He turned to the children.

'They have lost their tongues and no wonder, for they came here with some cooked-up tale to get their fairy godfather out of the mess. Isn't that so? Answer!'

'Is not true, Sir, we didn't even want to come.'

'What's your name?'

'Sista, Sir.'

'Who told you to come here to make a statement?'

'Nobody, Sir.'

'I don't think it will do much good taking down what they have to say, Corporal. You know our people. If these children had something worth knowing about the case, which would have been beneficial to us, they would never have come here. They all hate the police. I am sure they have been primed to come here and give us some cock and bull story. But still it won't do any harm to hear the tale.'

'Alright, you hear what the Sergeant said. We know you came here with a mouthful of lies, but we will hear what you have to tell us. You must learn that you cannot fool the police. Now, speak up, girl.'

'She don't have anything to say, now. None of we don't have anything to say. We shouldn't come. We was fool to come!'

The Sergeant intervened, 'Shut up, you little hooligan! Do you think you are speaking to one of your dirty street companions? I am not so sure I won't do something about your impudence.'

Mobel stood defiant before them, returning their scornful glances tenfold. Her bumpy plaits pointed upwards and outwards on her head, her very dark face filled with hatred, her lips parted with a sneer and her eyes smouldering. Her pride drew grudging admiration from the Officers. Almost behind Mobel, one on each side, stood Sista and Pazart, looking both brave and fearful at the same time.

It was the Sergeant of Police who looked away first.

'Corporal?'

'Yes, Sir?'

'I have to leave now. Let them go if they do not wish to speak, but get their names and addresses.'

The three did not speak.

'Mobel? You is sleeping?'

'Sista, you is a fool! How I can be sleeping when you big mouth just bawl out me name?'

'Awright, Mobel, I don't want no row. I just want to ask you if you hear like Pazart crying?'

'Yes, Sista! Sound like it! Make we go at him door and listen.'

'Without we frock, Mobel? Better make we wear something over we slip.'

'Come as you is, damfool! Maybe Pazart feeling sick!'

'Awright, make we go.'

'You hear it, Mobel? Him crying like a baby!'

'Yes, I hear him.'

'Pazart? You awright?'

'Him stop crying now, I can't hear him.'

'Pazart, you have pain?'

'Pazart! What wrong?'

'No need you do like you sleeping, Pazart! Me and Sista know you not sleeping!'

'Pazart, open the door. We want to talk to you!'

'Pazart?'

'What you want, Miss Sista and Miss Mobel?'

'You want to come in we room and sleep?'

'Go to hell!'

'Go to hell yourself Mister blooming Pazart, if you don't want we company, we don't want you company either! You hear? Come Sista, don't look like anything wrong with him!'

'Mobel and Sista?'

'What, Mister Pazart?'

'I sorry. I is awright . . . I was dreaming.'

'Damlie! Come Sista, make we go back to we bed and leave him. Is him own business if him telling lie . . .'

' . . .Is no use, Noname, him tell them him don't want to see anybody . . . not even me. Him say him don't want no lawyer. Him just give up and won't let anybody do a thing.'

'But him must be off him head, Ironman. Nobody can tell me poor Tip not off him head. Him would never kill a soul if him is in him right mind, and furthermore, I don't feel him kill Cap'n.'

'If you can say that, Noname, what 'bout me? The man was like him was me own blood brother. I never see anyone what I take to so much like Tip. Mind you, to tell you the truth, when I see him the very first time, I don't know why, but me 'ole body get stiff, just like when you meet somebody what you feel is you enemy. But, after that, I feel him was the kind of man I woulda like to be.'

'The 'ole town is talking 'bout him. Them did like Cap'n but them love Tip.'

'Only them three picnies 'gainst him. I can't understand it. Them picnies have good heart and nobody stick up for them friend more than them. And yet them bring back every single thing what them get from him since them know him. It don't make sense, Noname; Tip worship them. All the other picnies in the town turn 'gainst them three because of how them turn 'gainst Tip. But them don't change them mind!'

'I can't understand it meself. Is not like Mobel, Sista and Pazart to turn them back on a friend. One other thing funny I notice 'bout all this – Tip would say or do something, just as if him feel him was going to dead soon. 'Member how him get you to take charge of almost everything and make him will? And how, when him don't know anybody watching him, him face would look sad?'

'Yes, Noname, I 'member. I notice it meself plenty time and every time I ketch him looking so sad and ask him why him look so, him seem so confuse just like him was shame. Plenty time I make to ask him to tell me what make him look so sometime, but it would look like I want to know him business.'

'Is true. You know it make I wonder if Shepherd did know 'bout how Cap'n dead? Him did hate him and me never trust the man. It was him what kill Bangbelly and even though him beg for it, you can't get away from the fack that it was him what do the job.'

'Noname, you forget that Shepherd drown at sea the same night Cap'n dead? And you forget Tip say him is guilty? . . .'

'Wonder what happen to you cap, Ironman? Funny, last time you see it hanging on the nail on the verandah was the night when Shepherd come here. But him drown as you say, and Tip confess . . .'

'Mobel?'

'What?'

'How you going to tell them?'

'You wait and see.'

'Mobel?'

'What, Sista?'

'What you think Sonna would do if it was one of we and him was alive?'

'I don't business what Sonna would do. I know what I going to do.'

'But you always say Sonna use' to do the right thing all the time!'

'Awright, what I going to do is the right thing.'

'But suppose is not him, Mobel?'

'Is not him kill Sonna?'

'You know is not that I mean.'

'Well, all I want to know 'bout him is, him kill Sonna.'

'Yes, him did kill Sonna.'

'You know, Bugsie sister tell me everybody saying we live off him all this time, but now, because him get trouble we don't own him. She say all the picnies say them sorry for him 'cept we. I was going to beat her, but I didn't bother, for we going to laugh and laugh at them, when them hear who him is!'

'Mobel?'

'What?'

'You think Pazart awright?'

'Why you say so?'

'You know, from that night when him run in him room and lock up the 'ole night, him change. Him never vex anymore, and him so kind to we.'

'Yes, Sista, I think him awright, but you know what? It was better when him use to vex 'bout everything. You don't know what him thinking now, don't care what you say.'

'Is true, Mobel, is true . . .'

But next day they could not find Pazart. He had gone for one of his lone walks. Now darkness had fallen and the stars were hidden under banks of clouds while the sound of thunder could be heard in the distance. The girls went to town to search for him. They called at Ironman's twice, not letting him see they were anxious. They did not even stop to talk to anyone. They went back home feeling that by now he too might have returned, but everything was just as they had left it.

They looked to see if he had taken anything, fearing he might have decided to go away, but as far as they could tell he had taken nothing.

They sat in their room and waited and then went to the verandah. He was all they had left, and they were afraid to imagine how they would feel if he did not return. A storm began. They hardly spoke to each other as the noise of the water splashed on the galvanized roof, and then fell to the ground, but they would not go inside. The rain reminded them of the night they had lost another companion . . .

It was nearly midnight now. Despite the rain, the thunder and the pitch darkness – in spite of the spirits who loved such a night for prowling – they covered themselves with old hessian bags and stepped out into the downpour. They stumbled along the narrow lane, their bare feet splashing in the flood of water. They could see nothing until the lightning flashed. They felt that the evil spirits must be close behind, ready to claw at their backs, but they also remembered that good spirits, the spirits of their parents and of Sonna, were walking with them too.

A light shone on them suddenly. They had not seen the black uniform of the policeman in the darkness.

'What you doing out in the street at this time of night?'

'Going to see if we can find we friend, Sir.'

'What friend?'

'Him name is Pazart, Sir.'

'Man?'

'No Sir, boy thirteen year ol'.'

'What is he doing out this time of night?'

'Don't know, Sir. Him just don't come home.'

'Where do you live?'

'Mango Walk, Sir.'

'How do I know you telling the truth?'

'Don't say no more, Sista. Make him do what him like.'

'What do you say, girl?'

'I say make you do as you like.'

'Do you know I have the right to take you to jail?'

'Well, you woulda have to take me as well, Officer.'

Ironman loomed out of the darkness behind the children and as the light of the torch reached his face the two girls turned towards him. He looked so big standing there, with the water dripping from his head onto his black face as he placed his protecting arms around each child. The policeman moved his torch slowly down to Ironman's feet and decided that there was no bigger man in the whole world. Without a word, and with his hands still on the shoulders of the girls, Ironman turned his back on the policeman and walked away.

They heard with relief that Pazart was at Ironman's home. After their two visits, he had searched for the boy and had found him near the graveyard, dazed after a fit, clutching a mouth-organ and a crumpled piece of cardboard with a picture of snow and strange houses which Ironman knew to be a Christmas card. Each of the children had received one through the post from Tip.

Pazart had been ill. He was walking alone as he did so often now. He reached one of the back-streets of the city where many of his friends lived and found three of them playing with discarded ball-bearings as a substitute for marbles.

''Ello Pazart!'

'Awright Leslie.'

'Want to play?'

'No.'

'Where Mobel and Sista?'

'Home.'

'Don't talk to Pazart, Leslie! Come and play you marbles if you still playing!'

'Mister Cliffud, why Leslie mustn't talk to me?'

'You don't know, Mister Pazart?'

'No, I don't know. Tell me.'

'Don't listen to Cliffud, Pazart! Cliffud, why you always look for trouble?'

'If you 'fraid for Pazart and him Sparrow gang, Leslie, I not 'fraid!'

Pazart guessed now what the boy, Clifford, was driving at. He had heard the taunt several times of late. Sometimes it was a hint, sometimes his old friends passed him without acknowledging his greetings. The last person to treat him like this was Bugsie. But he did not fight Bugsie because, when Sonna had died, Bugsie had taken Sista's place several times on the march with the rope over his shoulder, and he could not fight with the boy who had shared in such a task. So Bugsie had taunted him and he had bitten his lip and walked away. And here it was again.

The boy called Clifford took up his marble of iron and was about to continue his game.

'You going to tell me, Mister Cliffud?'

'What you want me to tell you, Mister Pazart?'

'Why you say Leslie mustn't talk to me?'

'You playing you don't know?' Now the boy raised himself up from his crouching position over the marbles. He stood upright. Taller than Pazart by about an inch, with a more robust body, looking quite sure of himself against the boy who was still showing the effects of his past illness, he said:

'You better don't try to fight me, Mister Pazart, you weak like a rat, and you just come out of sickness as well!'

'You going to tell me what I ask you, Mister Cliffud? Or you want me to beat it outa you?'

'You hear that, Leslie? Mister Pazart get brave! God, boy you really brave!' mocked Clifford.

'You only taking on Pazart because you feel you can beat him, Cliffud, bet you wouldn't talk so to Sonna 'fore him dead, nor Mobel if she was here.'

'Think I would 'fraid to tell Miss Mobel so to her face?'

'You don't tell me nothing yet, Mister Cliffud!'

'Awright, since you want me to tell you, Mister Pazart. Everybody know how Marse Tip was good. Him was good to all of we, but him was good to you and Mobel and Sista the most. And now, just 'cause the poor man musta get off him head and say him kill Cap'n, you turn 'gainst him, all three of you don't want to know. Just 'cause the man not here to full you gut with food! So you all treat a friend?'

Pazart was panting with indignation and shame.

'You damlie Cliffud! Is not that why!'

'Tell me why then, Mister Pazart, tell me why?'

Silence.

'You see Leslie? Pazart can't even find a good lie now. Him just stand up like him dumb!'

Pazart struck Clifford's ear. Before he could recover from the shock of the blow, Pazart lashed out again, this time on the mouth. Clifford tried to retreat and fight at the same time but this was a new Pazart. The boy struck out blindly in defence and drew blood from Pazart's gum. But Pazart, fired by the taunt, charged his enemy again with hands flaying. In pain now and anticipating defeat, Clifford began to back away.

'Jesus, Cliffud, you running?' said one of the children.

'Lawd, wait till Bugsie hear how Pazart beat Cliffud!'

'Make him beg you, Pazart!'

'God! Right 'pon Cliffud nose aggen!'

It was as if Pazart wanted to unleash all he had suffered since the night when he had faced Tip with a gun in his hand. As Clifford ran, Pazart suddenly felt weak and the triumph of this, his greatest fight, gave him no thrill. He walked away as if he had lost the battle, without a word to the children who crowded around him.

He arrived home with swollen lips and a sadness which even the remarkable victory could not efface. Mobel said nothing but she was watching him and noting his bruises. Sista came out with her mending in her hand and seemed about to question him but she too decided to say nothing. Pazart took the supper she brought for him and went to his room. He never thought that eating could be so painful. 'People have two hand, two nosehole, two ear, two eye, two feet, why the hell we couldn't have two mouth as well?' he mumbled as he tried to swallow. He would have to face their questions sooner or later. He couldn't say he fell because they would be sure to hear about the fight from someone as soon as they went to town. This was the very first time he had fought and won yet he did not wish to speak about it, though he didn't know why. He went outside.

'Pazart!'

'What you want, Mobel?'

'You not going to tell we?'

''Bout what?'

''Bout the fight?'

'Boy trouble me and me and him fight, that's all.'

'Who win?'

'Me.'

'And you don't want to talk 'bout it, Pazart?'

'No.'

Ironman came once more to see the children. He tried to convince them that Tip could not have done wrong, but they would not listen to him. Their hardness surprised Ironman and he was hurt on Tip's behalf. Disappointed, he returned home, feeling sad that he had failed to soften them.

The children were relieved when he went. At least the questioning had ceased. But they knew that their secret was now a barrier between themselves and those around them and their sense of isolation brought an added sorrow.

CHAPTER FORTY

Tip was still refusing to allow any lawyer to act in his defence. His thoughts were centred on Ironman, who by now would know the truth and hate him for it.

On the day of his examination he was told he would be taken to court the back way in order to avoid the crowds that had gathered. He said to himself: 'Thank God! Them saving me from them. Them know who I is now. Oh God, I couldn't stand it. If only them could leave something with me so that I could get rid of meself, for I have to go back to trial next month when Home Circuit meet. That will bring the crowd. Them going to spit on me. Oh God, wish it was all over. I wish it was!'

They came for him and led him through the back door to the waiting car in handcuffs. His grey trousers and sky blue shirt were creased in a dozen places. His bare feet shuffled with each step and he blinked his one good eye as if the light was too much for him. He had lost some of the muscle he had started to gain and his face looked haggard. There was a large amount of grey in the curly mass on his head and also in his beard. He shrank between two detectives in the back of the car as they were driven through the side-streets. He thought of the ordeal to come and tried to steel himself for the examination which he knew well because of his past association with the law. He wondered if many would be waiting in the court to show their loathing. He remembered the hours he had spent with Pazart way up on the beach, where he had seen 'snappers' and 'jacks' darting to and fro in the clear pool, dotted with rocks. He remembered how the boy had made him feel that there was no need for words between them. He remembered Sista, who concealed nothing; her eyes said whatever her lips had not blurted. He loved her no less for this. Then there was Mobel. Unreadable, proud, hardened by the strain of being mother and father to children of her own age; bitter and sarcastic at the patience and fortitude of adults who buried their souls in hope and prayer. Yet he knew that Mobel cared. He had come across them once, each holding the Christmas card he had sent them. They had not seen him. He was just in time to hear Mobel say: 'I want to keep this till I grow up into a big woman, right till the day I dead.' As he crept back he heard the others vowing likewise. They never knew that he had heard them.

The detectives sitting on each side touched him. He opened his eye. They were in the rear of the Santa Lucia Court House. He barely glanced at the few people looking on as he unexpectedly appeared. The throng were the other side of the street watching the rest of the prisoners leave the Black Maria, thinking he was there among them. They seemed to protest when they did not see him and he feared that they would be all the more angry when he came out.

They brought him up, still handcuffed, to face the court. He glanced around nervously at the packed room. Neither the children, nor Ironman, nor Noname were there. He felt that it was better like this, yet it made him feel so very much alone. Then he remembered Ma Kuskus. Only she would think no worse of him for she had no illusions about him. She knew his past yet still looked upon him with affection. The thought cheered him so that when they called his name, he was able to say, 'I plead guilty, You' Honour', without faltering.

The date of the trial was arranged. The crowd remained outside, but once again the police outwitted them. Only when they had dispersed was Tip taken down the steps into another car. As they slammed the door, he felt eyes upon him. He looked up into the face of Ma Kuskus. The car shot out into the street and sped away, but it seemed that for the whole route, the eyes of Ma Kuskus were looking at the self-confessed murderer. He took heart, for in that brief glance she had told him that she understood.

It was almost dark when he reached the gate of the prison, now deserted by the crowd. One of the detectives stepped out of the car and opened the door, while the other held Tip's arm. He stepped out. On the far side of the street, their faces hidden by the gloom of the fast coming night, were the three he would have known anywhere. They stood in their shabby clothes and bare feet, as though they had come to gloat at his punishment. He turned and walked away with his head so low that his beard, though it was not long, touched his chest.

CHAPTER FORTY-ONE

Tip awoke at dawn on the day of his trial and tried to prepare himself to face the hatred of the crowd. He wished that a form of madness would take over and make him oblivious to their contempt until he realized that these would be his last days and every conscious moment was therefore precious. He concentrated on his will. Had anything been left undone? He had written requesting no visitors, no letters. Half of everything he had was to be kept in trust for the three children. Ten pounds was to go to Noname and his remaining assets were to be left in the hands of Ironman to help the poor in any way that he felt fit. His business had continued to prosper; he would leave more money than he had ever imagined possible. The saying was obviously true; when a man has a short time to live his business ventures always succeed.

Tip had heard through the warders that the campaign for raising wages in the various industries of Santa Lucia had been successful. The strike had been called off after only three days as the government and the employers had conceded to the workers' demands. Some of Tip's money had been used in support of the strike. He thought of Dimlight. The idea had been his, he had campaigned hard, risking arrest, believing that if the strike worked the people would be encouraged to have faith in themselves as well as in God. He had not lived to see his dream come true. No matter, the people would remember him.

The people! Tip's thoughts returned to the ordeal he must face before the crowd. The children – or Shepherd – would have told them by now. He tried to think of something else and Salome came into his mind. What would she feel when she heard he was Bangbelly? Perhaps she would not even want to keep the things his money had bought. He thought of her husband, Sonna and Ironman's wife. The harm he had

200

done as Bangbelly was not over yet. Like the Sparrows, people would feel angry and hurt and betrayed . . . he would be despised; he would die totally alone, and he was afraid. No, not quite alone; Ma Kuskus was with him, he had seen it in her eyes when she had waited for him outside the court.

It was no use, his mind kept returning to the themes he wanted to forget. He would drift from one thing to another but in the end, he always came to the same scene.

He had been to a prison once, miles from Santa Lucia, just to hear the trap-door thump as the condemned man died. There had been many people there. He recalled every detail now: the early morning sun coming over the mountain, the great gates studded with metal, the high walls. A large square surrounded the prison, capable of holding a crowd of thousands. Just before half-past seven some men had climbed the three tall coconut trees to look over the wall at the death-cell opposite. One had shouted: 'Them coming with him!' The crowd of three hundred or so had fallen silent. Then suddenly the voice of a man had reached them; 'I can't bear it! Oh God!' he had cried, 'I can't go to me death! Oh God, save me, save me!' The crowd had vibrated visibly at his terror, and had felt with him all the fear a strong and healthy man must feel, knowing that in the next few minutes his life would be taken away from him. He had cried all the way to the gallows, and the crowd had stood still, anticipating his last seconds, waiting for the great thump which would tell them that the trap-door had been sprung and the young man was hanging by his neck. Then it had come and the crowd had sighed as if they had been holding their breaths as one. The men who had watched from the trees had slithered down to the ground, looking from the distance like huge snakes. Afterwards a khaki-clad warder had come through the gates and had pinned a notice on the board to the effect that the death by hanging had been duly witnessed, and a black flag had been raised near the gate.

And now he had chosen this end for himself, could he still save himself? The thought came and went quickly. He hid his face in his hands and sat thus until they came to take him out for trial.

Again the police outwitted the crowd and Tip was not brought before them. As he stood in the dock, he longed to get it all over and done with, for he felt that the waiting would sap all his courage. He saw the blurred faces of judge, jury, policemen and lawyers in wigs, gowns and suits. He glanced at those present with one quick movement and then bowed his head and pleaded in a clear voice which surprised him in that it did not betray the emotion he felt.

'Guilty, You' Honour.'

The rest was just a formality.

He saw the judge reach for the black cap and only heard half the words as he stood between the two officers . . . 'By your neck until you are dead . . . and may the Lord have mercy on your soul.'

He heard a cry . . . one sharp cry, like the voice of a child, just as he turned to leave the court. He made as if to turn his head, then thought better of it. He could not look again. He did not want to see Ironman or the three children just behind him. Yet their faces still managed to meet his good eye as went unsteadily down the steps between the two warders. He avoided glancing into their eyes.

This time, in spite of the police efforts, they could not get away without spectators. People saw them as they reached the car and they all surged forward, just as it pulled away. Their shouts were drowned by the roar of the engine, and Tip could only see the upraised hands of men and women and guessed what they were saying. 'Oh God, oh God!' he said, and covered his face with his handcuffed hands. The two officers looked at him strangely but said nothing. There was no crowd at the prison gates, just the solitary figure Tip had felt would be there. He raised his head from between his hands and gazed for a few seconds into her face. The two coal-black eyes looked back at him, and his lips moved. The lips of Ma Kuskus moved also.

The officer on the right asked the other:

'You know that old woman?'

'Yes, I know her, she sell herbs and tell fortune,' his companion replied.

'Wonder what she waiting here for?'

'Don't know,' came the reply.

Only Tip knew and he kept his peace.

CHAPTER FORTY-TWO

They tried to pretend they had forgotten the scene. No one mentioned the cry which had escaped the lips of one of the three – Sista perhaps – they were not sure. They walked home through the side-streets hoping no one would ask them the result.

Nervously, Pazart would either walk ahead of the girls or linger behind them when they went out together. He still showed signs of his recent illness and he was far from being his old self. He would get into a temper over the least thing, hurting the girls with his taunts or sometimes acting as if he were sorry for himself. He spent long hours alone and would alternate between shouting at them and remaining completely silent.

Sista made excuses for him, but a few days after the trial it was she who brought matters to a head when he had been exceptionally rude.

'We want to know why you going on like this, Pazart?' she said. 'We want to know what we do you why you going on like you hate we? One night, Mobel and me hear you like you crying, so we come out to you door and ask if you want to come and stay in we room, for we know when you one in a place how you can feel bad, and you tell we to go to hell, you think is right?'

Pazart hung his head while he walked before them with his hands in his pockets. Then he suddenly started running, and they knew it was because he did not want them to see his face or hear his sobs. He ran straight to his room and locked the door and would not come out for the rest of the day.

Surprisingly, the next morning, Pazart was his old self again, joking with them, showing them consideration, looking for sticks for the fire and chopping them to size. The girls were surprised and relieved.

One day he came home and they knew, without asking, that he had heard something.

'Is next month,' he said, without their having to ask the question.

'What date?' asked Mobel softly.

'The twenty-first.' Silence. Then: 'Mobel, when you going to tell them?'

Mobel looked far away and said, 'The last week, we will wait till the last week, then we tell them.'

They sat down with their plates in their laps beside the vessel of rice and peas, cooked together with corned pork. They toyed with their spoons and took mouthfuls which they had trouble swallowing. They did not look at each other. Each had thoughts boxed-up within, and each seemed to wish only for their own company, despite knowing they would be more miserable in separation than they would be together. Sista got up and said she wanted to walk up the road; not long after Pazart got up, too. Mobel remembered that he had nearly died alone in a time of great stress and was reluctant to let him go; yet she, too, wanted isolation. When he went, Mobel sat until the night came down and the moon came over the hill. She forgot to be afraid of the dark; she forgot to wish for Bulla, who was now permanently at Ironman's. Her two companions met each other on the return journey and, as they entered the gate, they found Mobel lying on the ground, her face pressed to the earth as if she needed to feel something solid and hard and tangible beneath her.

Pazart and Sista were sitting in their small kitchen, not sure what to say to one another. Then Pazart asked:

'Sista, how much days left?'

'Fifteen. Why you ask, Pazart?'

'Nothing.'

'Where Mobel gone?'

'Don't know, she just say she want to go for a walk by herself.'

'Pazart?'

'What?'

'What going to happen?'

'Don't know.'

'Suppose is not him?'

'Suppose is not him what?'

'Kill Captain?'

'We couldn't do anything. You 'member how the police treat we?'

'Yes. All the same I know the cap what I kick with my foot that night belong to Marse Ironman.'

'And if them did find the cap, them would think is Marse Ironman kill Cap'n.'

'Oh God, then them would maybe hang Marse Ironman.'

'That's why we wasn't going to say anything to the police 'bout the cap.'

'But we was going to tell them we was with *him* that night, and him take up something off the table when I come in and tell him 'bout what I see. But the police didn't want to hear we . . . Pazart?'

'What?'

'You . . . you sorry?'

'Go to hell . . .'

CHAPTER FORTY-THREE

Tip lay on the prison bed with his face to the ceiling, his eye closed. He began to talk in his mind. *Them ask if there is anything I would like. Suppose I was to tell them yes. Not a single one of what I would like or what I want them could give me. Not a single one of the umpteen hundred things I would want.*

Anything you wish to have? Yes, Superintendent. I would like to be free again, even for one day after the time you preparing to hang me. Just one day! I can see how the Superintendent would look at me and shake him head, like I was asking for the world. But yet him ask me if there was anything I would like or anything special what I want!

Yes, I want something. I want to still see the sun after half-past seven Tuesday morning. I don't want to lay where the hangman put me, and can't get up any more . . . What him would say if I say that to him?

Is there anything you would like? I would like to live my second life over again. Not the first, just the second part. I would like to hear Salome' voice, sweet as a bell, say 'Tip' like when she say it before she go away on the bus. I would like to sit there in her little room, even with me one eye and bad foot, watching the light on her face and hear her talk 'bout the mountain when the sun come up . . . when it go down. When the moon come up over the hill, and . . . and the night jesmin and the other things smell like nothing you know, for nothing else smell like it. I would like to smell that smell, I would like to tell her how she lay inside of me, morning, noon and night, from the time I look 'pon her face and hear her talk. I would like to take her little girl on me knee and make up little stories 'bout Brer Ananse, Brer Tacuma and Brer Rabbit. I would like to see the child' face when she laugh, just like I see it that day when I bring the money and the little doll for her.

There was a long pause, then he opened his eye and continued talking in his mind: *I would like the three picnies to have them friend again. To see this boy Sonna, really see and know him. I would like to hear him call me Godfather just like the others call me that day. I would like to see how him face would look when I buy the nice things for him like what I buy for the others last year Christmas. But if I can't get him back from the dead, I would like the others . . . to meself . . . sitting down on the doorstep again, listening to the pigeons them raising in the coop behind the house, coo, and far up the road, somebody whistling a song, and me and them just sit down not saying a word, for we all too happy to talk . . . I would like to sit on Black Rock, just me and Pazart, like that day. We wouldn't care if fish bite or not. We don't care if crab or eel eat off all the bait or break we line. We just want to sit down there, not saying a single word, me and him, like father and son.*

O Jesus . . . I would like to walk along the street and into the market pushing my handcart and people won't make I pass without saying something nice. Hallo, Marse

Tip! How things? Awright Tip! Take it easy, Marse Tip. You know if it wasn't me little girl I would pass and don't see you? She always talking 'bout you, Marse Tip. Watch you, Tip! What you know? . . . Tip, you bugga, you promise me and my woman you would come and spend one Sunday with we! When you coming? Every day my wife ask after you, 'blige to tell her is me she married to, her name is not Mrs Tip! You must come nex' week, Sunday, Tip, try and come! . . . God bless you, Marse Tip . . .

I would like to know where I going after Tuesday morning . . . I would like to know, if when I pray with the minister, like I pray this afternoon, God really hear me. I would like to know if all this what we read and hear 'bout God is true. I would like to know if all this talk 'bout heaven and hell, 'bout God and the Devil, 'bout soul and eternity is true or not. I would like to know if Jehovah, God of the Jews, is God of the black man as well. I would like to know if Jehovah is the same God who call David a man after His own heart, though David grudge Uriah wife so much that him murder the innocent man. For if is so, God will pardon me for causing Sonna to dead . . . I would like to know if I going to come back on this earth as a different person . . .

Is there anything you would like? Superintendent ask. Suppose I say any of these things? Them couldn't help me with one . . . Even if I say, I would like Tuesday morning . . . since I must dead . . . to dead like a man, not as I know I going to dead. I would like to get courage to walk outside, with me head straight . . . without warders holding me up under me armpit . . . without me bawling like I did hear that man bawl when I come to listen that day . . .

'Anything you would like to have?'
'No, Sir, nothing . . . nothing at all . . .'

CHAPTER FORTY-FOUR

'You know dat ole woman what sell bush an' tell fortune?'
'You mean Ma Kuskus?'
'Yes, same one. You know how she did say dat brute Bangbelly was gwine to suffer, an' all de t'ings what was gwine to happen to him?'

'Yes, I 'member! None of what she say come true! Him would get away ef it was not fe Shepherd!'

'All dis talk 'bout him gwine bury 'live, an' him gwine to hang himself, an' him gwine to beg dem to hang him!'

'Yes, an' from dat time people stop gwine to her to make her read dem han' fe dem say she don't tell truth!'

'So I hear! An' I hear people cuss her to her face an' say she is a ol' liar 'cause of what she say would happen to Bangbelly an' it didn' happen!'

'I hear one woman tell her so to her face, meself!'

'An' you mean she never say anyt'ing to de woman?'

'No. She jus' stan' up an' look hard at de woman, but it seem like de woman get frighten', fe she walk fast to get outa Ma Kuskus sight afterwards!'

'An' to t'ink how people use to be 'fraid of Ma Kuskus!'

'I tell you, sister, I was surprise' to see how dem treat her now!'

Sunday night. The three sat on the steps of the girls' cottage, now almost without furniture. The prized iron beds had been given back to Ironman. They slept on home-made canvas cots as they had done before they had known Tip. Their wardrobes contained only the things which they had bought themselves. The night was dark and silent, except for the occasional bark from a dog. It was long past bedtime, but the three who sat side by side did not care. They seldom spoke. It had been so all through the week, and now it was Sunday night; only Monday and then *Tuesday morning*.

'Pazart and Sista, you know what I going to do?'

'What?'

'I going to tell them tomorrow. I going into the market and tell the market people what cussing we and calling we ungrateful. I going on the Dungle where them picnies play and tell them too, and watch how them going to look shame when we tell them who *him* is! Then I going to Marse Ironman and say: "You think we ungrateful because we give back or give away all the things we get from *him*, you know why? Because *him* is Bangbelly! *Him* kill Sonna! And we promise Sonna we would get revenge!" Then we will see them face! All of them will want to go to the prison gate tomorrow night to mock him Tuesday morning and hear when the trap-door fly. Everybody will want to go when them hear!'

'Yes, Mobel, everybody will want to go when them hear and we will go, too!'

'Yes, Pazart, me and you and Sista will go tomorrow night and stay the 'ole night with the crowd till Tuesday morning! Don't you think it is a good idea, Sista? After that people can't call we ungrateful no more, and all them picnies what won't speak to we now will have to come and beg we pardon!'

'Yes, Mobel, after that we won't need to feel shame because of what people saying 'bout we anymore. We have to tell them tomorrow.'

'Yes, Sista, we have to tell them! What you say 'bout it Pazart?'

'Yes, Mobel, we will tell them tomorrow, then them will stop call we ungrateful. I . . . I feel like I want to go to me bed now. Good-night Sista and Mobel.'

'Good-night, Pazart. We going to we bed now, too . . .'

It was long past midnight when the girls, still wide awake, heard a tap on their door.

'Who knocking?'

'Is me . . . Pazart! . . . Make I come in and stay with you?'

'Yes, Pazart, come and stay in here with we . . .'

Morning found the three, weary and red-eyed. They had not found sleep.

CHAPTER FORTY-FIVE

Monday night! Tonight is Monday night. My last night in this world! Tomorrow, this time, where I will be? Oh God! I don't know! No more night after this one. No more seeing the sun going down in the sea. No more hearing the birds singing. No more dreaming what it would be like to be with Salome up in that mountain to smell the things what make the place smell like nothing you know for nothing else smell like it! Oh God! No more talking with Ironman and fishing with Pazart. No more going to pictures with them, with all the children and the big people calling to me: Hello Tip! Hello Marse Tip! Watch you, Tip! God, and I was just learning how life can be sweet! I can't even walk to me dead tomorrow morning with the consolation that them still think I is a good man! And I going to me dead and still don't know what will happen to me after. I don't know if what the Bible say is true.

If what the white man teach we 'bout God is true. I still don't know if this white man God is a black man God as well. I still don't know whether is true or not that the black man can go to the white man heaven, or to the white man hell. I don't know whether my old people' belief that the dead turn into spirit and live on earth and know and see things and proteck them love' ones is right or not. I don't know enough 'bout my ancestor' belief, and what I know 'bout Christian belief is full of confusion, just like the Christian church where some say, I is the right church! and all the other' saying, We is the true church!

Noname say we black people take to the Bible because the things the Jews suffer is just like what we suffer. Him said that is why the black man and the Jews get on so well together, for in all history it is only the Jews who suffer like the black man. The Bible! It have such a lot of things. Some good, some bad. Some say one thing some say another thing. And me going to the gallows tomorrow without knowing what will happen to me after. Oh God! If I go on like this I will get mad! And I mustn't get mad for I would not know what was happening to me, and I prefer to know. If I could choose I would like what my ancestor' say happen after a man dead. I would like to come back as a spirit here on earth, so that I can look after and guard them what I love. I wouldn't feel bad if I know it was true . . . yes, I still would feel bad, but not like how I feel now, for I don't know where I will go after. I getting mad! I keep saying the same things over and over. I must think 'bout something else. I don't want them to carry me out mad tomorrow morning. I must recite poems. The warder hear me talking to meself and them thinking I is getting off me head. Them watching me so that if I rush and try to harm meself them can stop me. Them want to see I is fit and well tomorrow morning at half-past seven, so that them can hang me by me neck until I is dead . . . I must think 'bout something else. Yes, I did say I would recite poems what I know at school: I 'member one now. The Graves of an Household:

'They grew in beauty side by side,
They filled one' home with glee
Their graves are scattered far and wide
O'er mound and stream and sea . . .'

Jesus, why them teach we such things at school?

'Not a drum was heard
Not a funeral note
As his corpse to the . . .'

Good God, look like all the poems we learn at school is 'bout dead. Lucy Grey *more dead.* The Boy Stood on the Burning Deck *more 'bout dead. Better I turn to the Bible. Yes, maybe the Bible might take me mind off tomorrow . . .*

'Whither shall I go from Thy Spirit? Or whither shall I flee from Thy Presence?'

209

'If I ascend unto Heaven, Thou art there' – *wonder if it is true?* – 'If I descend into hell, Thou art present.'

'If I take the wings of the morning and dwell in the utmost part of the sea, even there shall Thy Hand lead me, and Thy Right Hand hold me.' *If I could only feel that when David write that it mean me, as well, it would cheer me up. But David was talking to him God, and we don't know if him is our God as well! Look how them people pray for the little boy what I kill. God never answer!* 'Yea the darkness hideth not from Thee' . . . *I 'member when I say these words the last time, it was in the hills, and the rain was pouring, and something tell me the child was going to dead . . .*

'But the night shineth as the day, and the darkness and the light are both alike to Thee.'

David, the man after God's own heart said them words. Maybe . . . maybe him feel like I feel now when him write that, for him was guilty of murder.

'He was despised and rejected of men, a Man of Sorrow and acquainted with grief' . . . *But God, it is hard to know tomorrow morning I will be strong and healthy and them will take me life, and perhaps if them did not have my life to take them would take poor Ironman' life. I glad that I could do this for him, but God, I feel 'fraid. I can't help it . . . tomorrow morning . . . I feel I will get mad and cry out in a minute.*

He heard without listening the talk between the warders . . .

'I tell you, it look like the whole town coming . . .'

'Never seen so much people in me twenty years as a prison officer. One of them chaps coming back from town on him bicycle said you couldn't stick a pin between the heap of men, women and even children, coming along the road.'

'Jesus! But man, must be near a thousand outside a'ready . . . Never see anything like it in all my life . . .'

Tip raised himself to a sitting position as the words of the men became significant to him. He sat on the edge of the bed, his one eye looking big and fearful, his hands resting palm downwards on his knees.

The death-watch warder eyed him, and a knowing sign passed between himself and his fellow guard.

Tip was saying to himself: *God A'mighty! Them coming! The bos'n say the road from town full of them – men, women and children. The other one said them is more than a thousand outside a'ready. Oh God, I going to get mad! I know I going to get mad. Them all coming to mock me and listen when I bawl out for mercy tomorrow morning. And I know I going to bawl. Oh God, I don't have the strength. I feel I getting off me head right now. I must say something, I must find something to say to the warder, it might keep me from getting off me head. Oh God, I can hear the sound of bus or truck stopping every few minutes outside. Them coming by foot, by bus, by car, by bicycle, tonight, to witness my shame tomorrow morning. I feel bad in me stomach, but I know is frighten' make I feel so. Inside empty and I feel I want to vomit. I must find something to say to the bos'n. If I can find something to say it might keep me mind from tomorrow and the crowd outside.*

'Officer!'

'Yes, friend, what you want?'

'Can . . . can you tell me the time?'

'Just quarter past nine, friend.'

'Thank you, Officer.' *Jesus help me to bear up, please Jesus.* 'Officer, you musta hate this kind of work, all of you. This death-watch I mean.' *Help me, God, please help me keep from bawling out. Me foot trembling, them won't stay still on the floor. I must tap me foot, it might help.*

'I don't think anybody could like the job of a death-watch, friend, but is all in the day's work, and somebody have to do it.'

'Yes, somebody have to do it, Officer, that's true.'

The warders watched the condemned man tapping his bare foot as he sat on the edge of the bed. It was just as if he was keeping time to a song or to some music. But they became wary. They said to themselves: *We going to have trouble in a minute. Is the first sign. We must get ready to keep him from dashing him brains out. Him must be in perfect condition when we hand him over tomorrow morning. It make you laugh! The man going to be a dead man one minute past half-past seven in the morning, but the law is that him must not have a chance to kill himself, not even a scratch him must have, or somebody pay for it. It would have been better for everybody if the law was to allow the poor bugga to kill himself. But no! Doctor will fight like hell to save the man' life if him take sick in the death-cell. Him must not dead until the hangman kill him. Hell of a vindictive thing this civilization and its laws. We going to have trouble with this one tonight. Poor fellow, you can see him trying to keep up conversation so that him might keep what coming to him out of him mind. Wonder how our ancestors in Africa would treat a man who commit murder? Bet them could not be more primitive, or as cruel as this! Give the condemned man anything he ask for, anything within reason, but not him life. Keep him under observation all the time. Torture him by telling him at intervals of the terrible end awaiting him. But see that him is physically fit for the hangman. Jesus, and them say this is civilization! Look at the one-eye' man on that bed. Now him start tapping him fingers on him knees. I know the sign. Will start rave in a minute. We have to watch him now.*

Tip tried to find something more to say, but failed. He could only hear the murmur of people outside the prison walls, like the hum which would come from maybe a thousand hives of bees. Every now and again a motor, perhaps a truck or a bus, would roar up then stop, and snatches of bargaining could be heard coming over with the slight comforting wind which took the heat out of the night. 'She only a little child . . . how much you say? . . . Thank you kinely . . .' The snatches came over time and again. So it was true as the warders had said: thousands of men, women and children were gathering out there, waiting to hear his cry, waiting to laugh and jeer. Without realizing it he was lifting the palms of his hands off his knees, then bringing them down again with a tap, tap, tap, tap, slowly at first, then the tempo became a little faster, then the hands raised higher and higher, until the tap, tap, became slap, slap, slap, slap. His one eye stared in front of him, big and frightened. Suddenly he stood up. The warders, within and without, became tense, ready to pounce on him should he try to harm himself. They prepared themselves for the shouts which they were sure were not far off. But when they came it was nothing like what they expected, for though it was an agonized cry, it came out as a mutter from deep inside of him, so that though they were not far away, they could not catch the words.

'Ma Kuskus? . . . Ma? You did say you love me! You did say so!'

It was like the cry of a tortured child instead of a man. The warders saw the look on the upturned face, and thought the time had come for action.

Across the road, on the far side of the prison under a coconut tree, sat an old woman, alone, except for a donkey. Even if there was light, there was no one there to see the perspiration gleaming on her wrinkled forehead, the head thrown back, the eyes closed. There was no one to look at the convulsions which took hold of the woman and shook her whole body. Only Ginny, the donkey, stood close to her mistress, pressing her great cheek against her face. After a little while, the convulsions ceased, and the old woman opened her eyes and looked across to where the outline of the prison could be seen. Then she spoke like a mother hushing tenderly the child of her womb.

'Tip, my son, go to sleep. Sleep Tip, my son, sleep till de sun come out aggen. I is here wid you, you know I love you. Sleep! Sleep! My son!'

The herb-seller ceased speaking. Then she stretched out her withered hands almost above her and drew the head of the donkey down against her face.

Back in the death-cell the warders stood ready to do their duty, every muscle tensed, with ears prepared for the shouts they felt would come. They saw the man stop just as he made ready to say something, perhaps to shout something. He stood listening, his lips moved, but they could not hear what he said. The wide eye became soft and a sad, half-smile seemed to touch his lips like a child smiling in his sleep. They saw him still listening – though he felt for the rough bed – they watched, fascinated, as he ever so slowly sat down. Then – as if he did not wish to disturb the atmosphere with a single rustling sound – he laid himself down on the bed, on his side, with the palm of one hand resting under his face. They stared unbelievingly, for as soon as the man had laid himself down on the bed, his even breathing told the watchers of the miracle.

'Jesus Christ,' whispered the warder, 'I just can't believe it! Sleeping like a babe . . . a innocent babe!'

They woke him, and yet he did not understand at first. He got up and they helped him to get ready, to see to his wants, to do what must be done. He still looked around bewildered, perhaps not wanting to believe this was reality, or perhaps not realizing how precious the minutes were. They had left him to sleep until it was absolutely necessary. Whatever had been said to him through the night – whatever had been said for his benefit, for the benefit of his soul, or for the satisfaction of the administrators of justice – he had no recollection of it. If they had woken him he had no knowledge of it. If he had responded to their words he could not remember. He only knew that he had slept after he thought of Ma Kuskus. And he had slept as he had never slept for years. He had had pleasant dreams – and these he was trying to remember now, trying to see which was which – and now they had woken him though he was still very sleepy.

Suddenly he was really awake. He remembered the day. He remembered why he was there, why they had woken him, why he could not rest before he thought of Ma Kuskus. 'Jesus Christ A'mighty! Them come to get me ready to take me out!' he whispered loudly.

No, he wanted nothing . . . Nothing they could give. He remembered the crowd outside as they made ready for his brief re-entry into the outside world for the last time. The light was outside, the sun was shining on the trees outside, on the coconut trees.

The coconut trees!

Oh God, the people waiting outside! Thousands of them. They are all here even the minister. Oh God, is not a dream. It going to happen this very morning. I going to cry out, and them going to hear me. I can't help it, I can't help it! Them is all there waiting . . . and the men high on top of the coconut trees, watching to tell them.

How long since them wake me? Not more than two minutes, no, less than that, one

213

minute, no, less, half minute. I don't even draw me breath two times yet, and them do and say all what them want to say. How time could fly so quick? Them cheat me, is not so late . . . see them cheating, is only a minute since the warder say it was half-past six, and now them trying to say is time! Them cheat me of me last few minutes of life, and now I must go out and make that crowd hear me beg for more time. I must get little time to prepare meself. If the crowd was not there listening, God, I wouldn't mind. I could bawl and I wouldn't shame, but what I saying? Dead man can't have any shame? Not after him dead? Jesus, I getting mad, I getting mad, if them wasn't outside to mock me. Oh God, I can't bear that, I can't bear that! Why you didn't make I dead in my sleep last night God? Couldn't you have pity on me? Them say you did have pity on the thief on the cross, and yet you wouldn't pity me and make I dead without them people here to mock me in my shame? You forsake me, God, just like everyone forsake me . . . 'cept Ma Kuskus, wherever she is . . .

The warders took him gently by the arms. He tried to stand like a man as the door of the condemned cell was ready for him to pass through . . . Plainly he heard the call from the trees:

'Them coming out now!'

And immediately his knees turned soft, so that almost all his weight rested on the warders who had him between them. As they started moving him forward with his feet dragging, he kept saying under his breath:

'Them waiting till I face the door then them will start to jeer and shout. Oh God, make I deaf so that I can't hear.'

He reached the door of the condemned cell with the warders almost bearing his full weight. There was no sound from outside the gate now, and the sun was in hiding, so that there were no morning rays to make the branches of the tall coconut trees shine and glitter.

The condemned man held his breath as he faced the walk across the prison yard towards the gate.

'Now I will hear them taunting me! I can't go! My knees too weak. I can't walk! Oh God! Oh God!' he whispered.

'God-fa-ther!'

'God-fa-ther!'

'Oh God-fa-ther!'

The heart-rending cries came to the ears of the condemned man, and to him the earth stood still, the gentle wind ceased, and every heart, and every breath stopped in sympathy with his. He heard the voices of his beloved children pouring out their very souls with each syllable. The wonder of it all brought a startling change to him.

'Pazart! Mobel! Sista! Oh bless you my children! Bless you!' he cried

214

at last, and even the officers taking him to the gallows felt too touched to move him for a moment. Another cry:

'Tip! My love! This is Salome! Sa-lo-me!'

'God bless you and keep you, Salome!' Tip shouted back, but something big welled in his throat so that he had to struggle with himself to clear it. Then out of the short silence that followed came the voices of countless children. Pure and moving came the hymn from the throats of wingless angels – alias hooligans, alias ragamuffins – led by three voices:

> 'God be with you till we meet again,
> By His Counsels guide, uphold you . . .'

Those in the procession looked at the face of the condemned man, and what they saw there would live with them for the rest of their lives.

> 'With His sheep securely fold you . . .
> God be with you till we meet again.'

'I don't deserve such goodness God! I don't deserve all this!' Tip whispered in a choking voice, as the thousands of adults joined the children in the chorus of the farewell hymn.

> 'Till we meet! Till we meet!
> Till we meet at Jesus' Feet . . .'

Gently the condemned man prised away the hands of the warders supporting him on both sides. They saw him suddenly grow taller and, when he strode off between them, it seemed he had added inches to his normal height. They saw that even his chest seemed broader, that he almost walked firmly on his crippled foot, and his smiling face was transfigured with happiness.

> 'Till we meet! Till we meet!
> Till we meet at Jesus' Feet . . .'

The sun came out of hiding suddenly, and a little wind played on the coconut branches so that they seemed to be waving a farewell, in tune with the singing. The great basses and baritones from the men now became reinforced with those of the hundreds of prisoners in the prison itself, so that the deep notes seemed to vibrate all around as if the sounds came from a number of mighty pipe organs. The women's and children's voices took the high notes to the skies and the wind took them so that they seemed to come from above as well as below.

Tip hastened to lead in the chorus this time, so that his strong bass reached them, assuring them that he understood and was happy:

>'Till we meet! Till we meet!
>Till we meet at Jesus' Feet . . .'

He sang, and the thousands answered back as one, with every word filled with a thousand meanings:

>'Till we meet! Till we meet!
>God be with you . . .
>Till we meet again . . .'

He saw them all as he walked along, just as if there were no wall and no gate. He saw his beloved children, Pazart, Sista and Mobel, standing in front of the gate with thousands of other children beside and behind them. He saw Salome with the sadness in her eyes and the strange beauty of her face, standing among the crowd, weeping. He saw Ironman, big and brave, gentle and kind. He saw the market women who smoked cigars with the lighted ends in their mouths, the handcart men, the dockers, the street-sweepers. He saw the fat woman who gave him that terrible job. He saw Noname, Paperman and countless others.

>'Till we meet! Till we meet!
>Till we meet at Jesus' Feet . . .
>Till we meet! Till we meet!
>God be with you, till we meet again!'

Even the skies seemed to be filled with the glory of that farewell. He walked with firm steps, with the padre and the procession of officials looking nervous and embarrassed. The crowd never stopped singing. They told the man walking towards the little shed-like house all that was possible for anyone to say when there was real love at a parting.

>'God be with you till we meet again,
>Keep loves banner floating o'er you,
>Smite death's threatening wave before you,
>God be with you till we meet again.'

Tip turned to those who were making the last arrangements:
'How can a man die better?' he asked.
And the crowd outside sung with all their souls and with all their might:

>'Till we meet! Till we meet!
>God be with you, till we meet again.'

And no one heard the thud of the trap-door.

'Marse Ironman?'

'Yes, Mobel?'

'That ole woman . . . under that tree . . . she sleeping! And the donkey lying down beside her like it dead. Maybe she travel all night to get here . . . What Marse Ironman? Why you looking so? Gosh! It's Ma Kuskus!'

'Hush, Mobel. Don't get frighten', don't wait. I will see 'bout her.'

'I must know, Marse Ironman! I must! She . . . she not sleeping? Tell me the truth!'

'You mustn't frighten', Mobel, is awright.'

'Awright, Marse Ironman, I understand. Look just like she was sleeping . . . poor Ma Kuskus . . .'

EPILOGUE

Pazart took the dead sparrow from where he had placed it beside him on the bench in the snow-covered park. He walked towards a corner where the whiteness was high on the ground, and there he buried the dead bird with great reverence.

HEINEMANN
CARIBBEAN WRITERS SERIES

A PAPERBACK ORIGINAL

Namba Roy has brought to life the colourful and historical crucible that was Jamaica in the 1930s. *No Black Sparrows* challenges social injustice, the use of capital punishment and orthodox Western religion at a time when 'we black people starting to think. And we starting to see de holes in you religion, and you democracy and you civilization'.

The novel focuses on 'God's Little Sparrows' – orphans Sonna, Pazart, Mobel and Sista – who scrape a living selling bootlaces, pins and needles. The rough warmth they share with the generous Ironman who feeds them, and Captain Dimlight who teaches them 'to speak English good', cannot however protect them from the sadistic community constable, Bangbelly: but an ironic twist ensures that the fates of both Bangbelly and Sonna are intertwined.

This compelling tale boils over with a vitality and an emotion that will appeal to readers everywhere.

'A remarkable book which contains much that is valuable, articulate, pertinent and positive.' *Anne Walmsley*

Cover design by Keith Pointing
Cover illustration by Namba Roy

ISBN 0-435-98812-3

9 780435 988128